Cycling in the UK

An introduction to the National Cycle Network

AA

sus**trans**

JOIN THE MOVEMENT

Commissioning Editor: Paul Mitchell
Editor: Donna Wood
Art Editor: Nick Otway @ Alphaforme
Copy Editor: Helen Ridge
Proofreader: Jennifer Wood
Picture Researchers: Alice Earle (AA) and
  Jonathan Bewley (Sustrans)
Image retouching and internal repro:
  Sarah Montgomery and James Tims
Cartography provided by the Mapping Services
Department of AA Publishing and Sustrans
Researched and written by: Lindsey Ryle, Nick Cotton,
Melissa Henry and Sustrans' regional staff
Production: Richard Firth

This product includes mapping data licensed from the Ordnance Survey® with the permission of the Controller of Her Majesty's Stationery Office. © Crown Copyright 2009. All rights reserved. Licence number 100021153.

This is based upon Crown Copyright and is reproduced with the permission of Land & Property Services under delegated authority from the Controller of Her Majesty's Stationery Office, © Crown copyright and database rights [2009] 100363. Licence number 90028.

Produced by AA Publishing
© Copyright AA Media Limited 2009
ISBN: 978-0-7495-6279-3 and (SS) 978-0-7495-6407-0

Published by AA Publishing (a trading name of AA Media Limited, whose registered office is Fanum House, Basing View, Basingstoke RG21 4EA; registered number 06112600).

A04068

The National Cycle Network has been made possible by the support and co-operation of hundreds of organisations and thousands of individuals, including: local authorities and councils, central governments and their agencies, the National Lottery, landowners, utility and statutory bodies, countryside and regeneration bodies, the Landfill Communities Fund, other voluntary organisations, Charitable Trusts and Foundations, the cycle trade and industry, corporate sponsors, community organisations and Sustrans' Supporters. Sustrans would also like to extend thanks to the thousands of volunteers who generously contribute their time to looking after their local sections of the Network.

We have taken all reasonable steps to ensure that the cycle rides in this book are safe and achievable by people with a realistic level of fitness. However, all outdoor activities involve a degree of risk and the publishers accept no responsibility for any injuries caused to readers while following these cycle rides. For advice on cycling in safety, see pages 268–269.

The contents of this book are believed correct at the time of printing. Nevertheless, the publishers cannot be held responsible for any errors or omissions or for changes in the details given in this book or for the consequences of any reliance on the information provided by the same. This does not affect your statutory rights.

Printed in Spain by Graficas Estella
theAA.com/shop

Sustrans
2 Cathedral Square
College Green
Bristol BS1 5DD
www.sustrans.org.uk

Sustrans is a Registered Charity in the UK: No 326550 (England and Wales) SCO39263 (Scotland).

CONTENTS

FOREWORD BY ALISTAIR McGOWAN

A few years ago, I was asked to visit some friends in Port Isaac in Cornwall. Not having a car, I asked them for the name of the nearest train station.

"Bodmin Parkway," they said. "And then jump in a cab. It's about twenty-five miles."

Twenty five miles in a taxi ? That sounded painful in every sense.

"Or could I cycle?"

"I don't know," they said, "I suppose so."

I looked into it and, a few days later, I found myself on the National Cycle Network (Route 32), under the warmth of the July sun, heading from Bodmin Parkway to Wadebridge. It was one of the most beautiful experiences of my life. So much so that I did it again the next year. Even in the pouring rain, it was a fabulous experience to be riding down a tree-lined, well-maintained route on the National Cycle Network, full of rivers, mini-waterfalls, trees, birds, history and the freshest of fresh air. It was the beginning of a beautiful relationship and I've since enjoyed many other routes elsewhere along the Network: in Sussex, Hampshire, Suffolk, Worcestershire and London.

I've always loved cycling: the feel of the world on my skin, the sound of the wind in my ears, the chance to stop and touch nature in all its green glory. One of the great rites of passage for me in my youth was spreading my wings, expanding my horizons and learning to ride a bike. That feeling of exhilaration, freedom, independence and achievement are, I expect, familiar to everyone who remembers their first time on two wheels – or indeed, their last time.

And here is a book dedicated to helping you to recreate (or discover) that feeling.

The National Cycle Network is fast becoming a national treasure and if you haven't yet had the pleasure of cycling (or walking) along its many thousands of miles, you've a real treat in store.

The National Cycle Network passes within a mile of over half of us (so it's never far away) and it caters for all kinds of people, from complete novices to cycling veterans. About a third of the Network is traffic-free, with the remainder of the routes signed along traffic-calmed streets and quieter roads. You feel safe. You feel free. You feel like the world has, at last, done something for you the cyclist, you the pedestrian and not, for once, for them, the car drivers.

The Network takes you along beautiful coastlines, over mountains and through valleys, across ancient viaducts and award-winning bridges, and into National Parks. It takes you to the heart of our cities, towns and villages. It passes great houses and monuments, bird and wildlife reserves and places of outstanding natural beauty. The Network itself is also home to many artworks – a public art gallery in its own right.

All of this adds up to a travel network (co-ordinated by the UK's leading sustainable transport charity, Sustrans) which is of great value to every man, woman, child and animal! Whether you want to get to work, to school, to the shops or to each other, whether you're planning a day out or a week's holiday, the Network exists for you.

And best of all, of course, cycling and walking are zero-carbon ways of getting about. So, any journey along the Network will only burn calories and not carbon. As the many challenges posed by climate change, obesity and the rising price of oil unfold, I suspect we will be even more glad of the existence of the National Cycle Network.

Try it! But I warn you: it could be the beginning of a beautiful relationship!

WELCOME TO THE NATIONAL CYCLE NETWORK

In the hot dry summer of 1979 a small group of volunteers laid down stone to build a smooth path for cyclists along five miles of abandoned railway leading into Bath. It took three months and became immensely popular overnight. Cyclists and walkers found it a convenient route for local journeys and a memorable trip through the countryside away from the traffic on the A4. It was a safe place to learn to cycle, or to brush up on forgotten skills.

Flushed with success, Sustrans embarked on a programme to make similar routes elsewhere in the West Country – Plymouth, Axbridge, Cheltenham, Swindon, Bradford-on-Avon and Devizes to name but a few – making use of every kind of corridor including not only former railways but canal towpaths, riverbanks, forest roads and urban parks. We always aimed to reach the centre of towns to enable people to take everyday journeys, the railway station to enable more integrated travel over distances and schools to enable the one sector of the population who really wanted to cycle to do so.

And we felt we had so little time – time to persuade the public to travel by foot and bike more, a commonsense response to resource depletion, environmental degradation and more recently the burgeoning consequences of a sedentary society short on fitness and health.

All this came to a head in 1995 with the launch of the National Cycle Network as the one lottery-funded project to span the whole of the UK. We saw this as a catalyst for change and a strategy for bringing at least one or two really good walking and cycling routes into every town. We saw the Network as a model of good practice and a way of making a statement that pedestrians and cyclists are valued travellers, just as they are elsewhere in Northern Europe.

We have had an exciting journey and one which still has a long way to go. I would be the first to acknowledge that we have often fallen short of our ambitions. But I hope that as you ride the routes in this book you will take pleasure in all that has been achieved, the travelling landscape, the

sculptural mileposts, the details on roads, even the signposting! All this is the result of the effort and commitment of tens of thousands of individuals – Sustrans supporters, staff and volunteer rangers, staff and councillors in almost every council and local authority in the land, numerous public bodies, landowners and funders including all the National Lottery players. In fact, all of you who use these routes have contributed in some way to its success.

I hope you enjoy the National Cycle Network and ride more often and more safely into the future and, if you do, you will consider supporting Sustrans and the valuable work we do.

John Grimshaw, CBE
President of Sustrans

Route Map Legend

National Cycle Network (Traffic Free)	National Cycle Network (On Road)	Cycling in the UK route (Traffic Free/On Road)	Cycling in the UK Start or Finish Point
AA approved campsite	Farm or animal centre	Viewpoint	
AA approved caravan site	Garden	Vineyard	
AA approved caravan & campsite	Hill-fort	Visitor or heritage centre	
AA recommended pub	Historic house	Windmill	
Abbey, cathedral or priory	Industrial attraction	World Heritage Site (UNESCO)	
Abbey, cathedral or priory in ruins	Marina	Zoo or wildlife collection	
Agricultural showground	Monument	AA golf course	
Air show venue	Museum or gallery	Stadium	
Aquarium	National Nature Reserve: England, Scotland, Wales	Indoor Arena	
Aqueduct or viaduct		Speedway	
Arboretum		Tennis	
Battle site	Local nature reserve	Horse racing	
Bird Collection	National Trust property	Rugby League	
Bird Reserve (RSPB)	National Trust for Scotland property	Rugby Union	
Cadw (Welsh Heritage) site	Picnic site	Football	
Castle	Roman remains	Ice hockey	
Cave	Steam railway	Athletics	
Country park	Theme park	Motorsports	
English Heritage site	Tourist Information Centre	County cricket	

INTRODUCTION

Welcome to *Cycling in the UK*, the first publishing collaboration between the AA, who have been producing books of cycle rides around Britain for many years, and Sustrans, the charity behind the award-winning National Cycle Network, a comprehensive network of signed cycleways and walking routes throughout the UK.

The National Cycle Network came into being following the award of the first ever grant from the National Lottery, through the Millennium Commission, in 1995. Funding for the Network also came from the bike retailers and manufacturers through the Bike Hub, as well as local authorities and councils UK-wide. It's interesting to note that dedicated walking and cycling routes cost about £200,000 a mile to build at today's prices, compared to over £29 million for a mile of motorway. Currently there are over 12,000 miles of Network throughout the UK, and it is growing every year.

Over a million journeys a day are made on the Network, taking people to school, to work, to the shops, to visit each other and to seek out green spaces. Half of the journeys are by foot and half by bike, with urban traffic-free sections of the Network seeing the most usage. One of the busiest sections of the National Cycle Network is the Bristol and Bath railway path, the first 'greenway' built by Sustrans along a disused railway line. Over 2.5 million journeys are made every year on the urban sections of route – this is more than 6,500 trips day-in-day-out, or the equivalent of the number of people needed to fill over 200 buses carrying an average of 30 people each.

Over 2,500 Sustrans volunteer rangers assist in the maintenance of the National Cycle Network by adopting sections of route in communities throughout the UK. They clean up glass, litter and dog mess, cut back vegetation and try to ensure routes are well signed, as well as reporting broken lights, poor surfaces and broken signage to local authorities. These efforts have also helped to make the National Cycle Network a haven for wildlife, particularly alongside greenways and waterside paths, which act as green corridors. Many of the UK's rarest species co-exist within the Network, including slow-worms, dormice, bats, owls, newts, skylarks, kingfishers, peregrines, otters and water voles.

The National Cycle Network is host to one of the UK's biggest collections of public artworks. Original earthworks, sculptures, benches, water fountains, viewing points and award-winning bridges enhance its pathways, adding interest and beauty to the routes so that they become even more pleasant and inspiring places to travel along. Due to this commitment to art in the travelling landscape, Sustrans is one of the biggest commissioners of public art (see feature on page 114).

About one-fifth of trips on the Network are made by young people under the age of 16. Many of these journeys are to school, but many more are for play and leisure. Sustrans pioneered the Safe Routes to Schools initiative in the UK, and the Network is one of the many ways to make safety for children possible. Sustrans looks forward to a world in which people are able to choose to travel in ways that benefit their health and the environment, and the National Cycle Network is one of many practical ways that seeks to make this a reality.

We hope that you enjoy using this book to explore the National Cycle Network and we would like to thank the many hundreds of organisations who have worked with Sustrans to develop the walking and cycling routes within these pages, including every local authority and council in the UK.

Malcolm Shepherd, Sustrans CEO, with TV crew △

National Cycle
Network Routes

Kirkwall
Thurso
Wick
Lerwick
Elgin
Inverness
Peterhead
Aberdeen
Fort William
Pitlochry
Oban
Dundee
Perth
St Andrews
Stirling
Glasgow
Edinburgh
Hamilton
Irvine
Berwick-upon-Tweed
Ayr
Galashiels
Campbeltown
Moffat
Dumfries
Coleraine
Londonderry
Newcastle upon Tyne
Antrim
Carlisle
Durham
Omagh
Belfast
Workington
Penrith
Enniskillin
Middlesbrough
Darlington
Newry
Kendal
Thirsk
Scarborough
Douglas
Bridlington
Lancaster
York
Blackpool
Leeds
Kingston upon Hull
Southport
Blackburn
Grimsby
Liverpool
Manchester
Doncaster
Holyhead
Sheffield
Lincoln
Conwy
Macclesfield
Skegness
Chester
Stoke-on-Trent
Caernarfon
Nantwich
Cromer
Nottingham
Shrewsbury
Stafford
Derby
King's Lynn
Newtown
Telford
Leicester
Norwich
Birmingham
Peterborough
Aberystwyth
Coventry
Ely
Newmarket
Worcester
Warwick
Northampton
Cambridge
Ipswich
Hereford
Milton Keynes
Felixstowe
Fishguard
Brecon
Cheltenham
Luton
Colchester
Carmarthen
Gloucester
Stroud
Oxford
Hertford
Newport
Watford
Chelmsford
Tenby
Swindon
London
Swansea
Bristol
Newbury
Reading
Canterbury
Cardiff
Bath
Basingstoke
Bideford
Andover
Guildford
Ashford
Dover
Taunton
Wells
Crawley
Folkestone
Bude
Salisbury
Winchester
Yeovil
Southampton
Hastings
Okehampton
Portsmouth
Brighton
Wadebridge
Exeter
Dorchester
Bournemouth
Eastbourne
Bodmin
Torquay
Weymouth
Truro
St Austell
Plymouth
Penzance
Falmouth

——— National Cycle Network
traffic-free routes

——— National Cycle Network
on-road routes

SOUTH WEST OF ENGLAND

Defined by its extensive coastline, rural character and a stunning variety of scenery from high moorland to lush pastures, the South West of England has much to offer every type of cyclist, whether you are a novice looking for an easy day ride or a well-travelled touring cyclist with several long-distance trips under your belt. This region is home to some of the best-known traffic-free rides in the country, such as the Camel Trail in Cornwall, the Tarka Trail in Devon or the Bristol & Bath Railway Path, Sustrans' first ever project, started almost 30 years ago.

The spine of the National Cycle Network in the West Country is Route 3, running all the way from Bristol, the region's largest city and home of Sustrans' headquarters, to the dramatic Atlantic cliffs at Land's End, a pilgrimage for any cyclist, even if you are not (yet) planning your Land's End to John o' Groats ride. Route 3 links together a remarkable diversity of landscapes, from the rugged Cornish coastline to the dark peat soils of the Somerset Levels via old tin-mining areas, the other-worldly white clay mountains around St Austell, high Exmoor and the Mendips. Shorter rides can be found on the series of traffic-free paths located along the course of Route 3, paths such as the coastal promenade around Mounts Bay near Penzance, the network of trails in Cornwall known as the Mineral Tramways and the Clay Trails, the Tarka Trail in Devon and the canal towpath from Taunton to Bridgwater.

Another principal route in the region is Route 27, running from Plymouth north to Ilfracombe and encompassing three popular family rides: the Plym Valley Trail which climbs steadily from the coast to the edge of Dartmoor, the Granite Way which skirts the northern edge of Dartmoor with amazing views out into the surrounding countryside and the Tarka Trail, dropping gently down to the North Devon coast at Bideford and Barnstaple.

Linking Bristol to London, Route 4 is almost entirely traffic-free for the first 40 miles as far as Devizes, using the Kennet & Avon Canal towpath eastwards from the end of the Bristol & Bath Railway Path, passing between honey-coloured houses built of Oolithic Limestone, most abundantly seen in the Cotswold villages from Bath to Cheltenham. Route 4 begins to the east of Bristol and Route 41 leads north up the Vale of Severn along quiet lanes and the Gloucester & Sharpness Canal to Gloucester.

Running along the South Coast from Cornwall to Kent, Route 2 is still a work in progress although there are already some notable success stories, such as the wide shared-use promenade along the coast at Bournemouth and the development of cyclepaths around the Exe Estuary and Exeter, one of the country's first 'cycle demonstration towns' (a government initiative to prove that increased funding and bespoke projects have a significant impact on levels of cycling).

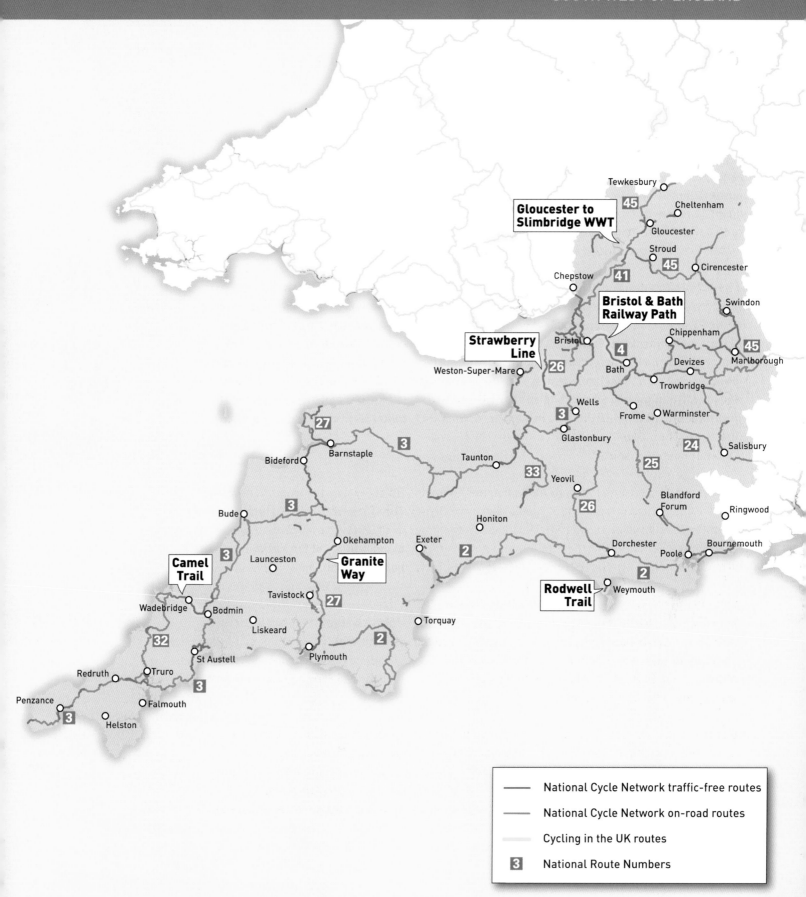

Tewkesbury

45

Cheltenham

Gloucester

Gloucester to
Slimbridge WWT

Stroud

45

Cirencester

Chepstow

41

Swindon

Bristol & Bath
Railway Path

Chippenham

Strawberry
Line

Bristol

4

45

Devizes

Marlborough

Weston-Super-Mare

26

Bath

Trowbridge

Wells

Frome

Warminster

3

Glastonbury

24

Salisbury

27

25

Barnstaple

3

Taunton

Bideford

33

Yeovil

Blandford
Forum

Ringwood

3

26

Bude

Honiton

Okehampton

Exeter

Dorchester

Bournemouth

Camel
Trail

3

Launceston

Granite
Way

2

Poole

Rodwell
Trail

Weymouth

2

Tavistock

27

Wadebridge

Bodmin

Liskeard

Torquay

32

Plymouth

2

St Austell

Redruth

Truro

3

Penzance

3

Falmouth

Helston

CAMEL TRAIL

Cornwall's spectacular Camel Trail is one of Britain's most popular recreational routes and, along with the Eden Project, a 'must-do' activity for visitors to the county. It runs for 18.5 miles (30km) along the course of the old London & South West Railway, from Wenfordbridge near the foot of Bodmin Moor and the wooded countryside of the upper Camel Valley down to Bodmin. The town gets its name from the Cornish 'bod meneghi', meaning 'dwelling of the monks' – St Petroc founded a monastery here in the 6th century.

A spur from Bodmin and the line from Wenfordbridge join and continue on to Wadebridge, which has always been an important settlement in north Cornwall, providing the first crossing of the River Camel. It is claimed that large sacks of wool were used to build the foundations of the medieval bridge. From Wadebridge, the trail runs alongside the picturesque Camel estuary as far as Padstow. This section is a paradise for bird-watchers: there are wonderful views of creeks, sandbanks and rocky shores. Wintering wildfowl include wigeons, long-tailed ducks and goldeneyes. Spring and autumn bring many migrants to the estuary, while in summer you will see little egrets, herons, cormorants, oystercatchers and many gulls.

National Routes: 3 and 32

START Bodmin Jail (former prison), Bodmin town centre.

FINISH Padstow harbour.

DISTANCE
12 miles (19km).
Other options, Wadebridge to Padstow: 6 miles (9.5km); from Wenfordbridge to Padstow, via Bodmin (the whole of the Camel Trail): 18.5 miles (30km)
You may wish to devise your own lane routes from the ends of the trail back to Bodmin. Be warned – it is hilly around here!

GRADE
The Camel Trail itself is easy, running along the course of an old railway line. The link from Bodmin Parkway train station to the start of the trail is fairly strenuous.

SURFACE
Variable, mainly gravel surface, suitable for mountain and hybrid bikes.

HILLS
The section between Bodmin and Padstow is flat. There is a gentle 61-m (200-ft) climb from Bodmin northeast along the Camel Trail to Wenfordbridge. The route between Bodmin Parkway train station and the start of the Camel Trail is hilly, with one particularly steep climb.

YOUNG & INEXPERIENCED CYCLISTS
The Camel Trail is ideal for young children, with lots to see along the way. You have to go through the centre of Wadebridge on streets but there are so many cyclists that traffic does not pose the normal threats. The (hilly) route from Bodmin Parkway train station to the Camel Trail is mostly on-road, and includes the Millennium bridge over the A30. Care should be taken crossing the A389 in Bodmin.

REFRESHMENTS
• Lots of choice in Bodmin, Wadebridge and Padstow.
• Tea shop near Boscarne Junction.
• Wine tastings at Camel Valley Vineyard.
• Borough Arms, Dunmere: cycle-friendly pub with direct

access from the Trail and a dedicated free car park for Trail users.

THINGS TO SEE & DO
BODMIN:
- Bodmin Jail: last county jail in Cornwall, eventually closing in 1927; 01208 76292; www.bodminjail.org
- Bodmin and Wenford Railway: steam train rides; 0845 125 9678; www.bodminandwenfordrailway.co.uk
- Bodmin Museum: 01208 77067; www.bodmin.gov.uk
- Pencarrow House: Georgian House with 50 acres of formal and woodland gardens; 01208 841369; www.pencarrow.co.uk
- Camel Valley Vineyard: wine tastings; 01208 77959; www.camelvalley.com
- Lanhydrock House and gardens: 01208 265950; www.nationaltrust.org.uk (see page 36)
- John Betjeman Centre, Wadebridge: celebration of the life and work of the poet laureate in a restored railway station; 01208 812392; www.johnbetjeman.org.uk

PADSTOW:
- National Lobster Hatchery; 01841 533877; www.nationallobsterhatchery.co.uk
- Prideaux Place: Elizabethan manor house; 01841 532411; www.prideauxplace.co.uk
- Rick Stein's Seafood School and restaurants, Padstow; 01841 532700; www.rickstein.com
- Boat and fishing trips, and ferry to Rock (carries bicycles)

TRAIN STATIONS
Bodmin Parkway.
Bodmin and Boscarne Junction are on the infrequent Bodmin and Wenford tourist line (www.bodminandwenfordrailway.co.uk).

BIKE HIRE
- Bodmin Cycle Hire: 01208 73192; www.bodminbikes.co.uk
- Trail Bike Hire, Padstow: 01841 532594; www.trailbikehire.co.uk
- Padstow Cycle Hire: 01841 533533; www.padstowcyclehire.co.uk

- Bridge Bike Hire, Wadebridge: 01208 813050; www.bridgebikehire.co.uk
- Bridge Cycle Hire, Wadebridge: 01208 814545

FURTHER INFORMATION

- To view or print National Cycle Network routes, visit www.sustrans.org.uk
- Maps for this area are available to buy from www.sustransshop.co.uk
- Dedicated Camel Trail information at www.destination-cornwall.co.uk
- Cornwall Tourist Information: 01208 265632; www.visitnorthcornwall.com

ROUTE DESCRIPTION

From the old jail in Bodmin, follow the Camel Trail along the course of an old railway line, through the wooded valley of the River Camel towards the busy market town of Wadebridge. From Wadebridge, the trail follows the sandy shores of the Camel estuary, with wonderful views of creeks, sandbanks and rocky shores, until the attractive harbour town of Padstow. If you lock your bike

in Padstow, you can continue on foot along the coast path to Stepper Point to experience magnificent views. Bikes can be taken on the ferry from Padstow to Rock to explore the lanes to Chapel Amble and on to Wadebridge to complete a circumnavigation of the estuary.

In addition to there-and-back rides along the Camel Trail, you could make loops using the network of country lanes, to explore the coastline east of the estuary at Port Isaac, Polzeath and Rock, or west of Bodmin to Ruthernbridge, Rosenannon and beyond. Bear in mind that you are likely to be faced with short sharp climbs!

NEARBY CYCLE ROUTES

The Camel Trail is part of the Cornish Way (National Routes 3 and 32) and the start/finish of the West Country Way (National Route 3), which runs from Padstow to Bristol and Bath.

The Camel Trail can be used to reach other options:
- Mountain bikers can access Bishop and Hustyn Woods from the Trail at Polbrock Bridge, 3 miles (5km) from

BODMIN

Wadebridge, towards Bodmin (National Route 32).
- Head south from Bodmin to Lanhydrock House, 3 miles (5km), and on to the Eden Project, 8 miles (13km), reached through the idyllic Luxulyan Valley (National Route 3).

- There are forest trails in Cardinham Woods, east of Bodmin, and also a signed link running from the Camel Trail to the Cornwall Showground, but this involves a strenuous climb.

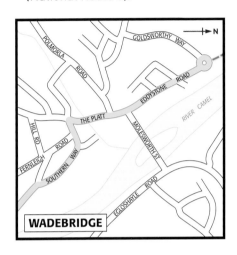

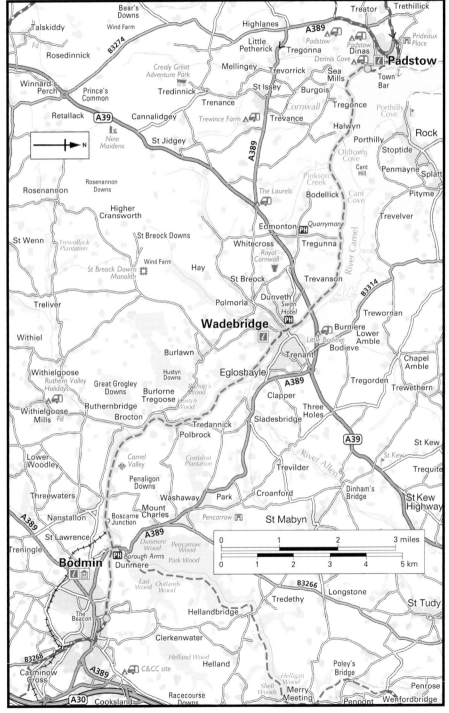

GRANITE WAY

Climbing gently to a highpoint of 290m (950ft) on the western flanks of Dartmoor, this long stretch of railway path offers wonderful views into the heart of the National Park and out over the rolling Devon countryside that lies to the north of Okehampton.

Set above the town, Okehampton train station is a wonderfully preserved time capsule from a bygone age. The ride starts from here and runs parallel with the railway line to the spectacular steel viaduct at Meldon, built in 1874 and spanning 104m (341ft). Southwest of Meldon, the trail continues past the largely 15th-century Sourton Church and over a second vast viaduct at Lake, this one made of stone.

The extensive granite plateau of Dartmoor is an ancient volcanic region where the rocks have been eroded into the dramatic profiles of the tors. The area is the setting for Sir Arthur Conan Doyle's famous novel *The Hound of the Baskervilles*.

National Route: 27

START Okehampton train station.

FINISH Lydford Castle.

DISTANCE 12 miles (19.5km).

GRADE
Easy on the railway path, which is the longest section. The lane section from Lake to Bridestowe is more strenuous.

SURFACE
Tarmac, except for a rough track leading down from Lake Viaduct to the main road.

HILLS
Gentle climb towards the centre of the ride (the highpoint is between Meldon Viaduct and Sourton church) from both ends. If you cycle to Lydford by lane, there is a steep climb south of Bridestowe.

YOUNG & INEXPERIENCED CYCLISTS
The route is traffic-free as far as Lake Viaduct. On the road section towards Bridestowe, great care is needed

crossing the A386 by the Bearslake Inn (Lake). The lane network through Bridestowe is relatively quiet. The A386 alternative between the end of the railway path and Shortacombe (about 1 mile/1.6km) should be attempted only by experienced cyclists and requires pushing your bike for the first 75m (82 yd) along a short linking section.

REFRESHMENTS
- Several pubs, cafes and restaurants in Okehampton.
- Highwayman Inn, just off the route in Sourton.
- Bearslake Inn, Lake; also does cream teas.
- White Hart Inn, Bridestowe.
- Castle Inn, Lydford.

THINGS TO SEE & DO
- Museum of Dartmoor Life, Okehampton; www.museumofdartmoorlife.eclipse.co.uk
- Okehampton Castle: remains of the largest castle in Devon; www.english-heritage.org.uk
- Sourton Church: 14th–16th-century church.
- Dartmoor Railway: 15-mile (24-km) long railway line operating on the route of the old Southern Railway, from Crediton to Okehampton and Meldon Quarry; 01837 55667; www.dartmoorrailway.co.uk
- Meldon Viaduct: a Victorian wrought and cast iron structure from 1874, re-opened in 2002; www.meldonviaduct.co.uk
- Lake Viaduct: built of local stone and offering

GRANITE WAY

spectacular views of the Moor;
www.meldonviaduct.co.uk
• Lydford Gorge: the deepest gorge in the Southwest, with a spectacular 30-m (99-ft) waterfall; reduced entrance fee for those arriving by bike; 01822 820320; www.nationaltrust.org.uk
• Ruins of a 12th-century castle in Lydford; www.english-heritage.org.uk

TRAIN STATIONS Okehampton.

BIKE HIRE
Devon Cycle Hire, Sourton Down: 01837 861141; www.devoncyclehire.co.uk

FURTHER INFORMATION
• To view or print National Cycle Network routes, visit www.sustrans.org.uk
• Maps for this area are available to buy from www.sustransshop.co.uk
• Okehampton Tourist Information: 01837 53020; www.okehamptondevon.co.uk

ROUTE DESCRIPTION
The ride starts from Okehampton train station and runs alongside the railway line as far as Meldon Viaduct. It continues along the course of the old railway line, past Sourton Church and over a second vast viaduct at Lake.

Beyond, there is a section of the old railway land still in private ownership, so if you choose to go on to Lydford, where there are attractive walks along Lydford Gorge, you will need to use the road network. You have four options:

• Stay on the railway path and stop for a picnic at Lake Viaduct or go just beyond Southerley Halt, then retrace your steps back to Okehampton;
• Drop down from Lake Viaduct on a track to the pub at Lake, then come back up to the railway path;
• Use waymarked National Route 27 on (fairly hilly) minor lanes via Bridestowe to rejoin the railway path and continue on to Lydford;
• If you are an experienced cyclist, use a 1-mile (1.6-km) section of the busy A386 to access the southernmost section of the railway path into Lydford.

NEARBY CYCLE ROUTES
This ride is part of National Route 27, the Devon Coast-to-Coast Cycle Route from Ilfracombe to Plymouth. North of Okehampton, the route uses lanes through Hatherleigh and Sheepwash to reach the Tarka Trail near Petrockstowe, where it links with National Route 3, the West Country Way. Beyond Lydford, Route 27 heads for Tavistock and Plymouth.

OTHER WAYMARKED OR TRAFFIC-FREE RIDES INCLUDE:
• The traffic-free Tarka Trail, which starts at Meeth, on the A386, about 10 miles (16km) north of Okehampton.

- Forest trails in Abbeyford Woods, just north of Okehampton.
- The Military Road, to the south of Okehampton Camp, a tough but spectacular 10-mile (16-km) loop on mainly tarmac roads into the very heart of Dartmoor.

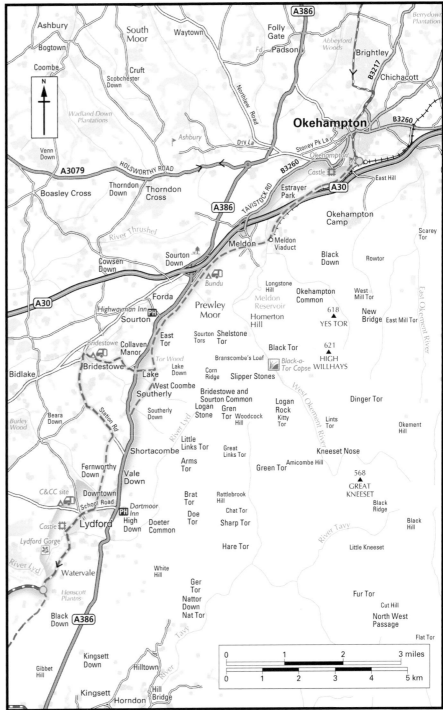

BRISTOL & BATH RAILWAY PATH

The Bristol & Bath Railway path was the first major project carried out by Sustrans and now, more than 20 years later, has over a million visits a year. The tarmac path runs from the heart of Bristol to the outskirts of Bath, climbing gently to pass through the tunnel at Staple Hill, skirting the old station at Bitton, with its fine array of steam trains, and crossing the River Avon several times as it approaches Bath. In springtime, the broad-leaved woodland of Kelston Woods is carpeted with bluebells. There are many remarkable sculptures along the way, such as a massive brick fish standing on its head, and a drinking giant.

The cities of Bristol and Bath stand in direct contrast to each other. Bristol is a 'muscular' city, the largest in the west of England, an ancient port built on trade and, latterly, on aerospace industries and financial services. Bath, on the other hand, is an elegant city dating back to Roman times, when it was a prosperous spa known as Aquae Sulis. In building its golden-stoned crescents in the 18th century, the architect John Wood created the prosperous city that 'Beau' Nash made the focus for high society in the Regency era. Today, it is a World Heritage City.

National Route: 4

START Castle Park, Bristol, or Bristol Temple Meads train station.

FINISH Bath Abbey.

DISTANCE
16 miles (26km).
Shorter options, from Bristol to Warmley: 6 miles (9.5km); to Bitton: 8.5 miles (13.5km); to Saltford: 11 miles (17.5km).

GRADE Easy.

SURFACE Tarmac.

HILLS None.

YOUNG & INEXPERIENCED CYCLISTS
Most of the path is traffic-free and ideal for children and beginners. The signposted approach roads from both Bristol and Bath city centres carry some traffic.

REFRESHMENTS
• Lots of choice in Bristol.
• Cafes on the railway path at Warmley (seasonal) and at Bitton Station (open daily all year round).
• The Midland Spinner pub, Warmley.
• Bird in Hand and Jolly Sailor pubs (0.5 mile/ 0.8km from path), Saltford.
• Dolphin pub, Locksbrook, Bath.
• Lots of choice in Bath.

THINGS TO SEE & DO
BRISTOL:
• Bristol Cathedral; 0117 926 4879; www.bristol-cathedral.co.uk
• Explore-At-Bristol: interactive science exhibits and activities, including a planetarium; 0845 345 1235; www.at-bristol.org.uk
• Arnolfini and Watershed Art and Media Centres: both situated on the docks, with exhibitions, cinema and cafe. Arnolfini: 0117 9172300; www.arnolfini.org.uk. Watershed: 0117 927 5100; www.watershed.co.uk
• Bristol Museum: houses a vast permanent collection,

with changing temporary programmes; 0117 922 3571; www.bristol.gov.uk
- Clifton Suspension Bridge: Grade I listed structure spanning Avon Gorge, designed by Brunel; 0117 974 4664; www.clifton-suspension-bridge.org.uk
- SS *Great Britain*: first launched in 1843 and built by Brunel, the ship is now an award-winning tourist attraction showing life on board in Victorian times; 0117 926 0680; www.ssgreatbritain.org
- Bitton station: steam railway, with themed days; 0117 932 5538; www.avonvalleyrailway.org
- Artworks en route: there are a number of sculptures to spot between inner Bristol and Bitton.

BATH:
- Thermae Bath Spa: day spa, offering pools with natural thermal waters and spa treatments; 0844 888 0844; www.thermaebathspa.com
- Roman Baths: magnificent temple and bathing complex, which still flows with natural hot water; 01225 477785; www.romanbaths.co.uk
- Assembly Rooms: Georgian public rooms and home to the Fashion Museum; 01225 477173; www.nationaltrust.org.uk
- Bath Abbey: founded in 1499 and completed in 1611; 01225 422462; www.bathabbey.org
- Sally Lunn's House: the oldest house in Bath and home of the original Bath bun; 01225 461634; www.sallylunns.co.uk
- No.1 Royal Crescent: restored Georgian town house; 01225 428126; www.bath-preservation-trust.org.uk

TRAIN STATIONS
Bristol Temple Meads; Bath Spa.

BIKE HIRE
- Blackboy Cycles, Bristol: 0117 973 1420; www.blackboycycles.co.uk
- Webbs of Warmley Cycle Hire: 0117 967 3676; www.bristolcycles.co.uk
- Specialized Concept Store, Bristol: 0117 929 7368

FURTHER INFORMATION
- To view or print National Cycle Network routes, visit

BRISTOL & BATH RAILWAY PATH

www.sustrans.org.uk
- Maps for this area are available to buy from www.sustransshop.co.uk
- Bristol Tourist Information: 0333 321 0101; www. visitbristol.co.uk
- Bath Tourist Information: 0906 711 2000; www. visitbath.co.uk

ROUTE DESCRIPTION

Pick up the route at Castle Park in the centre of Bristol. Alternatively, from Temple Meads train station, cross the new bridge, which is reached via the car park at the rear of the station, into Avon Street. The route then goes through the Dings Home Zone and an industrial area before joining the railway path near Lawrence Hill. From Lawrence Hill, it then loops north towards Fishponds, travelling through east Bristol and continuing through Staple Hill Tunnel, which is lit from 5am to 8.30pm.

The path then continues through Mangotsfield, Warmley and Bitton, running parallel for a while with the steam railway line. The final section goes through Saltford before reaching Newbridge, in Bath. You follow a riverside path that takes you into the centre of Bath and towards Bath Spa train station. There are local cycle routes that will take you into the city centre.

From Bath, you could continue on the canal towpath to Bradford on Avon or follow the Colliers Way to Radstock and Frome.

NEARBY CYCLE ROUTES

National Route 4 runs from South Wales to London and uses the whole of the railway path. Together, National Routes 4 and 41 form the Severn & Thames Cycle Route from Gloucester to Newbury. National Route 3, the West Country Way and the Cornish Way, heads southwest from Bristol to the furthest tip of Britain at Land's End.

OTHER WAYMARKED OR TRAFFIC-FREE RIDES INCLUDE:
- The section of the railway path between Saltford and Mangotsfield, which forms a part of the Avon Cycleway, an 85-mile (137-km) signposted route using the network of quiet lanes around Bristol.

- The 5-mile (8-km), traffic-free Pill Riverside Path, which runs from the Bristol Harbourside along Cumberland Road, then alongside the River Avon to Pill, passing beneath the Clifton Suspension Bridge. There is also a link to this path through Leigh Woods.

- The Kennet & Avon Canal Towpath, a beautiful route from Bath to Devizes via Bradford-on-Avon.
- The canal towpath from Bath to Dundas Aqueduct, which joins National Route 24 to Radstock and Frome on the Colliers Way.

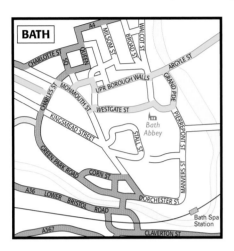

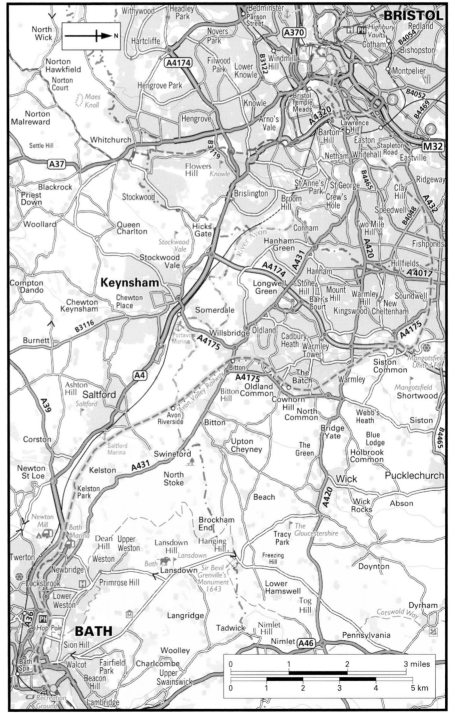

GLOUCESTER TO SLIMBRIDGE WILDFOWL & WETLANDS TRUST (WWT)

To the south of the cathedral city of Gloucester, the towpath of the Gloucester & Sharpness Canal offers an excellent escape route into the countryside, with the Cotswold Hills running parallel away to the east. Opened in 1827 to bypass a treacherous and winding stretch of the River Severn, the canal was at the time the widest and deepest in the country. This greatly increased construction costs but with the result that the canal remains in use today, and Sharpness Docks and Gloucester are still commercial ports.

From the Rea Bridge, you have a choice of two routes: one on quiet lanes with fine views across the Severn to the Forest of Dean or, if you are on a mountain bike, of continuing along the canal towpath, which can be rough at times. Both options take you to Frampton on Severn, with its vast village green, attractive old houses, pubs and shops. South from here, an improved section of the towpath leads directly to Shepherd's Patch and the minor road to Slimbridge Wildfowl & Wetlands Trust, one of the most important wildfowl sites in Britain.

National Route: 41

START Gloucester Docks (Llanthony Road), in the heart of the city.

FINISH Slimbridge Wildfowl & Wetlands Trust.

DISTANCE 14 miles (22.5km).

GRADE Easy.

SURFACE
Good-quality stone towpath from Gloucester to Rea Bridge, but beyond here it can be quite rough. The alternative is to use the waymarked National Route 41 on quiet lanes to Frampton on Severn.

HILLS None.

YOUNG & INEXPERIENCED CYCLISTS
The towpath section from the centre of Gloucester to Rea Bridge is traffic-free. The lane option south from Rea Bridge to Frampton on Severn has very little traffic.

REFRESHMENTS
- Lots of choice in the centre of Gloucester.
- The Anchor Inn, Epney.
- Ship Inn, Upper Framilode.
- The Bell Inn and village shops at Frampton upon Severn.
- Cafe at the Wildfowl & Wetlands Trust, Slimbridge.
- Tudor Arms, Slimbridge.

THINGS TO SEE & DO
GLOUCESTER:
- Gloucester Cathedral: dating from 1089; 01452 521957; www.gloucestercathedral.org.uk
- National Waterways Museum; 01452 318 200; www.nwm.org.uk
- Gloucester Docks; www.visit-gloucestershire.co.uk
- Wildfowl & Wetlands Trust HQ, Slimbridge: home to the world's largest collection of swans, geese and ducks; ample bike parking and impressive visitor centre and cafe; 01453 891900; www.wwt.org.uk
- Severn Bore: a form of tidal wave, caused by each incoming tide funnelling into shallower water, which

can result in a bore up to 2m (6.5ft) high, travelling at speeds of 10 miles/hour (16km/h). The road at Stonebench is an excellent site to see the Bore at its most impressive. Check times in advance. 01452 421188; www.environment-agency.gov.uk

TRAIN STATIONS

Gloucester; Cam & Dursley.

FURTHER INFORMATION

- To view or print National Cycle Network routes, visit www.sustrans.org.uk
- Maps for this area are available to buy from www.sustransshop.co.uk
- Gloucester Tourist Information: 01452 396572; www.gloucester.gov.uk/tourism

ROUTE DESCRIPTION

From Llanthony Road at the Gloucester Docks, take the traffic-free path, on the west of the water, southwards. You follow this towpath through the outskirts of Gloucester towards the residential area of Quedgeley. Where the path ramps up to Rea bridge after passing under the new bridge carrying the Gloucester by-pass, you have the choice of using the waymarked National Route 41 on quiet lanes or, if you are on a mountain bike, continuing along the canal towpath.

Both options take you through the village of Frampton on Severn from where you rejoin the canal towpath to Slimbridge and the Wildfowl & Wetlands Trust. From here, you can continue on minor roads through Slimbridge village to Cam & Dursley train station and catch a train back to Gloucester.

NEARBY CYCLE ROUTES

This route is on National Route 41, which runs from Bristol to Gloucester, and will eventually continue to Stratford-upon-Avon and Rugby.

OTHER WAYMARKED OR TRAFFIC-FREE RIDES INCLUDE:
- National Route 42 from Gloucester Docks to the village of Highnam or until Telford's old humpback stone bridge and take the diversion to Maisemore village.

From here, quiet lanes could be followed north towards Tewkesbury.
- A traffic-free circuit in the Forest of Dean, about 15 miles (24km) southwest of Gloucester.
- The Stroud Valleys Cycle Trail, a 5-mile (8-km) railway

path running north from Nailsworth. The trail is part of National Route 45 to Cirencester, beyond which there are several traffic-free trails in Cotswold Water Park, to the south of Cirencester.

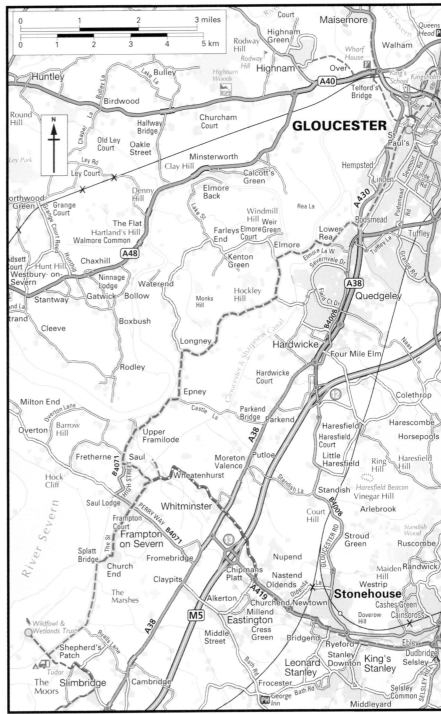

STRAWBERRY LINE

The branch line between Yatton and Cheddar was built in 1869 as part of the Great Western Railway and is known as the Strawberry Line because of its delicious cargo from the strawberry fields of Cheddar. The line was well used by passengers and to carry freight until it was closed in 1965, and since then a wealth of wildlife habitats have been allowed to flourish. Volunteers from the Cheddar Valley Railway Walk Society started work on converting the line to a walking and cycling route in 1983 and now it forms a 10-mile (16-km), almost traffic-free route through the picturesque villages of north Somerset.

Parts of the route have recently been re-surfaced, and on-going improvements will see the current road section through Sandford replaced with a traffic-free path behind Thatchers cider farm in 2009. This ride has no steep gradients and takes in a variety of landscapes, including the flat marshes and cider apple orchards around Yatton, a steep wooded cutting and a tunnel through the Mendips to historic Axbridge, with its picturesque streets. A magnificent perpendicular church and timbered houses surround Axbridge's spacious market square. The route ends in Cheddar, near the foot of spectacular Cheddar Gorge.

National Route: 26

START Yatton train station.

FINISH Cheddar Gorge.

DISTANCE
10 miles (16km).
Shorter options, from Yatton to Axbridge: 8 miles (13km); from Axbridge to Cheddar: 2 miles (3km).

GRADE Easy.

SURFACE
Generally firm compacted grit. Some muddy sections near Yatton when wet.

HILLS None.

YOUNG & INEXPERIENCED CYCLISTS
The route is mainly traffic-free, although care is needed on crossing and using short sections of busy roads at Congresbury, Sandford and Axbridge, and crossing the A38 after Winscombe.

REFRESHMENTS
- Pubs and cafes in Yatton, Winscombe, Axbridge and Cheddar; also in Congresbury (slightly off route and care needed on main road into the town).
- Thatchers Cider Shop and pub in Sandford.
- Good picnic area on Millennium Green, Winscombe.

THINGS TO SEE & DO
- Biddle Street: Site of Special Scientific Interest (SSSI) just outside Yatton, drained by a network of ditches that act as wet fences between the fields; look out for dragonflies and reed and sedge warblers; www.english-nature.org.uk
- Thatchers cider shop: try or buy Thatchers cider, made in Sandford from local apples; 01934 822862; www.thatcherscider.co.uk
- Millennium Green, Winscombe: picnic area converted

DRAU

5 LITR

WITH CONT

2·5 LITRES

WITH CONTA

1 GALLON

5 GALLON BARREL £25·

BARREL DEPOSIT £1

DRAUGHT CIDER WILL

APPROX 7·10 DAYS

from the old station, largely by a group of volunteers; includes sculpture crafted from local limestone and a timeline of brass plaques along the old platform edge; a May Fair is usually held on the green each year.

• Axbridge: picturesque town that has changed little over the centuries; visitors can wander around the medieval streets and soak up hundreds of years of history.

• King John's Hunting Lodge, Axbridge: local history museum in a 16th-century wool-merchant's house; 01934 732012; www.nationaltrust.org.uk

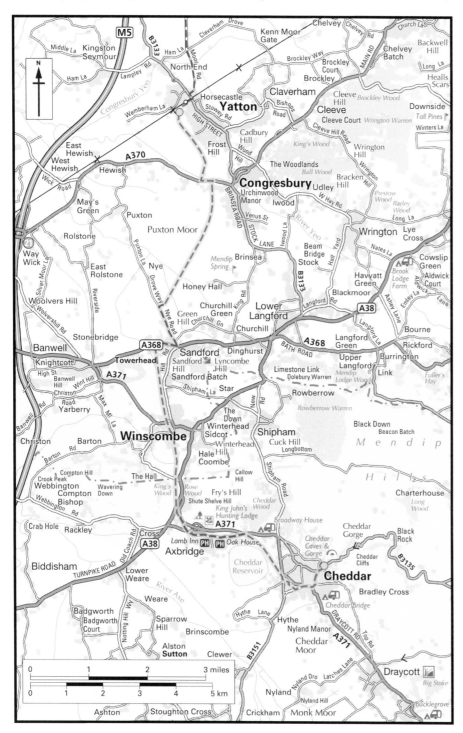

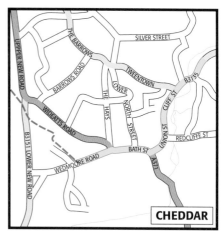

CHEDDAR

- Cheddar Gorge and Caves: highest inland cliffs in the country, reaching 152m (500ft); Cheddar Caves were inhabited by our early ancestors 40,000 years ago, and Britain's oldest complete skeleton, Cheddar Man, is on display; 01934 742343; www.cheddarcaves.co.uk

TRAIN STATIONS Yatton.

BIKE HIRE
Cheddar Cycle Store: 01934 741300; www.cheddarcyclestore.co.uk

FURTHER INFORMATION
- To view or print National Cycle Network routes, visit www.sustrans.org.uk
- Maps for this area are available to buy from www.sustransshop.co.uk
- www.thestrawberryline.co.uk

- Cheddar Tourist Information: 01934 744071; www.visitsomerset.co.uk

ROUTE DESCRIPTION
Exit Yatton train station from Platform 1 and turn right. At the end of the car park, you will see the artworks that mark the start of the path – it's a fairly straightforward route from here. The track is a little rough and can be muddy after rain, but surface improvements are in the pipeline. After crossing the River Yeo, the path comes out onto the main A370 on the approach to Congresbury and you need to turn left onto the main road for a few metres before using the pedestrian crossing to rejoin the traffic-free route. (For refreshments or toilets, you can continue on the main road into Congresbury but be careful, as there may be fast and heavy traffic.)

Continue through green and leafy woodland before emerging into the open countryside. You reach a quiet road taking you into Sandford, where you turn right onto the A368 for a short distance. Rejoin the traffic-free path indicated by the sign just after the pedestrian crossing.

After a pleasant stretch, you come to the old station at Winscombe, with its Millennium Green. A little further on is Shute Shelve Tunnel – although there is some lighting to guide you, you may want to switch on your bike lights. Soon after, you need to cross the A38 with care. Follow the signs on the path and then on roads to Axbridge, and rejoin the path after the town. The path winds through a housing estate before ending rather unceremoniously in an industrial estate. Continue by road into the town of Cheddar, with its famous Gorge and cave system, and even more famous cheese!

NEARBY CYCLE ROUTES
National Route 2 runs from Purbeck to Dorchester, then continues westward some way inland from the coast. The route is mainly on quiet roads, but the section past Maiden Castle is off-road and quite rough. National Route 26 runs west and north from Dorchester to Yeovil and Sherborne. The route is mostly on quiet roads, but the first 8 miles (13km) to Maiden Newton includes off-road sections up the River Frome valley.

RODWELL TRAIL

The Rodwell Trail connects Weymouth to Portland and is a pleasant route along the course of a dismantled railway. It stops at the Ferrybridge Inn on the Portland Road, and currently onward travel to Portland Bill is recommended only for experienced cyclists.

Some people have called the Isle of Portland Dorset's very own Rock of Gibraltar; a limestone peninsula jutting 4 miles (6.5km) out into the English Channel. The area has been heavily quarried over many centuries – Portland stone is highly prized, and has been used for many important public buildings, including St Paul's Cathedral, Buckingham Palace and even the headquarters of the United Nations in New York.

Portland Castle was built by Henry VIII in the 16th century to protect Weymouth against possible attack from France and Spain. In the Victorian era, it was the private residence of Charles Mannering, who was responsible for building the breakwater harbour, the largest of its kind in the world. The harbour is a popular spot for windsurfing and sailing, and will host sailing events in the 2012 Olympics.

START The Esplanade, Weymouth.

FINISH Ferrybridge Inn, at the Weymouth end of Portland Road.

DISTANCE 2.25 miles (3.5km).

GRADE Easy.

SURFACE Tarmac.

HILLS None.

YOUNG & INEXPERIENCED CYCLISTS
The trail itself is ideal for novices and young children. From Weymouth train station, there is an on-road section with a short section on a busy road, which you may want to walk. Continuing on to Portland Bill, the cycle path is narrow and adjacent to the road, with fast-moving traffic between Southwell and Portland Bill, and very steep through Fortuneswell.

REFRESHMENTS
• Ferrybridge Inn, Weymouth.

THE SEA COW
Free House
Bar
licensed restaurant
KODEN
W214 JJT
L213 MSK
WH 296

- Cafe on old Castle Road next to Sandsfoot Castle (seasonal opening).

THINGS TO SEE & DO

- Radipole Lake, Weymouth: nature reserve, with a good bird-watching site in the centre of the town; www.rspb.org.uk
- Sandsfoot Castle and Gardens: remains of castle, which dates back to 1539; beach close by; www.weymouth.gov.uk
- Whitehead's Torpedo Factory: built in 1891 by the 'father' of the underwater torpedo, Robert Whitehead; www.weymouth.gov.uk
- Portland Castle: 16th-century fortress overlooking Portland harbour; can be seen from the end of the Trail but access requires you to continue on the busy Portland Road alongside Chesil Beach; www.english-heritage.org.uk

TRAIN STATIONS

Weymouth.

BIKE HIRE

Weymouth Bike Hire: 01305 834951; www.weymouthbikehire.com

FURTHER INFORMATION

- To view or print National Cycle Network routes, visit www.sustrans.org.uk
- Maps for this area are available to buy from www.sustransshop.co.uk
- Weymouth Tourist Information: 01305 785747; www.visitweymouth.co.uk

ROUTE DESCRIPTION

From King's Statue on the Esplanade in Weymouth, take Westham Road to the bridge by the marina. Cross it and continue straight, taking the underpass under the A353 to reach Abbotsbury Road.

Alternatively, from the Swannery car park, go under Swannery Bridge and along the Backwater to reach Westham Bridge and follow the route as above.

From Abbotsbury Road, cycle along the path until you reach Newstead Road, where you will have to leave and rejoin the trail (Sustrans is working on a scheme that will solve this problem).

Shortly after this you will pass the World War II gun emplacement viewing point. At Wyke Road, you go through a tunnel and then pass by what used to be Rodwell train station. At Sandsfoot Halt, you could take

a detour to Sandsfoot Castle and Gardens. A little further on, there are great views of Portland Harbour from the sailing club. Towards the end of the trail, you pass the site of Whitehead's Torpedo Factory. The trail ends at the Ferry Bridge Inn on Portland Road.

NEARBY CYCLE ROUTES

National Route 2 goes from Wareham via Dorchester to Axminster. From Dorchester, National Route 26 goes north to Castle Cary.

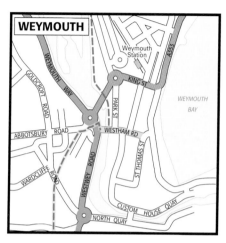

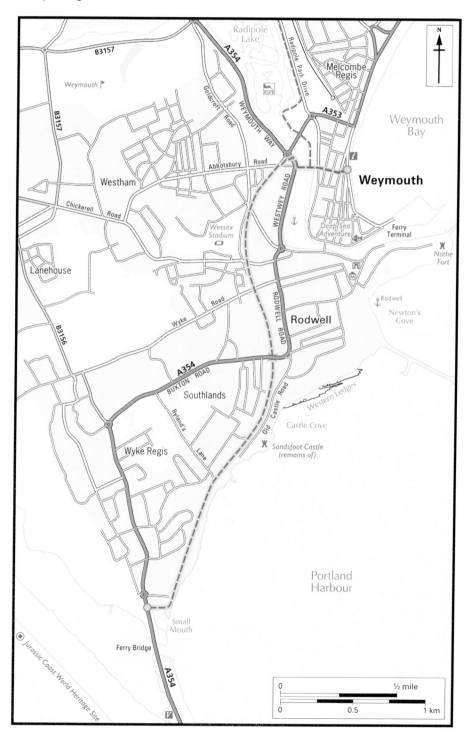

CYCLE ROUTES TO NATIONAL TRUST PROPERTIES

The National Trust was founded in 1895 as a guardian for the nation in the acquisition and protection of threatened coastline, countryside and buildings. More than a century later, the Trust cares for over 612,000 acres of beautiful countryside in England, Wales and Northern Ireland, plus more than 700 miles (1,126km) of coastline and more than 200 buildings and gardens of outstanding interest and importance. The Trust looks after places that connect the present and future with the past: from ancient stone circles and Victorian cotton mills to gardens, village streets and castles, these places are alive with history. The National Trust is a registered charity and completely independent of Government, relying on the generosity of its 3.5 million members.

CYCLING & THE NATIONAL TRUST

The majority of Trust properties are easily accessible by bike, with many now linked to the National Cycle Network. Most properties have cycle parking on-site or nearby. A link to a map of cycle routes in the area is held in each property's individual web pages. Just click on 'Getting there' and the 'Local cycle routes' link to access a property-centred map on the Sustrans website. Look out for the bicycle icon in the property information to see which properties have cycle routes.

LANHYDROCK

Located to the southeast of Bodmin in the heart of Cornwall, and just off National Route 3 (the Cornish Way), Lanhydrock is the perfect historic country house and estate. Explore the high-Victorian interiors of this wealthy but unpretentious home and discover evidence of the Robartes family all around the house. Generations of the family have walked in the Long Gallery, contemplating historic events such as the English Civil War, the Jacobite Rebellion or World War I. The gatehouse and north wing, housing the Long Gallery with its biblical plasterwork ceiling – children enjoy spotting all the familiar stories and characters – are 17th century, while the rest of the house was restored after a fire in 1881, to include the

latest advances in design and technology. There are 50 rooms to explore, with the servants' quarters and 'below stairs' particularly evocative. The garden is Victorian, with a magnificent collection of magnolias, camellias and rhododendrons, and it is full of colour all year. Beyond, you can follow numerous paths through woods and parkland down to the banks of the River Fowey, haunt of otters and kingfishers. There is also an adventure playground, with a wobbly bridge. There are reduced admission charges when arriving by bike.
Tel: 01208 265950
Email: lanhydrock@nationaltrust.org.uk
www.nationaltrust.org.uk/main/w-lanhydrock

LINDISFARNE

Lying 10 miles (16km) south of Berwick-upon-Tweed, just off National Route 1 (the Coast & Castles Cycle Route) and connected to the beautiful Northumberland Coast by a causeway that is covered at high tide, Lindisfarne is a romantic 16th-century castle, transformed by the young Edwin Lutyens in 1903 into an Edwardian holiday home. Perched dramatically on a rocky crag, the island castle presents an exciting and alluring aspect. The small rooms are full of intimate decoration, with windows looking down on the charming walled garden planned by Gertrude Jekyll. There are fantastic views of Farne Island and Bamburgh Castle. The property also has several extremely well-preserved 19th-century lime kilns.
Tel: 01289 389244
Email: lindisfarne@nationaltrust.org.uk
www.nationaltrust.org.uk/main/w-lindisfarnecastle

POWIS CASTLE

Situated just to the west of Welshpool in Mid Wales and lying right on the course of National Route 81 (Lôn Cambria), medieval Powis Castle rises dramatically above its celebrated garden. Overhung with enormous clipped yews, the garden shelters tender plants and sumptuous herbaceous borders. Italian and French styles have influenced its design, and it retains its original lead

1 Veteran beech trees on the estate at Lanhydrock, Cornwall 2 The kitchen scullery at Lanhydrock, Cornwall 3 View of the rocky crag and causeway below Lindisfarne Castle 4 Upturned boats converted into huts at Lindisfarne Castle 5 Statue of a shepherd by John Van Nost at Powis Castle 6 View from the terrace at Powis Castle 7 Kings Room, Falkland Palace 8 Falkland Palace and gardens

statues, an orangery and an aviary on the terraces. In the 18th century, an informal woodland wilderness was created on the opposite ridge. High on a rock above the terraces, the castle, originally built c.1200, began life as a fortress of the Welsh Princes of Powys and commands magnificent views towards England. Remodelled and embellished over more than 400 years, it reflects the changing needs and ambitions of the Herbert family, with each generation adding to the collection of paintings, sculpture, furniture and tapestries. A superb collection of treasures from India is displayed in the Clive Museum.
Tel: 01938 551944 (Infoline) or 01938 551929
www.nationaltrust.org.uk/main/w-powiscastle_garden

NATIONAL TRUST FOR SCOTLAND

The National Trust for Scotland was established in 1931, to act as guardian of the nation's heritage of architectural, scenic and historic treasures.

FALKLAND PALACE

Located in Fife, midway between Edinburgh and Dundee and right on the course of National Route 1, Falkland Palace is the only Royal Palace in the care of the National Trust for Scotland. It is an impressive Renaissance building, set in the heart of the town at the foot of the Lomond Hills. Built by James IV and James V between 1450 and 1541, the Palace was a country residence of the Stuart monarchs of Scotland for over 200 years. Lush green lawns, colourful herbaceous borders and many unusual shrubs and trees complete the setting for this memorable property.
Tel: 0844 493 2186
www.nts.org.uk/Property/93

SOUTH EAST OF ENGLAND

As the South East of England is the most densely populated and wealthiest region of the United Kingdom there is higher car ownership and more traffic here than in any other part of the country, hence the importance of the National Cycle Network in the area, offering attractive alternatives to the busy roads. It is a region full of pretty villages and some of the country's most stunning buildings such as the Oxford colleges, Windsor Castle, the Royal Pavilion at Brighton or the cathedrals at Winchester, Chichester and Canterbury, not to mention the architectural splendours of London. The good news is that the National Cycle Network takes you safely to all of these places.

The South East should not be judged just by its towns and villages, however: the rolling chalk hills of the North and South Downs offer some wonderful walks and rides, the New Forest is criss-crossed with trails allowing you to explore the broadleaf woodlands and get up close to the New Forest ponies and the Chiltern Hills are a delight all year round but especially so in the autumn with the changing colours. The gently flowing River Thames, another natural feature, is a linking theme for much of the Network to the west of the capital.

For those looking for long-distance challenges there are two routes to the south of London that together describe a circuit from Greenwich in central London, eastwards through Kent past Canterbury's famous cathedral and the Garden of England's fruit orchards to the coast at Sandwich Bay. Ever more of the route is traffic-free south from Deal to the white cliffs of Dover then west towards Brighton. The main exception to the traffic-free trails is the wonderful network of quiet lanes that cross the level pastures of Romney Marsh. From Brighton the route heads north over the South Downs, the Sussex Weald and North Downs to return to Greenwich. An alternative cuts inland from the seaside resort of Eastbourne, north to Heathfield along the Cuckoo Trail, the most popular traffic-free railway path in the South East. After a short hilly lane section to the north of the Cuckoo Trail, the Forest Way and Worth Way railway paths whisk you through East Grinstead to rejoin the Brighton to London route in Crawley.

Route 4 to the west of London starts from Putney Bridge. The route closely follows the River Thames past the magnificent buildings of Hampton Court Palace as far as Egham, before diverting via Windsor Great Park with its stunning views of Windsor Castle. The Chilterns are crossed to the north of Reading before the river is rejoined for the last section into the heart of Oxford.

Three other highlights of the National Cycle Network in the South East of England should be mentioned: the cyclists' paradise around Milton Keynes (if you don't believe it, just go there and try it!), the smooth towpath of the Kennet & Avon Canal west of Reading to Newbury and the various traffic-free trails on the Isle of Wight, including the UK's easiest coast to coast ride from Cowes to Sandown.

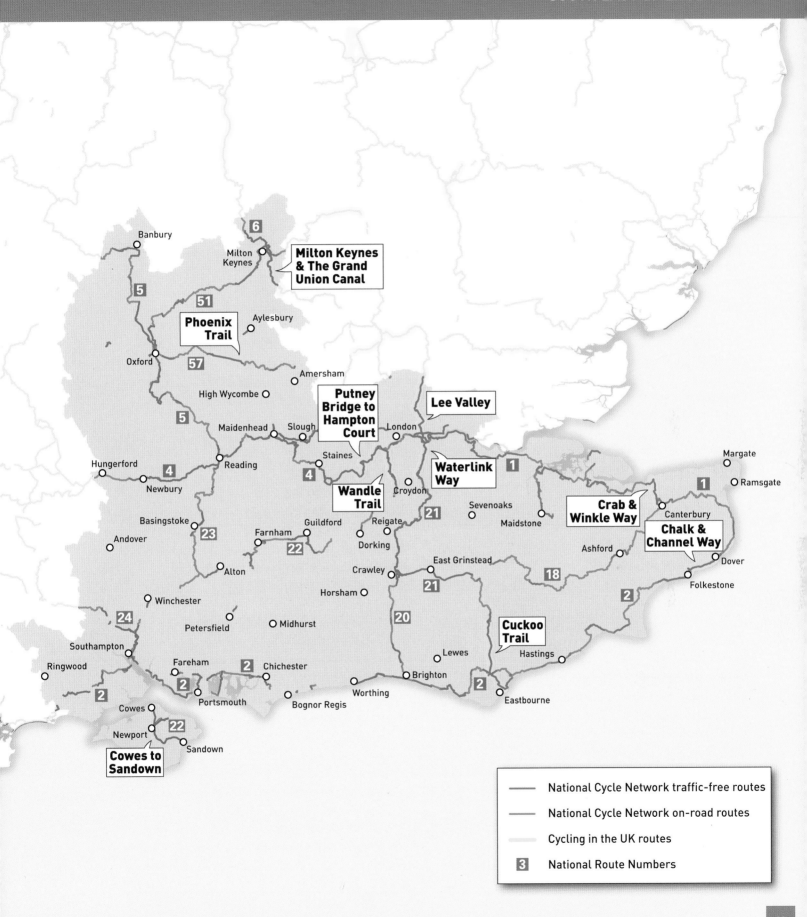

Banbury

6

Milton
Keynes

**Milton Keynes
& The Grand
Union Canal**

5

51

Aylesbury

**Phoenix
Trail**

Oxford

57

Amersham

High Wycombe

**Putney
Bridge to
Hampton
Court**

Lee Valley

5

Maidenhead

Slough

London

Staines

Margate

Hungerford

4

Reading

4

**Waterlink
Way**

1

Ramsgate

Newbury

**Wandle
Trail**

Croydon

**Crab &
Winkle Way**

Canterbury

Basingstoke

23

Guildford

Reigate

Sevenoaks

Maidstone

**Chalk &
Channel Way**

Andover

Farnham

22

Dorking

21

Ashford

Dover

Alton

Crawley

East Grinstead

18

Folkestone

Winchester

Horsham

21

2

Petersfield

Midhurst

24

20

Cuckoo
Trail

Southampton

Fareham

2

Chichester

Lewes

Hastings

Ringwood

Brighton

2

Portsmouth

Bognor Regis

Worthing

2

Eastbourne

Cowes

22

Newport

Sandown

**Cowes to
Sandown**

National Cycle Network traffic-free routes

National Cycle Network on-road routes

Cycling in the UK routes

3 National Route Numbers

COWES TO SANDOWN

Starting in Cowes in the north of the Isle of Wight and finishing in Sandown in the south east, this might be considered the easiest 'coast-to-coast' ride in the country. Included in the ride are two long sections of railway path. The first starts just south of West Cowes, runs parallel with the River Medina, which is filled with yachts, and finishes on the northern outskirts of Newport. The second, much longer railway path is joined at Shide on the south side of Newport. It takes you through lovely countryside – pasture, woodland and wildflowers – to the outskirts of Sandown, a popular seaside resort with fine sandy beaches.

At 13 x 23 miles (21 x 37km), the Isle of Wight is an ideal size for exploring by bike. It is also blessed with a mild climate, the countryside is largely unspoiled and the local authority has adopted a very positive attitude towards cycling. There are also good transport connections to the English mainland, with ferries sailing from Portsmouth, Southampton and Lymington.

National Route: 23

START Chain ferry terminal in West Cowes.

FINISH Sandown train station.

DISTANCE 16 miles (25.5km).

GRADE Easy.

SURFACE A mix of good-quality tarmac roads and tracks and gravel paths.

HILLS None.

YOUNG & INEXPERIENCED CYCLISTS

The section from south of Cowes to the north of Newport is ideal for families, as is the longer section from the southern edge of Newport to the western edge of Sandown. Care should be taken on the streets in Sandown, Newport and Cowes, particularly on the one-way systems.

REFRESHMENTS

• Lots of choice in Cowes, Newport and Sandown.
• Pointer Inn, just off the route in Newchurch (this involves a steep climb).

• There is often a tea tent at Old Merstone train station.

THINGS TO SEE & DO

Nearly half of the island is designated an Area of Outstanding Natural Beauty (www.wightaonb.org.uk). The Isle of Wight is also one of the few places in England where you can still see red squirrels and Glanville Fritillary butterflies.

COWES:
• Osborne House: Queen Victoria's island retreat; 01983 200022; www.english-heritage.org.uk
• Maritime Museum; 01983 823433; www.iwight.com

NEWPORT:
• Remains of a Roman villa, discovered in 1926 and painstakingly restored; 01983 529720; www.iwight.com
• Museum of Island History; 01983 823433; www.iwight.com
• Quay Arts Centre; 01983 822490; www.quayarts.org
• Classic Boat Museum; 01983 533493; www.classicboatmuseum.org
• Carisbrooke Castle, off the route near Newport; 01983 522107; www.english-heritage.org.uk

SANDOWN:
- Dinosaur Isle; 01983 404344; www.dinosaurisle.com
- Amazon World; in Newchurch, near Sandown; 01983 867122; www.amazonworld.co.uk

TRAIN STATIONS
Portsmouth Harbour; Ryde Pier Head; Sandown.

FERRIES
There are three passenger vehicle ferry routes operating to and from the mainland, all of which carry bikes free of charge.
- Southampton to East Cowes; www.redfunnel.co.uk/cycling. A chain ferry (floating bridge) connects East Cowes and West Cowes (bikes and foot passengers travel free of charge); www.iwight.com/council
- Portsmouth to Fishbourne; www.wightlink.co.uk
- Lymington to Yarmouth; www.wightlink.co.uk

There are also catamaran services for foot passengers running from Southampton to West Cowes (Red Funnel), and from Portsmouth to Ryde Pier Head (Wightlink). Bikes are allowed only on the Portsmouth crossing.

If you do this ride in reverse, you can take the catamaran from Portsmouth Harbour to Ryde Pier Head, where there is a direct train connection to Sandown (maximum of four bikes); www.wightlink.co.uk for catamaran; www.island-line.co.uk for train link.

BIKE HIRE
- Isle of Wight Hire: 01983 299056 (Cowes) or 01983 400055 (Sandown); www.isleofwighthire.co.uk
- TAV Cycles, Ryde: 01983 812989; www.tavcycles.co.uk
- Wight Cycle Hire, Yarmouth: 01983 761800; www.wightcyclehire.co.uk

FURTHER INFORMATION
- To view or print National Cycle Network routes, visit www.sustrans.org.uk
- Maps for this area are available to buy from www.sustransshop.co.uk
- Tourist Information in Cowes, Newport and Sandown; 01983 813818; www.islandbreaks.co.uk

ROUTE DESCRIPTION

Leaving the car ferry terminal in East Cowes, follow the signs on your right via Castle Street to the chain ferry to West Cowes. At West Cowes, follow the Route 23 signs from the chain ferry, left into Bridge Road, left again into Pelham Road and right and then left once more onto Arctic Road to the beginning of the railway path to Newport. You are now on the railway path skirting the western banks of the tidal River Medina towards the market town of Newport. Here, there are wonderful views across the river estuary, with a glimpse of Osborne House on your left. This easy-to-ride tarmac path is well used by walkers and cyclists, and crosses the rebuilt bridge at Dodnor Cottages.

You now enter the historic capital of the Island, Newport. After threading your way through the streets and looking out for the route signs, you join the second, much longer railway path at St Georges Approach towards Shide. This takes you through open countryside and a marshland nature reserve, and becomes part of the Sunshine Trail at Merstone. Continue towards Sandown adjacent to the River Yar via Horringford, Langbridge and Alverstone and under the railway by Sandown station. The route continues via the railway trail, finishing at the popular seaside resort of Sandown, with its fine sandy beaches.

NEARBY CYCLE ROUTES

The Cowes to Sandown route is the southernmost section of National Route 23, which starts in Reading, Berkshire, while Route 22 runs east to west across the island from Ryde to Yarmouth and Freshwater Bay.

It is possible to make a circular trip using the Isle of Wight Steam Railway from Wootton to Smallbrook Junction. Cycle from Sandown to Newport, then take Route 22 beside the main road to Wootton and back by steam train. There are two other short railway paths on the Isle of Wight: Shanklin to Wroxall and Yarmouth to Freshwater Bay.

For mountain bikers, there are plenty of fine chalk byways and bridle paths on the western half of the island, including the spectacular Tennyson Trail, with views out to the English Channel and back over the Solent to the mainland. The Round the Island Cycle Route is a mix of coastal and inland roads and paths.

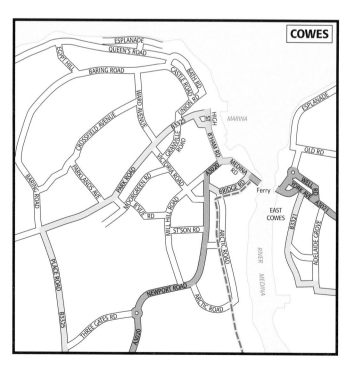

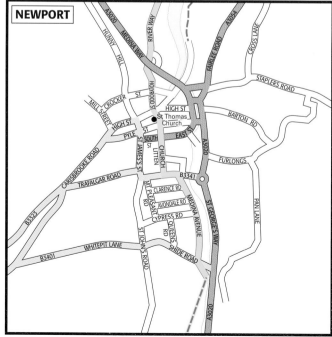

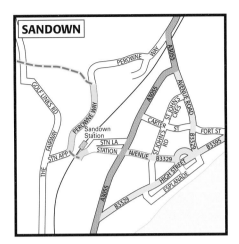

The Sunshine Trail is a 12-mile (19.5-km) circular route from Sandown, via Lake and Shanklin train stations, to the picturesque village of Godshill and on to Merstone, where you join Route 23 back to Sandown, as described in the main ride.

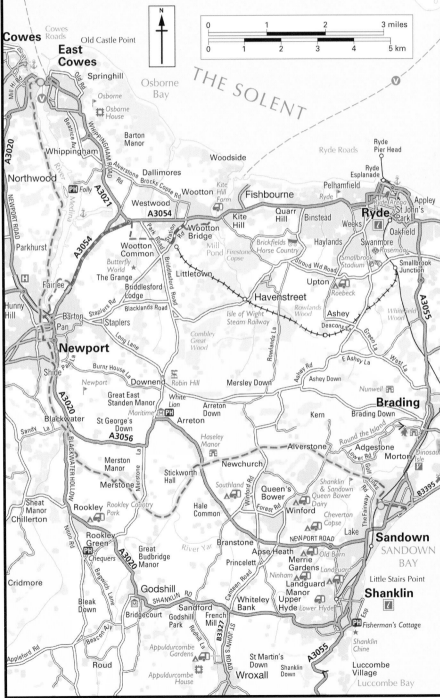

CUCKOO TRAIL

The Cuckoo Trail, from Hampden Park to Heathfield, is one of the longest and most popular railway paths in the south east of England. According to Sussex tradition, the first cuckoo of the year was released from a cage every spring at Heathfield Fair, hence the name Cuckoo Line given to the original railway line. The trail offers superb traffic-free cycling through a mixture of broad-leaved woodland, open grassland, arable farmland and pasture. There is a gentle 122-m (400-ft) climb up from Polegate to Heathfield, so that you can look forward to a gravity-assisted return journey! As you head back down towards Polegate, you can see the rolling chalk hills of the South Downs ahead of you.

There are lots of sights, sounds and smells to experience along the way: metal sculptures, an arch in the form of a Chinese pagoda roof, a claw-like hand and plenty of carved wooden seats with a variety of motifs, made from local oaks blown down in the Great Storm of 1987. In May, look out for butterflies such as the orange-tip. You might even see bullfinches, lesser whitethroats, cuckoos and weasels. There's also pungent wild garlic growing between Hellingly and Horam, and, in early summer, orchids near path edges. The route can be followed in either direction, but the climb from Polegate to Heathfield is easier heading south.

National Route: 21

START
Eastbourne seafront, near Sovereign Leisure Centre, 1 mile (1.6km) east of the Pier; or Hampden Park train station, 2 miles (3km) north of Eastbourne town centre; or Polegate train station, centre of Polegate village, 4 miles (6.5km) north of Eastbourne.

FINISH Heathfield.

DISTANCE
16 miles (25km) from Eastbourne seafront to Heathfield; 13 miles (21km) from Hampden Park train station; and 11 miles (17.5km) from Polegate train station.

GRADE Easy.

SURFACE Tarmac roads and fine gravel paths.

HILLS
There is a gentle 122-m (400-ft) climb over 11 miles (17.5km) from Polegate up to Heathfield, and two short climbs at bridges over the railway and the A27.

YOUNG & INEXPERIENCED CYCLISTS
The link from Eastbourne seafront to Hampden Park is not suitable for very young children so we advise young families to start from Hampden Park or Polegate, where the traffic-free Cuckoo Trail begins.

REFRESHMENTS
- Lots of choice at Sovereign Harbour.
- Various options in Hampden Park, Polegate, Hailsham and Heathfield.
- Cafe in Horam.
- Tea shop on the trail at the Old Loom Mill Craft Centre (2 miles/3km north of Polegate, just before crossing the B2104).

THINGS TO SEE & DO
- Sovereign Harbour, east of Eastbourne: one of the largest marinas in the UK, with five separate harbours, and restaurants and shops overlooking the water.

- Sussex Farm Museum, Horam; 01435 813352; www.sussexmuseums.co.uk
- Pevensey Castle, just off the route: a history stretching back over 16 centuries; www.english-heritage.org.uk
- Shinewater Country Park: Eastbourne's newest park, with landscaping completed as part of the Golden Jubilee Way; www.eastsussex.gov.uk/leisureandtourism
- A number of artworks line the route, including metal sculptures by local artist Hamish Black, and carved wooden seats, made from local oaks blown down in the Great Storm of 1987, by sculptor Steve Geliot.
- Good examples of Victorian engineering are the brick arch bridges between Hellingly and Horam, and the Heathfield Tunnel (open only in summer).

TRAIN STATIONS

Polegate; Hampden Park.

BIKE HIRE

- Cycleman, Eastbourne: 01323 501157
- M's Cycle Hire (five or more bikes, delivered and collected): www.m-cyclehire.co.uk

FURTHER INFORMATION

- To view or print National Cycle Network routes, visit www.sustrans.org.uk
- Maps for this area are available to buy from www.sustransshop.co.uk
- Sussex Tourist Information: 01243 263065; www.visitsussex.org

- Eastbourne Tourist Information: 0871 663 0031; www.visiteastbourne.com

ROUTE DESCRIPTION

From Eastbourne seafront, near Sovereign Leisure Centre, 1 mile (1.6km) east of the Pier, take the traffic-free path on the west side of Lottbridge Drove. Follow this all the way through the built-up area, across the A2280 roundabout to the next roundabout, where you take the right-hand turn onto Willingdon Drove. (Hampden Park is just a stone's throw from here: carry on up Lottbridge Drove to the next roundabout and turn left on Mountfield Road). From Willingdon Drove, look out for Edward Road on the left at the next roundabout. This will lead you into Shinewater Country Park, where after a left and a right turn, you reach a bridge. This will take you to Route 21, signed all the way to Polegate. Between Polegate and Heathfield, the route follows the old railway line with a very gentle climb. In places where bridges have been dismantled and houses built on the old line, the route continues on short sections of estate roads through Hailsham and Horam, rejoining the railway path, which continues to Heathfield. On wider stretches, an equestrian track runs parallel to the route, separated by grass with picnic tables and cycle parking hoops.

NEARBY CYCLE ROUTES

The Cuckoo Trail is part of National Route 21, which runs south from London through Redhill and East Grinstead to Eastbourne. From Polegate, the South Coast Cycle Route (Route 2) runs east through Pevensey to Bexhill and west

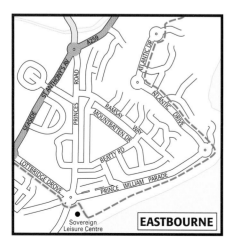

EASTBOURNE

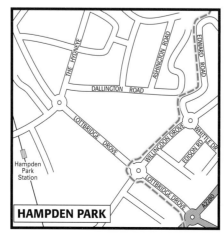

HAMPDEN PARK

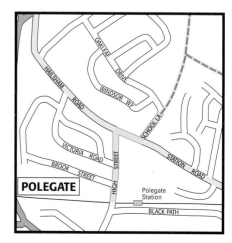

POLEGATE

to Newhaven and Brighton. The Forest Way and Worth Way start in East Grinstead, running west to Crawley and east to Groombridge. There are tracks along part of Eastbourne, Hastings, Brighton and Hove promenades.

The South Downs Way is suitable for mountain bikers. There is also a route around Bewl Water, southeast of Tunbridge Wells (summer only).

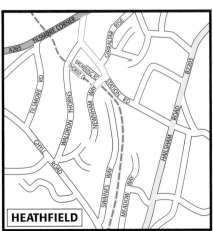

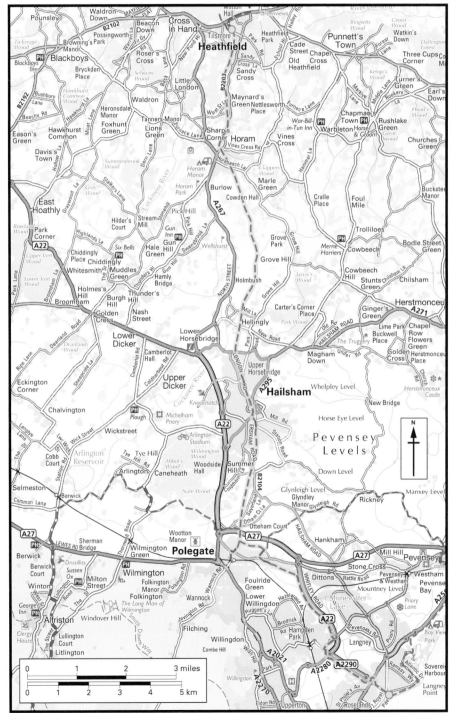

HEATHFIELD

CRAB & WINKLE WAY

Forming part of National Route 1, the 7-mile (11-km) Crab & Winkle Way links the beautiful cathedral city of Canterbury with the harbour in Whitstable. A section of the trail runs along the course of a dismantled railway, past fruit farms and through the ancient broad-leaved woodland of Blean Woods. There are fine views over Whitstable Bay from the highpoint of the ride, and Whitstable itself offers a wide range of places to eat and drink – its speciality is the local oysters, which have been harvested in the area since at least Roman times.

The Crab & Winkle line was the first regular steam-hauled passenger railway in the world. It had connections with the 19th-century's most celebrated engineers: the plans were drawn up by William James; George and Robert Stephenson built the engine *Invicta* for it; Thomas Telford constructed the harbour at its Whitstable terminus, and Isambard Kingdom Brunel visited the tunnel, which was the first in the world for passenger trains. The line was closed in 1953 and it became overgrown until, in 1997, the Crab & Winkle Line Trust was set up to bring it back into public use. The trail eventually opened in 2000.

National Route: 1

START Guildhall, Canterbury.

FINISH Whitstable train station.

DISTANCE 7 miles (11km).

GRADE Easy.

SURFACE
Streets at the start and finish; a fine stone-based path between the university and South Street, on the edge of Whitstable.

HILLS
The route is hillier than you'd expect from a railway path: there's a 61-m (200-ft) climb out of Canterbury and an undulating middle section before the drop down to the coast at Whitstable.

YOUNG & INEXPERIENCED CYCLISTS
The route through Canterbury and Whitstable uses traffic-calmed streets or cycle paths. The rest of the ride is on a traffic-free path.

REFRESHMENTS
- Lots of choice in Canterbury and Whitstable.
- Winding Pond is a great place to picnic.

THINGS TO SEE & DO
CANTERBURY:
- Now a UNESCO world heritage site, the city of Canterbury became a place of pilgrimage after the murder of the Archbishop of Canterbury, Thomas à Becket, in the cathedral in 1170.
- Canterbury Cathedral; 01227 762862; www.canterbury-cathedral.org
- St Augustine's Abbey: founded shortly after AD 597, the abbey was originally a burial site for the Anglo-Saxon kings of Kent; part of the world heritage site; 01227 378100; www.english-heritage.org.uk
- Canterbury Roman Museum; 01227 785575; www.canterbury.gov.uk
- Canterbury Tales Visitor Attraction; 01227 479227; www.canterburytales.org.uk.
- The alleyways and streets around the cathedral are also worth exploring but this is best done on foot, as cycling here is allowed only between 10.30am and 4pm.

MILLESIMO QV

- Blean Woods: a large area of broad-leaved woodland; look out for the rare heath fritillary butterfly; www.english-nature.org.uk; www.rspb.org.uk
- Clowes Wood: listen out for woodpeckers, warblers and nightingales.

WHITSTABLE:
- Whitstable Museum & Gallery; www.canterbury.gov.uk
- Oyster Festival; www.whitstableoysterfestival.co.uk
- Druidstone Park: animal park with a bluebell woodland trail; 01227 765168; www.druidstone.net

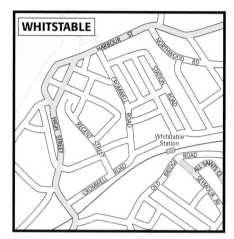

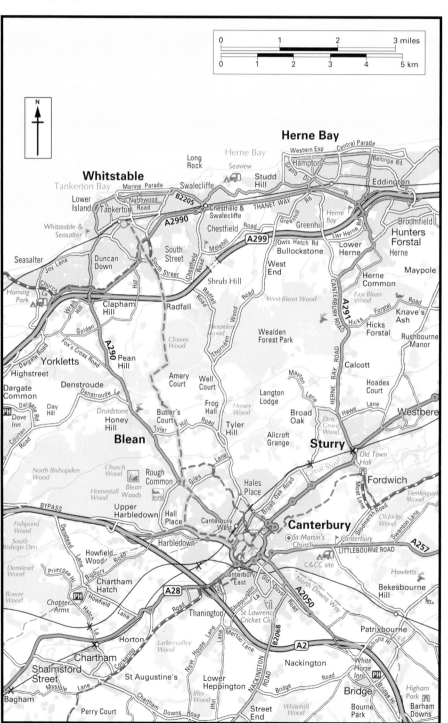

TRAIN STATIONS Canterbury West; Whitstable.

BIKE HIRE

Downland Cycles, Canterbury: 01227 479643;
www.downlandcycles.co.uk

FURTHER INFORMATION

- To view or print National Cycle Network routes, visit
  www.sustrans.org.uk
- Maps for this area are available to buy from
  www.sustransshop.co.uk
- Canterbury & Whitstable Tourist information:
  01227 378100; www.canterbury.co.uk;
  www.seewhitstable.com

ROUTE DESCRIPTION

The ride is signed on-road from Canterbury West train

station and joins National Route 1 in Canterbury near
the river at Pound Lane. As it climbs steadily out of the
city, wonderful views will open up behind you. From
Harbledown, the route is mostly traffic-free, following
the railway line from Winding Pond to the outskirts
of Whitstable. On the way, you'll travel through Blean
Woods and Clowes Wood. The route ends at Whitstable
train station, but is signed right through to the harbour.
If you don't feel up to the ride back, you can get the train
from Whitstable to Canterbury East, although you will
have to change at Faversham.

NEARBY CYCLE ROUTES

Canterbury lies at a crossroads of the National Cycle
Network. National Route 1 runs east–west from London
to Dover. To the south, National Route 18 goes to Ashford.
To the north, the Viking Trail on Regional Route 15
links to Route 1 and runs along the North Kent coast
via Ramsgate and Margate. Another option from the
centre of Canterbury is to follow the traffic-path east to
Fordwich, where you join a delightful network of lanes
meandering across rich agricultural country towards
Sandwich and the coast. The Cathedral to Coast Ride
is a waymarked 50-mile (80-km) circular route linking
Canterbury, Folkestone and Dover.

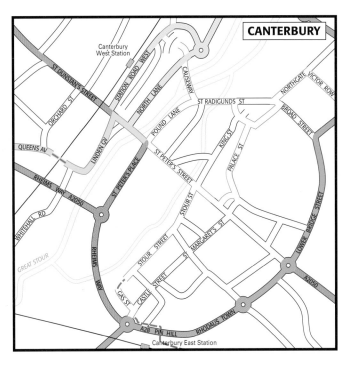

MILTON KEYNES & THE GRAND UNION CANAL

It may come as a surprise to some that there is an excellent network of recreational cycle routes in and around Milton Keynes, including circuits of lakes, tree-lined canal towpaths and well-made paths across parkland. Other surprises include a Buddhist pagoda and lots of adventure playgrounds. This route largely follows the course of the Grand Union Canal towpath from the centre of Milton Keynes, south to Leighton Buzzard and passing through Bletchley, which was made famous as the headquarters of the Enigma code-breakers during World War II.

When integrated in 1929, the Grand Union Canal was an amalgam of at least eight separate canals, and of these the Grand Junction Canal from Braunston near Daventry to the Thames at Brentford, to the west of London, was by far the most important. Built in the late 18th century, it cut a full 60 miles (96km) off the canal journey between the Midlands and London – until then, the exisiting canal had joined the Thames at Oxford. In 1929, the various canals were integrated with the aim of establishing a 70-ton barge standard throughout the waterways of the Midlands, widening locks wherever necessary. However, the money ran out by 1932, the task remained unfinished and broad beam boats never became common on the Grand Union Canal – many of the canals are still passable only by narrowboats, 2m (6.5ft) wide.

National Routes: 51 and 6

START Milton Keynes Central train station.

FINISH Leighton Buzzard train station.

DISTANCE 14 miles (22.5km).
Shorter option, from Bletchley to Leighton Buzzard:
7 miles (11km).

GRADE Easy.

SURFACE Tarmac.

HILLS None.

YOUNG & INEXPERIENCED CYCLISTS

In Milton Keynes, all busy roads are crossed via underpasses or bridges. There are on-road sections south of Woughton on the Green and through Bletchley, but these are all minor roads. As an alternative, the ride can be started at Bletchley, following the towpath all the way to Leighton Buzzard.

REFRESHMENTS

- Lots of choice in the square by the train station and elsewhere in central Milton Keynes.
- Ye Olde Swan pub and shop in Woughton on the Green (just off the route).
- Caldecotte Arms (windmill pub) by Caldecotte Lake.
- The Grand Union pub at Stoke Hammond and Globe Inn at Linslade (both on towpath).
- Good picnic spots at Willen Lakeside Park (just off the route) and Caldecotte Lake.

THINGS TO SEE & DO

- Peace Pagoda, Willen Lakeside Park (just off the route): the first of its kind in the West, with a frieze telling the story of the Buddha; a Circle of Hearts Medicine Wheel (a Native American stone circle and symbol of peace); and Tim Minett and Neil Higson's turf maze with bronze roundels representing the four races of mankind.
- Walton Lake nature reserve (just off the route).
- Children's play area near Caldecotte Arms (windmill pub) by Caldecotte Lake; www.mkparks.co.uk
- Ancient churches of St Mary's at Woughton and St

Thomas's at Simpson; www.woughton.org/churches
- Leighton Buzzard: this charming old market town is well worth exploring.

TRAIN STATIONS

Milton Keynes Central; Bletchley; Leighton Buzzard.

BIKE HIRE Willen Lake: 01908 691620

FURTHER INFORMATION

- To view or print National Cycle Network routes, visit www.sustrans.org.uk
- Maps for this area available to buy from www.sustransshop.co.uk
- Milton Keynes Tourist Information: 01908 677010; www.destinationmiltonkeynes.co.uk

ROUTE DESCRIPTION

Go straight ahead from Milton Keynes Central station and follow Route 51 along Midsummer Boulevard. Cross the overbridge into Campbell Park, where there are splendid views of the surrounding countryside. Keep following the Route 51 signs until you meet Route 6 at the canal. For a short detour, continue straight on, following Route 51 to Willen Lakeside Park, which offers a good picnic spot and a chance to explore the Peace Pagoda, Circle of Hearts Medicine Wheel and turf maze.

To continue on the ride, return to the canal and Route 6 and follow the towpath south towards Woughton on the Green. There is a short section on minor roads through Woughton when you pass close to the Open University.

The 13th-century church of St Mary's and the Walton Lake nature reserve are also both close by. (Walton Lake was dried out when it was no longer needed to cope with floodwater, which is now taken by Willen and Caldecotte Lakes.) At Simpson, where there is another 13th-century church, join the path alongside the River Ouzel – companion waterway to the canal – and cycle past Caldecotte Lake, another good picnic spot, with its windmill pub and children's play area.

The route follows minor roads through Bletchley before rejoining the canal towpath for 6 miles (9.5km), all the way to Leighton Buzzard. Here, you could visit the Georgian high street and market square before turning back to the station (all within easy reach of the towpath).

NEARBY CYCLE ROUTES

The section of this ride that goes through Milton Keynes is part of the 170-mile (273-km) long Redway network, named after its red tarmac surface, with routes throughout the town.

Milton Keynes is at a crossroads of the National Cycle Network. Route 6 passes through Milton Keynes on its way south from Leicester and Northampton to St Albans and London. Route 51 runs from Oxford to Bedford, Cambridge and the east coast.

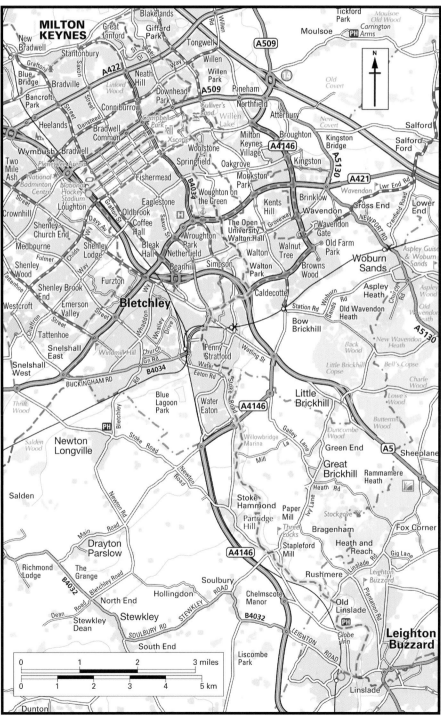

PHOENIX TRAIL

Passing through the countryside on the border between Oxfordshire and Buckinghamshire, the Phoenix Trail links the attractive market towns of Thame and Princes Risborough, providing an ideal traffic-free ride for novice cyclists and families with young children. Sit on the sculptures, which are dotted along the trail, to admire the magnificent views of the nearby Chiltern Hills and observe red kites, the impressive birds of prey that thrive in the area. Keep an eye out for the sculptures of strange animals perched high up on poles about halfway along the ride.

Running along the base of the Chilterns southwest from Bledlow, near the Princes Risborough end of the ride, is the Ridgeway; a reasonably level, broad, stone and chalk track that offers easy off-road riding for mountain bikes through the summer and early autumn. This ancient trading route is over 5,000 years old and claimed to be the oldest in Europe. It used to link the flint workings at Grimes Graves in Norfolk with the Dorset coast. The Chilterns themselves are criss-crossed with bridleways and byways, and also offer excellent mountain biking, but obviously the rides are a lot tougher than the Phoenix Trail.

National Route: 57

START Princes Risborough train station.

FINISH Upper High Street, Thame.

DISTANCE 7 miles (11km).

GRADE Easy.

SURFACE Part tarmac, part limestone dust.

HILLS None.

YOUNG & INEXPERIENCED CYCLISTS
The route allows you to enjoy the countryside without tackling hills or long distances. There is a 2-mile (3-km) section on-road from Princes Risborough to Horsenden, where the 5-mile (8-km) traffic-free path starts and goes all the way to Thame.

REFRESHMENTS
• Variety of choices in Princes Risborough.
• Red Lion pub at Longwick, just off the route.

PHOENIX TRAIL

ROUTE DESCRIPTION
From Princes Risborough, after leaving the station approach road, follow the National Cycle Network Route 57 signs to the start of the traffic-free path in Horsenden.

The route is then traffic-free all the way to Thame and passes through the countryside on the border between Oxfordshire and Buckinghamshire. The terrain is largely flat, but the Chilterns make an impressive backdrop to the ride towards Thame.

The market towns of Princes Risborough and Thame are both worth a potter, so add in extra time to your ride.

NEARBY CYCLE ROUTES
National Route 57 continues, mainly on-road, west of Thame to Oxford: go past Lord Williams's School and follow the signs.

For the more energetic, the Ridgeway (a national walking trail and Britain's oldest road) is nearby, and a 9-mile (14.5-km) section west of Bledlow is open to cyclists.

- Three Horseshoes pub at Towersey.
- Variety of choices in Thame.

THINGS TO SEE & DO
- Princes Risborough: market town with a history stretching back over 5,500 years.
- Thame: historic market town with an attractive centre and unique shops.
- Look out for a rich variety of wildlife, including red kites.
- There is a wide selection of artworks along the route.

TRAIN STATIONS Princes Risborough.

BIKE HIRE
Risborough Cycles, Princes Risborough: 01844 345949; www.risboroughcycles.com

FURTHER INFORMATION
- To view or print National Cycle Network routes, visit www.sustrans.org.uk
- Maps for this area are available to buy from www.sustransshop.co.uk
- Princes Risborough Tourist Information: 01844 274795; www.visitbuckinghamshire.org
- Thame Tourist Information: 01844 212833; www.visitsouthoxfordshire.co.uk

PRINCES RISBOROUGH

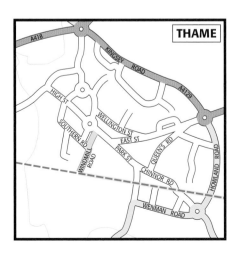

THAME

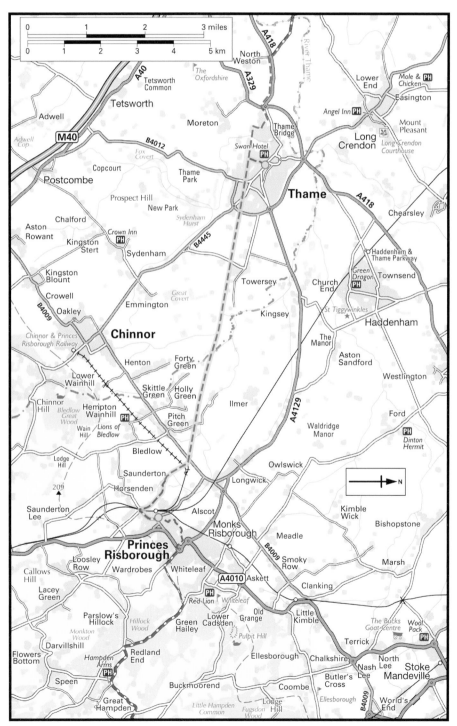

CHALK & CHANNEL WAY

The Chalk & Channel Way is a walking and cycling path along the top of the famous White Cliffs overlooking the English Channel. On a day of good visibility, you may be able to see right across to France. Crossing the Kent Downs Area of Outstanding Natural Beauty, the trail links the harbours of Dover and Folkestone and is part of National Route 2 of the National Cycle Network that connects the towns of the south coast, going through areas of great natural beauty and historical significance.

A whole series of artworks along the trail gives you every reason to stop and admire the views. *Samphire Tower* is a huge oak-framed and larch-clad structure that reflects nautical architecture around the UK coastline. *Coccoliths*, inspired by the microscopic skeletons left by the millions of extinct algae forming the white cliffs, is a collection of giant concrete forms nestled into the hillside overlooking Folkestone. *On the Crest of a Wave* is two Portland stone blocks, white like the cliffs of Dover, each one supporting the figure of a swimmer in sea-green Kirkstone slate.

National Route: 2

START
Dover Promenade by the *Crest of a Wave* sculpture.

FINISH
Folkestone Harbour.

DISTANCE
8 miles (13km).

GRADE
Medium. Some parts are easy but there are a couple of sections with steep hills.

SURFACE
Mainly dust paths or tarmac.

HILLS
Steep climbs at both ends but spectacular views.

YOUNG & INEXPERIENCED CYCLISTS
Around half the route is on-road and half on traffic-free trails or designated cycle lanes. Families with young children travelling from Dover may prefer to start from Samphire Hoe and avoid the on-road climb out of the city. If you're starting from Folkestone, the scarp of the Downs at the beginning is long and steep and therefore not suitable for young children.

REFRESHMENTS
- Lots of choice in Folkestone & Dover.
- Seafood stalls and pubs at Folkestone Harbour.
- The Lighthouse bar at Capel-le-Ferne.
- Halfway along the route, there's a cliff-top cafe with spectacular views.
- Drinks and light refreshments available at Samphire Hoe, along with a good picnic spot; this is at sea level, with a steep climb back up to route.

THINGS TO SEE & DO
The Chalk & Channel Way travels along the top of the famous White Cliffs of Dover, where there are good views over the English Channel – on a clear day, you can see the coast of France. The route is punctuated by a series of artworks.

DOVER:
- Dover Castle (just off the route), www.english-heritage.org.uk
- Dover Docks & Harbour; www.dover-kent.co.uk
- Knights Templar Church: foundations of a small medieval church, traditionally the site of King John's submission to the papal legate in 1213; www.english-heritage.org.uk
- Western Heights: huge fortification begun during the Napoleonic Wars and completed in the 1860s, designed to protect Dover from French invasion; only the moat can be visited; www.english-heritage.org.uk

- Samphire Hoe picnic site and visitor centre; 01304 225688; www.samphirehoe.com
- Battle of Britain memorial at Capel-le-Ferne.
- Listening Ears: large concrete listening devices, known as sound mirrors, built along the coast in the 1930s to detect enemy aircraft.

FOLKESTONE:
- Sunday market by the start of the route at the harbour.
- Old High Street: this cobbled street leading up to the town centre is part of the Creative Quarter and is lined with galleries and cafes.
- Entertainment at the Leas Cliff Hall.
- East Cliff Sands at Folkestone forms the only natural sandy beach in the area. There is also an adventure playground about half a mile (0.8km) to the west of Folkestone Harbour and nearby a cafe overlooking a small, man-made and sheltered sandy beach.

TRAIN STATIONS
Dover; Folkestone Central; Folkestone Harbour.

BIKE HIRE
Dover White Cliff Tours: 01303 271388; www.doverwhiteclifftours.com

FURTHER INFORMATION
- To view or print National Cycle Network routes, visit www.sustrans.org.uk
- Maps for this area are available to buy from www.sustransshop.co.uk

- Dover Tourist information: 01304 205108;
  www.whitecliffscountry.org.uk
- White Cliffs of Dover: www.nationaltrust.org.uk
- Folkestone Tourist Information: 01303 258594;
  www.discoverfolkestone.co.uk

ROUTE DESCRIPTION

Start at the *On the Crest of a Wave* sculpture by Ray Smith on Waterlook Crescent by the docks in Dover. Follow Route 2 west on the traffic-free path to reach a short on-road section in Aycliff before rejoining the traffic-free path. For a good picnic site, take a detour to Samphire Hoe, a peaceful site with wildflowers and birds, made from the chalk marl dug to create the Channel Tunnel. Back on the route, from here onwards, you'll come across a series of artworks (see right).

You can make this a circular route by going inland at Capel-le-Ferne to join Regional Route 17 (blue sign) and cycle east through West Hougham and Maxton and back to Dover.

NEARBY CYCLE ROUTES

The Chalk & Channel Way is part of National Cycle Network Route 2, which connects the towns of the south coast. To the northeast, Route 2 continues to Ramsgate and is mainly traffic-free from St Margaret's at Cliffe. To the southeast, the route, which is initially along the sea front, is flat and traffic-free most of the way to West Hythe. Part of the route travels alongside the Royal Military Canal – boats are available for hire at Hythe.

There are also local cycle routes to Canterbury, but access to them means crossing busy roads that have inadequate facilities for cyclists at present.

ARTWORKS ON THE ROUTE

The Chalk & Channel Way cycle route is particularly rich in artworks. Along the way you will pass *Samphire Tower* by Jony Easterby and Pippa Taylor: a large oak-framed and larch-clad structure that reflects nautical architecture around the UK coastline. Inside is a sound installation by Geir Jenssen and Jony Easterby, where a brass telescope triggers sounds and compositions relating to the acoustics of the English and French coasts. There are also paintings by Sax Impey on a navigational theme.

Coccoliths, by Tim Clapcott, nestles into the hillside overlooking Folkestone. This collection of giant concrete forms is inspired by the structure of microscopic skeletons left by the millions of extinct algae that form the white cliffs.

Stepping Stones, also by Tim Clapcott, was created with the help of local children. Colourful paving stones line the entrance to the Samphire Tower, echoing the coccolith forms.

Flora Calcarea by Rob Kesseler consists of blocks, discs and seats, each with a cast bronze page carrying a

sketch of a local flower and its grains of pollen. There is also a series of poems by Ros Barber, one for each of ten locations along the route. They refer to something individual about each site, linked to the land itself, its flora and fauna or the human history of the area.

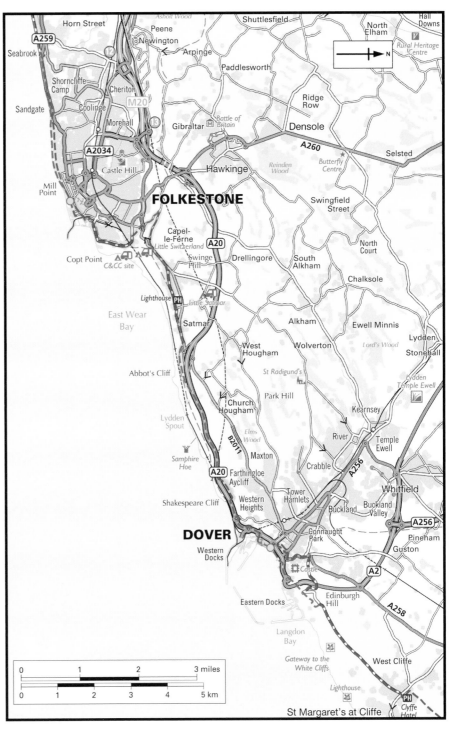

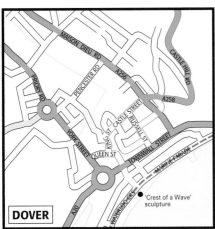

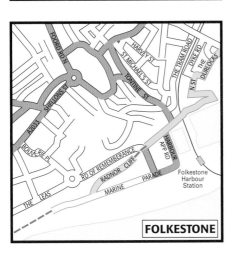

BIRDWATCHING ROUTES

Many of the National Cycle Network routes pass close by areas that are ideal for observing birds and other forms of wildlife. Here is a selection of some of the best. For more information, visit www.sustrans.org.uk

SOUTH WEST OF ENGLAND
HAYLE, CORNWALL
National Route 3
In cold winters, as many as 18,000 birds are seen here because this most southwesterly estuary in the UK never freezes. During spring and autumn, it is an ideal place to see migrant wading birds, gulls and terns. Look out for curlews, little egrets, oystercatchers, teals and wigeons.

SOUTH EAST OF ENGLAND
BARNES WILDFOWL & WETLANDS TRUST (WWT)
National Route 4
This international award-winning visitor attraction and Site of Special Scientific Interest (SSSI) is the best urban site in Europe for watching birds. Located on the banks of the River Thames, the 104-acre site is home to bitterns, kingfishers and a colony of endangered water voles.

LANGSTONE HARBOUR (RSPB), HAYLING ISLAND
National Routes 2 and 22
A muddy estuary that attracting large numbers of birds. Terns, gulls and wading birds breed here in spring and summer, while thousands of waders and Brent geese migrate from the Arctic to feed and roost in safety.

MIDLANDS
SANDWELL VALLEY (RSPB), SOUTH OF WALSALL
National Route 5
The hedgerows are full of finches and thrushes in winter, and warblers in summer, including whitethroats and lesser whitethroats. From the lakeside hide, flocks of ducks, geese, swans and wading birds can be seen.

EAST OF ENGLAND
WELNEY WILDFOWL & WETLANDS TRUST (WWT), SOUTH OF DOWNHAM MARKET
National Route 11
Each autumn sees 8,000 wild whooper and Bewick's swans travel to the Fens as they escape the Arctic cold.

8

Whooper swans travel 1,200 miles (1,930km) from their summer home in Iceland, while Bewick's swans travel 2,500 miles (4,000km) from Arctic Russia. The air is filled with the distinctive sound of their calls.

NORTH OF ENGLAND

BLACKTOFT SANDS (RSPB), EAST YORKSHIRE
National Route 65
The tidal reedbed is the largest in England and shelters bearded tits and bitterns. A breathtaking sight in summer is pairs of marsh harriers, passing food from one to the other in mid-air during their acrobatic courtship display.

WALES

VALLEY LAKES (RSPB), ANGLESEY
National Route 8
From these reed-fringed lakes you can see tufted ducks, pochards, shovelers, gadwalls and grebes. In winter, you'll also see wigeons and goldeneyes. In spring and early summer, the reed beds come alive with reed and sedge warblers. You may even glimpse water rails, marsh harriers and Cetti's warblers.

SCOTLAND

FORTH ESTUARY
National Route 76
The Firth of Forth stretches 60 miles (96km) from Stirling to the open sea. The shoreline and mudflats of the inner

Forth are rich feeding areas for wading birds. The open water beyond the Forth Bridges is home to a variety of seabirds, with spectacular breeding colonies on some of the islands.

NORTHERN IRELAND

LOWER LOUGH ERNE ISLANDS (RSPB), COUNTY FERMANAGH
National Route 91
Lough Erne is one of the largest freshwater lakes in the UK. You might see lapwings, curlews and snipe – or perhaps the unique inland colony of breeding sandwich terns. You may also see pine martens, badgers, red squirrels, otters, hares and stoats in the woodlands.

PORTMORE LOUGH (RSPB), COUNTY ANTRIM
National Route 94
During the summer, the traditional hay meadows alongside the lake attract a bewildering variety of butterflies, dragonflies and damselflies, while in the winter, greylag geese, whooper swans and thousands of ducks can be seen from the hide on the lake's edge.

1 Geese on Swan Pool at dusk, Sandwell Valley 2 Little Tern at Langstone Harbour 3 The London Wetland Centre at Barnes 4 Portmore Lough RSPB reserve 5 Common Shelduck (*Tadorna tadorna*) male attacking rival in water, Norfolk 6 Canada Geese on Forge Mill Lake in Sandwell Valley 7 Brent Geese (*Branta bernicla*), Langstone Harbour 8 Northern Lapwing (*Vanellus vanellus*) in courtship, North Kent Marshes

LONDON

London is one of the world's great cities and as time goes on it is becoming an ever-better place to cycle: the congestion charge for private vehicles and increasingly crowded public transport makes these options less attractive; in addition, the development of a cycle network and the pro-cycling stance taken by the last two mayors have all conspired to boost levels of cycling. This has been great news for commuters and regular cyclists but there have also been new routes built that offer fun rides for families and novices. Waterways and parks hold the key to finding routes through London that give cyclists attractive alternatives to the busy streets of the capital. Clearly the River Thames is the main corridor but there are also routes that make the most of the Lee Navigation, the Grand Union Canal and its branches, the River Wandle through Wandsworth and the River Ravensbourne to the south of Greenwich.

Route 4 enters London from the southwest following the splendid towpath alongside the River Thames from Weybridge. At Teddington Locks the character of the Thames changes dramatically: up to this point the river has been a place of pleasure craft and anglers, a river controlled and prettified; to the north and east of Teddington it widens and becomes tidal, there are more working boats and there is a more industrial feel to Old Father Thames. In Ham, Route 4 turns away from the river and cuts through Richmond Deer Park, home of hundreds of red and fallow deer. There is also a traffic-free trail all around the perimeter of the park (the Tamsin Trail). A highlight along this section of the ride is Barnes Wetlands Centre, an oasis for wildlife in the centre of the capital.

Greenwich, home of the *Cutty Sark*, the O2 Arena (ex-Millennium Dome) and the Greenwich Meridian, is the main crossroads of the National Cycle Network in London. Route 4 starts here and heads west for almost 300 miles to end at Fishguard in Pembrokeshire; Route 1 heads up the Lee Valley on its even longer journey north to John o' Groats; to the east Route 1 runs along the Thames towards Dover; to the south the Waterlink Way carries Route 21 down towards Brighton.

Creating continuous, high-quality routes in London presents enormous challenges and often requires major investment. As you ride around London on the National Cycle Network you will notice many special road crossings, traffic-calming measures and other features. For example, major junction modifications at Lambeth Bridge and dedicated walking and cycling bridges, such as the ones in Ravensbury Park on the Wandle Trail, have been installed to improve safety and access for cyclists and walkers.

The London Cycle Network Plus is being developed by Transport for London in partnership with the boroughs. 500 miles of routes will provide direct access to railway stations and to every major centre of employment, education and leisure.
Get hold of the free London Cycle Guide maps from www.tfl.gov.uk/cycling

PUTNEY BRIDGE TO HAMPTON COURT

Forming part of Route 4, which runs all the way from the capital to West Wales, this splendid green and leafy corridor offers plenty of interest, including the Wetlands Centre at Barnes, deer in Richmond Park, boating at Teddington Lock and Hampton Court Palace. The Palace was originally built for Cardinal Wolsey but it passed to Henry VIII when he fell out of favour with the king. It was at Hampton Court Palace that the King James Bible has its origins, and during the Civil War, Charles I was held prisoner here for three months before escaping. There is a striking contrast between the wide, untamed tidal Thames from Putney Bridge as far west as Teddington Lock and the highly managed pleasure boat section beyond.

Just off the route but connected to Route 4 via traffic-free paths are the Royal Botanic Gardens at Kew and Ham House, owned by the National Trust. Kew Gardens were started in 1759 by Princess Augusta, the mother of George III. They now cover more than 300 acres, and contain over 25,000 species and varieties of plants, as well as statues, glasshouses and an 18th-century pagoda. Ham House is a 17th-century mansion famous for its decorative interiors and restored formal gardens.

National Route: 4

START Putney Bridge, south bank.

FINISH Hampton Court Palace.

DISTANCE 12 miles (19.5km). Shorter options, from Putney Bridge to Richmond Park: 6 miles (9.5km); or to Kingston upon Thames: 9 miles (14.5km).

GRADE Easy.

SURFACE Tarmac and good-quality gravel paths.

HILLS Steady climb in Richmond Park.

YOUNG & INEXPERIENCED CYCLISTS
The route is a mixture of quiet streets and cyclepaths. The best traffic-free section alongside the river runs west from Kingston Bridge and crosses to the other side at Hampton Court.

CHISWICK
A316
A4
A4
A316
Hammersmith Bridge
B350
A306
River Thames
A219
Fulham Palace Road
A3218
London Wetland Centre
FULHAM
BARNES
A306
River Thames
Bull's Head
Church Road
A3003
Fulham FC (Craven Cottage)
PH
Barnes Bridge Station
Castelnau
Station Road
Road
Fulham Palace
M
PH
Idle Hour
Rocks Lane
Mill Hill Road
B349
Barnes Common
Lower Richmond Road
Putney Bridge
Vine Road
Barnes Station
B306
Queen's Ride
Upper Richmond Road
A205
Putney High Street
Putney
PUTNEY
Roehampton Lane
Dover House Road
East Putney
Priory Lane
Roehampton
A306
Putney Hill
A219
Roehampton Gate
Clarence Lane
Roehampton Gate
Putney Heath
Tibbet's Ride
Putney Heath
West Hill
A3
Sutherland Grove
Beverley Brook
Richmond Park
Kingston Road
A219

0 ½ mile
0 0.5 1 km

REFRESHMENTS All along the way.

THINGS TO SEE & DO

- Wildfowl & Wetlands Trust (WWT) at Barnes; 020 8409 4400; www.wwt.org.uk (see page 64)

- The National Archives, containing almost 1,000 years of history, is just off the route in Kew; 020 8876 3444; www.nationalarchives.gov.uk
- Royal Botanic Gardens, Kew, just off the route; 020 8332 5655; www.kew.org

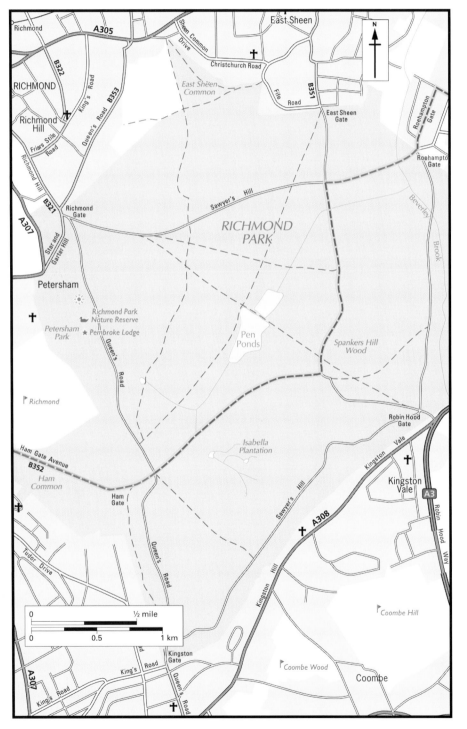

- Richmond Park: the largest Royal Park in London and home to around 650 free-roaming deer and other wildlife. The Park is designated a National Nature Reserve (NNR), a Site of Special Scientific Interest (SSSI) and a Special Area of Conservation (SAC);

020 8948 3209; www.royalparks.org.uk
- Ham House, Ham; 020 8940 1950; www.nationaltrust.org.uk
- Hampton Court Palace; 0844 482 7777; www.hrp.org.uk

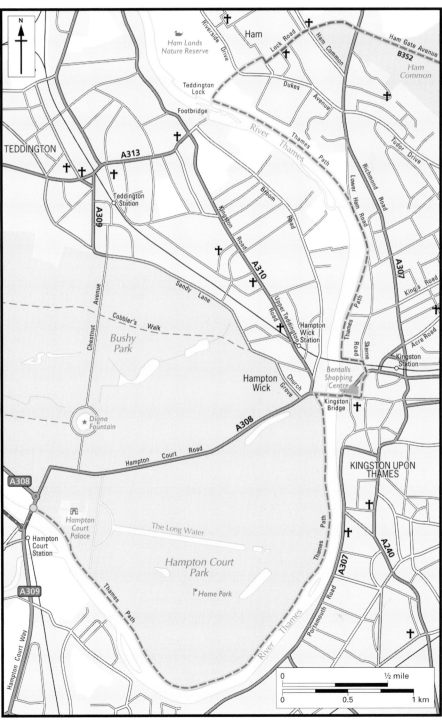

TRAIN STATIONS
Putney; Barnes; Kingston upon Thames; Hampton Court.

BIKE HIRE
- Go Pedal!: delivery to most areas of London; 07850 796320; www.gopedal.co.uk
- London Bicycle Tour Company, Gabriels Wharf: 020 7928 6838; www.londonbicycle.com
- Smith Brothers, Wimbledon: 020 8946 2270

FURTHER INFORMATION
- To view or print National Cycle Network routes, visit www.sustrans.org.uk
- Maps for this area are available to buy from www.sustransshop.co.uk
- Transport for London Cycle Guides: a series of free guides covering Greater London, with routes recommended by experienced cyclists. Available from: 020 7222 1234; www.tfl.gov.uk/cycling, as well as bike retailers, leisure centres, Travel Information Centres.
- Transport for London Journey Planner: detailed information to help you plan your travel anywhere in Greater London, by bike, on foot or on public transport; 020 7222 1234; www.tfl.gov.uk
- London Cycling Campaign: provides information and advice on cycling in London; 020 7234 9310; www.lcc.org.uk
- London Tourist Information; www.visitlondon.com

ROUTE DESCRIPTION
Starting on the south bank at Putney Bridge, the route follows the embankment for a mile or so before bearing away from the river, past the Wetlands Centre at Barnes, alongside Barnes Common and then towards Richmond Park (where you have the option of completing the Tamsin Trail, a totally traffic-free circuit of the park).

The route rejoins the river to the west of Richmond Park at Teddington Lock, threading its way through Kingston upon Thames. Near Kingston train station, you cross Kingston Bridge to travel along Barge Walk, from where you can get into Hampton Court Park to visit majestic Hampton Court Palace.

For a longer ride, cross back over the river on Hampton Court Bridge and follow the Thames closely on another traffic-free path for the next 6 miles (9.5km), passing Sunbury Lock and finishing at Weybridge.

NEARBY CYCLE ROUTES
The ride described here is the first section of the Thames Valley Cycle Route, which runs from Putney Bridge to Oxford (Route 4 to Reading, then Route 5 from Reading to Oxford). East from Putney Bridge, the London Thames Cycle Route runs right through the heart of London to Greenwich and on to Dartford. There is also a traffic-free circular ride around Richmond Park.

WATERLINK WAY

The Waterlink Way starts in Greenwich, where there is plenty to see and do. Visit the Old Royal Naval College, designed by Sir Christopher Wren; the National Maritime Museum, which traces the seafaring history of Britain from Tudor times to the 19th century; look in on the Royal Observatory, and take in the stunning panoramic views from the top of the hill in Greenwich Park across Docklands to the City. Sadly, the *Cutty Sark*, launched in 1869 and the fastest tea clipper in her time, is undergoing conservation, following the fire in 2007, and is open to visitors from summer 2010.

From Greenwich, the route goes south through Lewisham, Bromley and Croydon, following the valley of the little-known Ravensbourne River. You'll ride through many delightful parklands, both new and rejuvenated, making at least half of the ride traffic-free. At Catford, where the route picks up the River Pool, keep an eye (and an ear!) out for the parakeets that have taken up residence in the area. Cycle from park to park before entering the borough of Croydon at Elmers End. Here, you can catch a train back to London or head on south into South Norwood Country Park.

National Route: 21

START Greenwich (*Cutty Sark*).

FINISH South Norwood Country Park.

DISTANCE 8 miles (13km).

GRADE Easy.

SURFACE All tarmac, with a mixture of traffic-free paths, quiet lanes and some sections of road.

HILLS None.

YOUNG & INEXPERIENCED CYCLISTS
The route is suitable for novice cyclists and families, provided care is taken at a few points. It is ideal for young children where it passes though parkland. However, there are also several sections of road that are suitable only for older children (aged 10+).

REFRESHMENTS

- Lots of choice near the *Cutty Sark* in Greenwich.
- Various pubs near the route on the way south.
- Cafe in Ladywell Fields.

THINGS TO SEE & DO

GREENWICH:

- Old Royal Naval College: 020 8269 4799;
  www.greenwichfoundation.org.uk

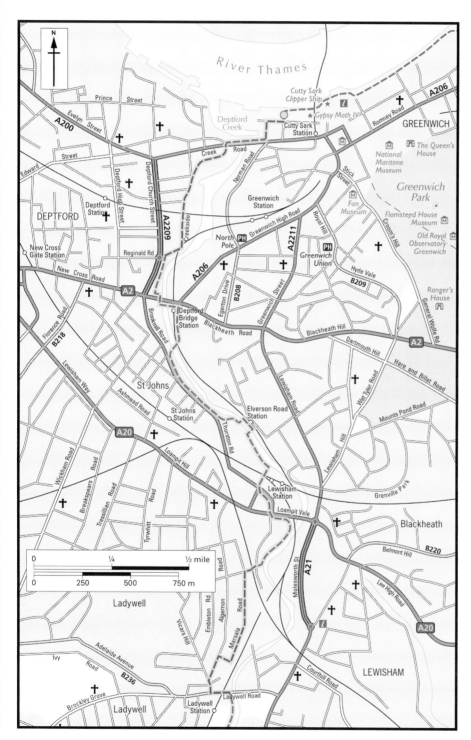

- Royal Observatory/Planetarium: 020 8858 4422; www.nmm.ac.uk/places/royal-observatory
- National Maritime Museum: one of the greatest maritime museums, containing models, displays, paintings and trophies from all over the world;

020 8312 6565; www.nmm.ac.uk
- Ladywell Fields: park with a small cafe, nature reserve, a children's play area and toilet facilities; www.lewisham.gov.uk/leisureandculture/ parksandrecreation

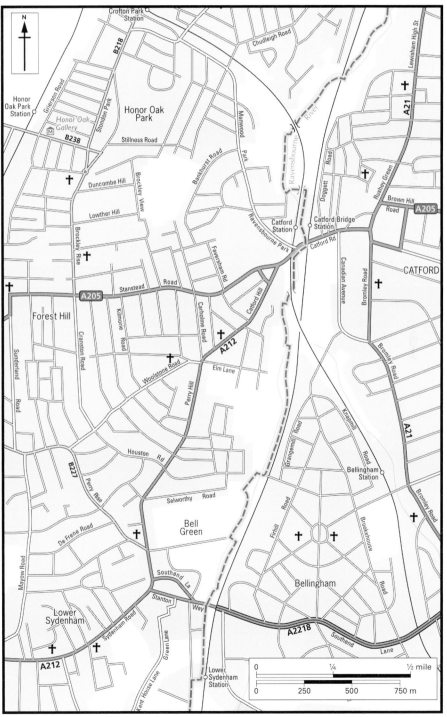

• South Norwood Country Park: www.croydon.gov.uk/
leisure/parksandopenspaces

and there are several others in between: Lewisham;
Ladywell; Catford; and Lower Sydenham.

TRAIN STATIONS

Greenwich and Clockhouse are at either end of the ride,

BIKE HIRE

• Go Pedal!: delivery to most areas of London;

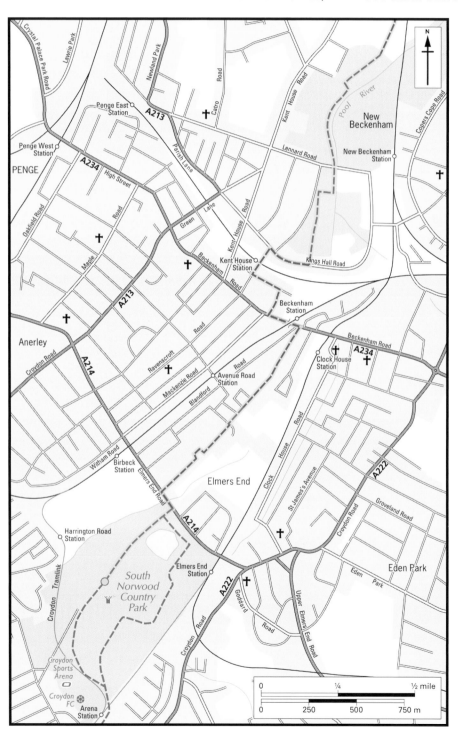

07850 796320; www.gopedal.co.uk
- London Bicycle Tour Company, Gabriel's Wharf: 020 7928 6838; www.londonbicycle.com
- On Your Bike, London Bridge: 020 7378 6669; www.onyourbike.net

FURTHER INFORMATION
- To view or print National Cycle Network routes, visit www.sustrans.org.uk
- Maps for this area are available to buy from www.sustransshop.co.uk
- Transport for London Cycle Guides: a series of free guides covering Greater London, with routes recommended by experienced cyclists. Available from: 020 7222 1234; www.tfl.gov.uk/cycling, as well as bike retailers, leisure centres, Travel Information Centres.
- Transport for London Journey Planner: detailed information to help you plan your travel anywhere in Greater London, by bike, on foot or on public transport; 020 7222 1234; www.tfl.gov.uk
- London Cycling Campaign: provides information and advice on cycling in London; 020 7234 9310; www.lcc.org.uk
- Greenwich Tourist Information; 0870 608 2000
- London Tourist Information; www.visitlondon.com

ROUTE DESCRIPTION
From the Greenwich Foot Tunnel, take the traffic-free path by the *Cutty Sark* and follow it as it dog legs towards Norway Street. Join a cycle path for a short stretch before turning left and crossing over the A200 along Copperas Street and Creekside to the roundabout at Deptford Bridge.

There are some excellent paths through Brookmill Park before Thurston Road and the path that runs once again alongside the River Ravensbourne. Pass through the new traffic-free section south of Lewisham station before reaching Marsala Road and Algernon Road. To avoid the traffic from Vicars Hill along Ladywell Road, stay on the pavement and push your bike for this short stretch. (Sustrans is currently working with the London Borough of Lewisham to improve this busy section of the route for cyclists.)

Take care on the humpback bridge and the short section of busy road before you reach Ladywell Fields, one of Lewisham's most popular green spaces. This is where the route rejoins the river, and it's a good place to stop for a rest. At the end of Ladywell Fields, go under the railway. From Adenmore Road, there are signs that mark the way under the Catford Road.

From the shopping centre, between Catford and Southend Lane, the route follows the river along good-quality shared paths. Cross Southend Lane, then join a traffic-free section to just north of Lower Sydenham Station before cycling a short on-road section past some industrial units. The route then takes you along the River Pool to just north of Lennard Road. Follow the Waterlink Way and Route 21 signs through Cator Park. Turn right onto Kings Hall Road and left to pass Kent House train station. There is then an on-road section along Barnmead Road, Beckenham Road, Churchfields Road and Beck Lane before you arrive at South Norwood Country Park.

NEARBY CYCLE ROUTES
The following are all part of the National Cycle Network:
- The Waterlink Way is part of Route 21, which goes from London to Hastings.
- North of Greenwich, Route 1 runs across the Isle of Dogs and Victoria Park, to join the Lee Valley.
- Route 4 runs west through London to Putney Bridge, to join the Thames Valley Cycle Route.
- East of Greenwich, Route 1 goes past The O2 arena (formerly the Millennium Dome) and the old Woolwich Arsenal on its way to Erith and Dartford.

LEE VALLEY

From the River Thames at East India Dock Basin to Ware in Hertfordshire, the Lee Valley Regional Park stretches 26 miles (42km) along the banks of the River Lee. The 10,000-acre park provides a kaleidoscope of countryside areas, urban green spaces, country parks, nature reserves and lake- and riverside trails. The route starts in maritime Greenwich, a World Heritage site, and crosses under the Thames via the Foot Tunnel to the Isle of Dogs, formerly the thriving London dock area. Beyond East India Dock Road, the Regent's Canal towpath passes through Mile End Park, where a 'green' bridge over busy Mile End Road offers fine views of Canary Wharf. Victoria Park is the oldest municipal park in the world, opened to the public in 1900, while Hackney Marshes hosts the largest collection of football fields in Europe. Walthamstow Marsh Nature Reserve – a Site of Special Scientific Interest (SSSI) – is one of the last remaining marshes along the River Lee and home to over 300 species of plants. Looking over the River Lee and Springfield Marina is the attractive Springfield Park. It was built on the grounds of three 19th-century houses (one of which still stands and has a fine cafe).

National Route: 1

START Greenwich Foot Tunnel, next to the *Cutty Sark*.

FINISH Waltham Abbey.

DISTANCE 13 miles (21km).

GRADE Easy.

SURFACE Tarmac, grit, gravel.

HILLS None.

YOUNG & INEXPERIENCED CYCLISTS

This route is mainly traffic-free and suitable for young children. Once you join the Regent's Canal, the route becomes entirely traffic-free all the way to the North Circular Road.

REFRESHMENTS

• Lots of choice in Greenwich.

• Cafe at Mudchute Farm, Isle of Dogs.
• Cafe in Victoria Park, Hackney.
• Cafe at Springfield Marina by Walthamstow Reservoirs.
• Cafe by Stonebridge Lock in Tottenham Marshes.

THINGS TO SEE & DO

• Greenwich Foot Tunnel; www.greenwich.gov.uk
• Museum of London, Docklands: learn about the fascinating trading history of the Isle of Dogs and London Docklands; 020 7001 9844; www.museumindocklands.org.uk
• Mudchute Park & Farm, Isle of Dogs: the largest urban farm in Europe; 020 7515 5901; www.mudchute.org
• Mile End Park: redeveloped park with views of Canary Wharf.
• Victoria Park, Hackney.
• Hackney Marshes.
• Olympic Park: the route runs adjacent to the park, which will be the focus of the London 2012 Olympic Games; www.london2012.com

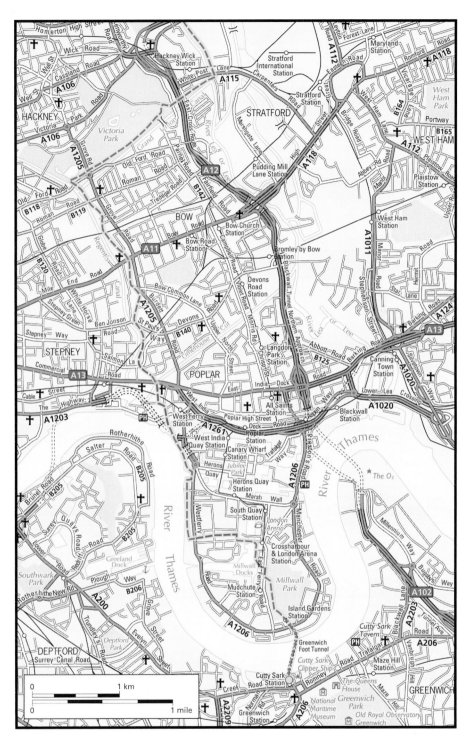

- Walthamstow Marsh Nature Reserve; www.leevalleypark.org.uk
- Springfield Park, Hackney.
- Tottenham Marshes: wide open space, with toilets, canoe and cycle hire, and a cafe at Stonebridge Lock; www.leevalleypark.org.uk

- Waltham Abbey Gatehouse & Bridge; 01992 702200; www.english-heritage.org.uk

TRAIN STATIONS

Greenwich; Limehouse; Hackney Wick; Clapton; Tottenham Hale.

LEE VALLEY

BIKE HIRE

- Go Pedal!: delivery to most areas of London; 07850 796320; www.gopedal.co.uk
- London Bicycle Tour Company, Gabriel's Wharf: 020 7928 6838; www.londonbicycle.com
- On Your Bike, London Bridge: 020 7378 6669; www.onyourbike.net
- City Bike Service: good for exploring the East End of London; 020 7247 4151; www.citybikeservice.co.uk

FURTHER INFORMATION

- To view or print National Cycle Network routes, visit www.sustrans.org.uk
- Maps for this area are available to buy from www.sustransshop.co.uk
- Transport for London Cycle Guides: a series of free guides covering Greater London, with routes recommended by experienced cyclists. Available from: 020 7222 1234; www.tfl.gov.uk/cycling, as well as bike retailers, leisure centres, Travel Information Centres.
- Transport for London Journey Planner: detailed information to help you plan your travel anywhere in Greater London, by bike, on foot or on public transport; 020 7222 1234; www.tfl.gov.uk
- London Cycling Campaign: provides information and advice on cycling in London; 020 7234 9310; www.lcc.org.uk
- London Tourist Information; www.visitlondon.com
- Lee Valley Park; 01992 702200; www.leevalleypark.org.uk

ROUTE DESCRIPTION

Starting in Greenwich, the route takes you under the Thames via the Greenwich Foot Tunnel – please walk your bike through the tunnel. You emerge to find yourself on the Isle of Dogs, home to Canary Wharf and the Mudchute Park and Farm: Europe's largest city farm.

After crossing Millwall Dock and passing the edge of the Canary Wharf development, you soon join the path of Regent's Canal and Mile End Park, crossing the Mile End Road via a 'green' bridge covered with grass and lined with trees.

Leave Regent's Canal to cross Victoria Park before joining the Lee Navigation canal towards Hackney Marshes. The route then continues through Walthamstow Marshes Nature Reserve. North of here, Lee Valley Park offers miles of traffic-free cycling.

NEARBY CYCLE ROUTES

The following are all part of the National Cycle Network.

- To the east of the Thames Barrier, Route 1 continues along the Thames estuary as far as Gravesend, where it heads inland through Kent, then on to Canterbury and

Dover. To the north, Route 1 continues to Roydon and Chelmsford.

• Route 21 links London with the south coast via the Waterlink Way, running down through Deptford and Lewisham towards Croydon and Redhill (see page 73).

There are also miles of enticing traffic-free cycling in Lee Valley Park, which continues north from the end of the route. London Cycle Network Routes 11, 14, and 54 intersect with the route, providing good on-road options if you wish to travel further.

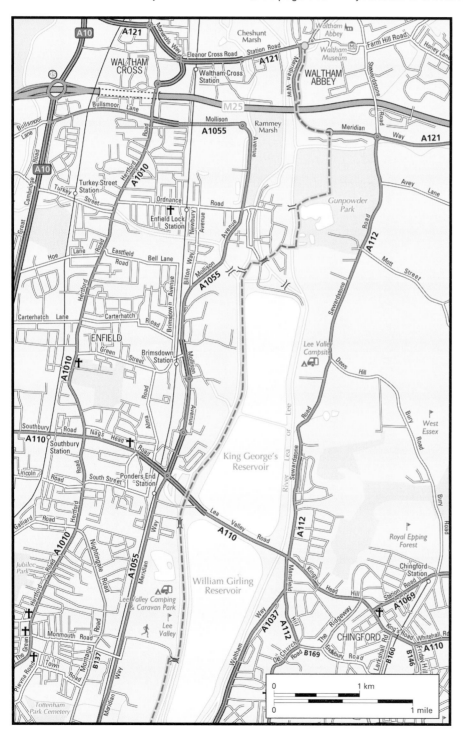

THE WANDLE TRAIL

The Wandle Trail follows the River Wandle, really just a chalk stream, from its junction with the Thames in Wandsworth through a series of small riverside parks south to Carshalton. In its industrial prime the River Wandle was known as Britain's 'hardest working' river, with over 90 mills positioned along its banks. It is one of those rides that seems to improve each time you do it as you begin to memorize the sequences of left, right and straight on that link the green, traffic-free stretches.

There is an excellent coffee/tea stop at the National Trust property in Morden Hall Park, a former deer park with a network of waterways including meadow, wetland and woodland habitats. Morden Hall was built in the mid 18th century by Richard Garth, lord of the manor of Morden. The park also boasts a spectacular rose garden with over 2000 roses, particularly fragrant from May to September. The historic mills and the 19th-century estate buildings house craft workshops including wood turning and furniture restoration.

National Route: 20

START Junction of the River Wandle with the Thames, west of Wandsworth Bridge.

FINISH Carshalton train station.

DISTANCE 11 miles (17.5km).

GRADE Easy.

SURFACE Tarmac or fine gravel and dust path.

HILLS None.

YOUNG & INEXPERIENCED CYCLISTS

There are several traffic-free sections through parkland linked by short road sections, many of which have safe crossings via pelican crossings. The longest traffic-free stretch runs south from Merton High Street to Ravensbury Park, passing through Morden Hall Park.

Please be aware that the Wandle Trail does includes busy sections that younger and less confident cyclists may find challenging, in particular Wandsworth Town and Earlsfield town centres. If necessary, these can easily be navigated on foot. (Sustrans is working to improve cycle facilities not only here but also along the entire Trail.)

REFRESHMENTS
- Lots of choice in the centre of Wandsworth.
- Lots of choice on Merton High Street.
- Cafe at Morden Hall.
- Surrey Arms pub, Morden Road, just south of Morden Hall Park.

THE WANDLE TRAIL

Tony Trude
Moored his houseboat
'Land of Cockaign'
And watched river life
The boat sunk
In 2001

- Lots of choice in the centre of Carshalton.
- Merton Abbey Mills.

THINGS TO SEE & DO
- Morden Hall Park: former deer park, now a National

Trust property, with a network of waterways, meadows and wetlands. The historic snuff mill and 19th-century estate buildings house craft workshops, including wood turning and furniture restoration; 020 8545 6850; www.nationaltrust.org.uk

- Merton Abbey Mills: bustling weekend market specializing in Arts & Crafts, with live music, theatre and craft workshops; www.mertonabbeymills.org.uk
- Deen City Farm: farm and riding stables offering children's events and educational programmes; 020 8543 5300; www.deencityfarm.co.uk

TRAIN STATIONS

Wandsworth Town; Earlsfield; Haydons Road; Mitcham Junction; Carshalton.

BIKE HIRE

- Go Pedal!: delivery to most areas of London; 07850 796320; www.gopedal.co.uk
- London Bicycle Tour Company, Gabriel's Wharf: 020 7928 6838; www.londonbicycle.com
- On Your Bike, London Bridge: 020 7378 6669; www.onyourbike.net
- Smith Brothers, Wimbledon: 020 8946 2270

FURTHER INFORMATION

- To view or print National Cycle Network routes, visit www.sustrans.org.uk
- Maps for this area are available to buy from www.sustransshop.co.uk
- Transport for London Cycle Guides: a series of free guides covering Greater London, with routes recommended by experienced cyclists. Available from: 020 7222 1234; www.tfl.gov.uk/cycling, as well as bike retailers, leisure centres, Travel Information Centres.
- Transport for London Journey Planner: detailed information to help you plan your travel anywhere in Greater London, by bike, on foot or on public transport; 020 7222 1234; www.tfl.gov.uk
- London Cycling Campaign: provides information and advice on cycling in London; 020 7234 9310; www.lcc.org.uk
- London Tourist Information; www.visitlondon.com

ROUTE DESCRIPTION

Starting at the Spit, at the mouth of the River Wandle, follow the river past Bell Lane Creek. Follow the route carefully around the Wandsworth one-way system and onto Garratt Lane. Cross the river to enter King George's Park. Leave the park at the end on Acuba Road, follow Penwith Road towards Earlsfield Station, turning right once again onto Garratt Lane. Turn right onto Summerley Street, then right again to cross Trewint Steet Bridge into Garratt Park, where you follow the river. Cross Plough Lane to continue through the park and go under the railway into the Wandle Meadow Nature Reserve.

Join Chaucer Way and then turn right onto North Road, to follow a road route along East Road, Hanover Road and Leyton Road before rejoining the riverside path. The path passes by Merton Abbey Mills and Deen City Farm and into Morden Hall Park.

Follow the route through the park before crossing Morden Road to reach Ravensbury Park, where once again the route follows the river. There is a short section along Bishopsford Road, left onto Peterborough Road and left again onto Middleton Road to take you around Poulter Park (the walking route goes through the park). Enter Watercress Park and follow the river until you reach Nightingale Road, where you turn right and then left on to The Causeway and left again onto River Gardens past Wilderness Island. Take a right along Denmark Road to reach Carshalton Station.

NB: The Wandle Trail for cyclists does not always follow the Wandle Trail for walkers. Please pay close attention to the cycle signs.

NEARBY CYCLE ROUTES

Route 4 of the National Cycle Network, joined at the northern end of the Wandle Trail, runs west from Wandsworth to Putney Bridge, the start of a long, mainly traffic-free section to Weybridge (see page 68).

Route 20 joins Route 22 which, when completed, will continue south and west through Dorking, Guildford and Farnham, down to the south coast at Portsmouth.

The Tamsin Trail in Richmond Park is a traffic-free circuit around the park's perimeter. The Wandle Trail also forms part of the SW Greenways, a cross-borough network of routes across southwest London.

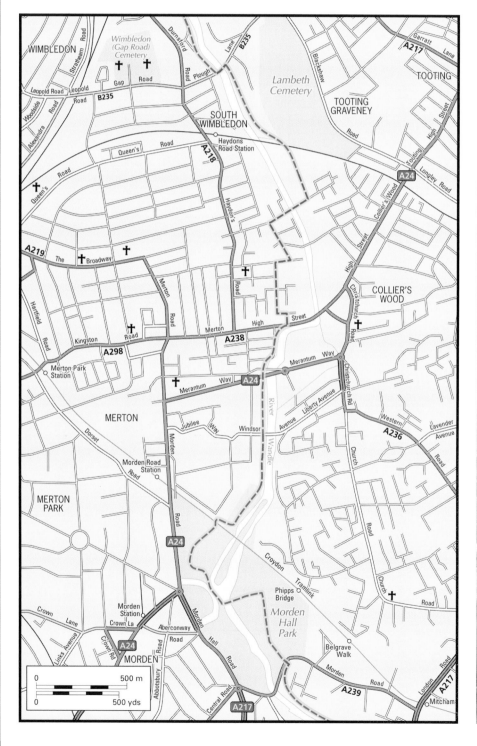

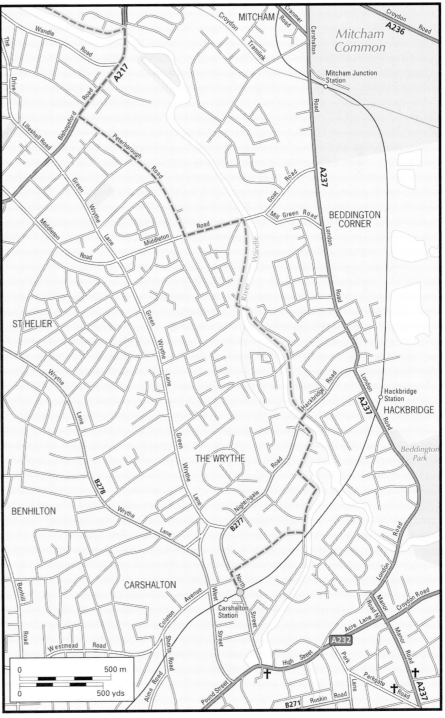

EAST OF ENGLAND

Mention the East of England and one thinks of a land without hills, a land of gentle gradients and few major conurbations, making it an ideal place for recreational cycling. Another major advantage for cyclists is that it is also the driest region in the UK, with less than half of the rainfall of some of the tourist areas on the west side of the country. From Gainsborough country in the south, on the Essex/Suffolk border, to the sandy beaches of the north Norfolk coast, there is a vast network of quiet lanes carrying little traffic linking attractive villages, many of which can boast a flint church and a distinctive village sign. Architectural glories visited on the National Cycle Network include the Roman remains at Colchester, the colleges of Cambridge University, the medieval core of Norwich and the cathedrals at St Albans, Peterborough and perhaps most extraordinary of all, the astonishing sight of Ely Cathedral rising up out of the Fens.

The area closest to London is clearly the most densely populated but it is here that you will find the best network of traffic-free trails, especially in Hertfordshire, including the towpath of the Lee & Stort Navigation through Ware and Hertford, the Albanway from the Roman settlement at St Albans to Hatfield, the Grand Union Canal near Watford and several other railway paths or purpose-built trails ideal for novices and family rides, such as the Cole Green Way (Hertford), the Ayot Green Way (Wheathampstead) or the Nickey Line (Harpenden).

There are plenty of other opportunities for easy traffic-free rides throughout the region: Bedford to Sandy, the Flitch Way near Braintree, the Marriott's Way to the northwest of Norwich and on the many trails around the cathedral town of Peterborough in a project known as the Peterborough Green Wheel; a visionary idea with 'spokes' radiating out from a hub connected by an attractive circuit around the edge of the town. There are also easy Forestry Commission rides in the extensive woodlands around Thetford, in the centre of the region, or on the Suffolk Coast at Rendlesham. Mention should also be made of the Peddars Way, an ancient trading route and now a broad chalk or sandy track from Bridgham Heath (east of Thetford) north through Castle Acre to the coast at Holme next the Sea.

As for long-distance routes, Route 1 runs parallel with the Suffolk coast as far as Beccles, turning inland to visit the cathedral city of Norwich and continuing west across the fertile landscape of Norfolk and Cambridgeshire through the attractive towns of Burnham Market, King's Lynn and Wisbech.

For wildlife enthusiasts there are excellent reserves to be found at Minsmere on the Suffolk Coast, the Norfolk Broads and several along the north Norfolk Coast, such as Titchwell and Cley. The Fens are served by the reserves at Welney and Ouse Washes. A more unusual wildlife reserve is the Otter Trust at Bungay.

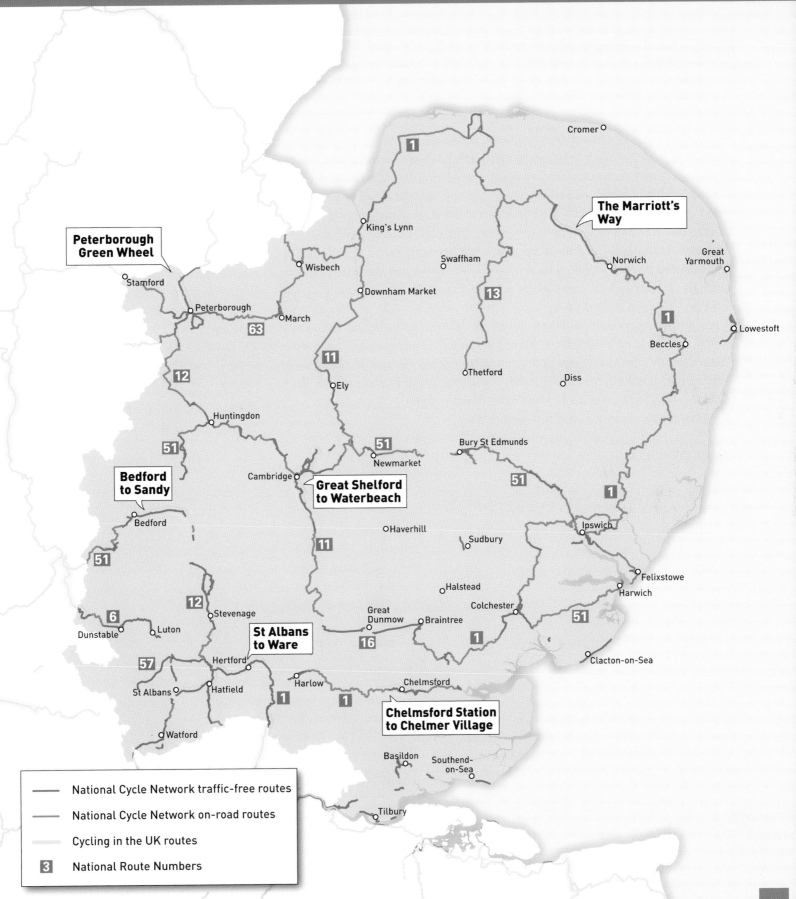

Peterborough Green Wheel

The Marriott's Way

Cromer

King's Lynn

Swaffham

Great Yarmouth

Stamford

Wisbech

Norwich

63

Peterborough

March

Downham Market

13

Lowestoft

Beccles

12

11

Ely

Thetford

Diss

Huntingdon

51

Bury St Edmunds

51

Newmarket

Bedford to Sandy

Cambridge

Great Shelford to Waterbeach

51

1

Bedford

Haverhill

Sudbury

Ipswich

51

11

Felixstowe

Harwich

12

Halstead

6

Stevenage

Colchester

1

51

Dunstable

Luton

St Albans to Ware

Great Dunmow

Braintree

Clacton-on-Sea

57

Hertford

16

1

St Albans

Hatfield

Harlow

1

Chelmsford

1

Chelmsford Station to Chelmer Village

Watford

Basildon

Southend-on-Sea

Tilbury

National Cycle Network traffic-free routes

National Cycle Network on-road routes

Cycling in the UK routes

3 National Route Numbers

ST ALBANS TO WARE

This 16-mile (26-km) linear route joins the attractive cathedral city of St Albans to Ware at the northern end of the Lee Valley by linking two railway paths and a canal towpath. The first railway path, known as the Albanway, runs along the former route of the Hatfield to St Albans branch line of the Great Northern Railway. All that is left of Verulamium, once the most important Roman town in Britain, lies to the west of the present city of St Albans. There are the remains of a great amphitheatre and part of an underground heating system. Modern St Albans takes its name from Alban, the first Christian martyr in Britain. The famous abbey was founded on the hill where he was beheaded. The Albanway passes through deep wooded cuttings with occasional glimpses back to the abbey.

A route skirting around the fringe of Welwyn Garden City takes you to the next railway path, which, at first, is open with views across arable fields but soon becomes wooded. Hertford Town's football ground comes at the end of the second railway path and the start of the urban section through the centre of Hertford, with its many refreshment stops. A short linking section between the two traffic-free rides drops you on the lovely towpath of the Lee Navigation canal, which is followed to Ware.

National Route: 61

START St Albans Abbey train station.

FINISH Ware train station.

DISTANCE 16 miles (26km).

GRADE Easy.

SURFACE Tarmac and fine gravel paths.

HILLS None.

YOUNG & INEXPERIENCED CYCLISTS

The two long sections of railway path, from St Albans to Hatfield and from Welwyn Garden City to Hertford, and the Hertford to Ware towpath, are all ideal for novice riders and children. The linking sections are mainly on cycleways and quiet residential roads but children will need supervision, particularly at road crossings.

REFRESHMENTS

- Lots of choice just off the route in St Albans, Hatfield and Welwyn Garden City.
- Cowper Arms pub in Cole Green (between Welwyn and Hertford).
- The widest choice is in Hertford, as the route goes through the town centre.

THINGS TO SEE & DO

ST ALBANS:
- Verulamium Museum and Museum of St Albans: www.stalbansmuseums.org.uk
- St Albans Abbey: founded in the 4th century; 01727 860780; www.stalbanscathedral.org.uk
- Section of Roman wall built between AD 265 and 270, to defend Verulamium; www.english-heritage.org.uk
- Hatfield House: built in 1607; the grounds include gardens, nature trails, national collection of model soldiers and the Old Palace where Princess Elizabeth

wooded cuttings and past a little lake before going under the mainline railway. Continue along the route, passing several disused platforms from the former railway. Take care crossing the road just past the old platform at Hill End station.

As you approach Hatfield, you pass The Galleria shopping mall, with shops, restaurants and leisure facilities.

A complicated but well-signposted route around the fringe of Welwyn Garden City drops you at the start of the second long, traffic-free section. Hertford Town's football ground marks the end of the railway path and the beginning of the urban section through the centre of Hertford.

This time the link section between the two traffic-free rides is much shorter and before long you are on the Lee Navigation towpath, which can be followed from Ware (beyond the end of the ride described here) all the way into London.

NEARBY CYCLE ROUTES
National Route 61 goes from Windsor to the Lee Valley; Route 12 from Hatfield to Stevenage; and Route 6 from

learned that she had become Queen, following the death of Queen Mary in 1558. Cycles are not allowed in the grounds but you can lock your bike at the train station. 01707 287010; www.hatfield-house.co.uk
- Welwyn Garden City: one of the first garden cities, with green space extending right into the town centre.
- Hertford Castle: close to the route in the town centre; www.hertford.gov.uk

TRAIN STATIONS
St Albans Abbey; Hatfield; Welwyn Garden City; Hertford North; Hertford East; Ware.

BIKE HIRE
Enquire locally.

FURTHER INFORMATION
- To view or print National Cycle Network routes, visit www.sustrans.org.uk
- Maps for this area are available to buy from www.sustransshop.co.uk
- St Albans Tourist Information: 01727 864511.

ROUTE DESCRIPTION
Leaving St Albans Abbey station, you soon join the railway path known as the Alban Way. This runs through deep

Watford to Luton and Milton Keynes.
Other waymarked or traffic-free routes include The
Nickey Line, a railway path running north from the
edge of Hemel Hempstead to Harpenden, and The Ayot
Greenway, going east from Wheathampstead to Ayot St

Peter. The Grand Union Canal can be followed northwest
from London through Watford and Hemel Hempstead,
while the Lee Navigation can be taken all the way south
from Ware to London.

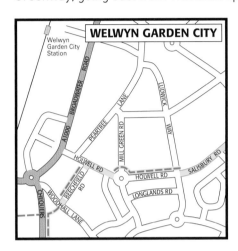

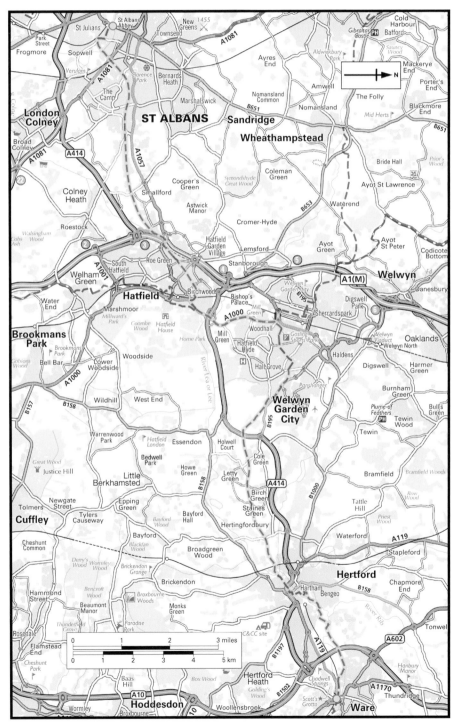

PETERBOROUGH GREEN WHEEL

The concept of Peterborough's Green Wheel is a 45-mile (72-km) network of routes in and around the city, including a 'rim', a 'hub' and 'spokes'. The ride described here initially runs west from the city centre, following the River Nene to Ferry Meadows Country Park, the entrance to which is marked by a wonderful centurion/frog/kingfisher/swan statue.

You'll also visit the pretty villages of Marholm and Etton. Marholm's village sign represents all sectors of Marholm's community under the Fitzwilliam family coat of arms and motto – *Appetitus Rationi Pareat* ('May your desires be reasoned').

Before you set off, or on your return, make the effort to visit Peterborough's splendid cathedral, one of England's finest Norman buildings, begun in 1118, and with a magnificent west front.

National Route: 12; Regional Routes 21 and 63

START/FINISH
The south end of Bridge Street in the centre of Peterborough at the junction of Routes 12, 53 and 63. The route can also be easily accessed from Peterborough train station, by heading north beside the railway and following signs leading to Route 12.

DISTANCE 21-mile (34-km) circular route.

GRADE Easy.

SURFACE Tarmac or fine gravel paths.

HILLS None.

YOUNG & INEXPERIENCED CYCLISTS
The best section for novice riders and young children is from the riverside path in the centre of Peterborough to the old stone bridge over the River Nene at the western end of Ferry Meadows Country Park. This is traffic-free and flat.

REFRESHMENTS
- Lots of choice in Peterborough.
- The Boathouse pub, near the rowing lake.
- Two cafes at Ferry Meadows Country Park Visitor Centre.
- Fitzwilliam Arms pub, Marholm.
- Golden Pheasant pub, Etton.
- Bluebell pub, Glinton.

THINGS TO SEE & DO
- Peterborough Cathedral; 01733 343342; www.peterborough-cathedral.org.uk
- Peterborough Sculpture Park: close to the route near the rowing lake, the park includes an early Antony Gormley piece; www.peterboroughsculpture.org
- Ferry Meadows Country Park: situated in a large meander of the River Nene, with lakes, meadows and woodlands; 01733 234193; www.nene-park-trust.org.uk
- Nene Valley Railway: steam train rides from Peterborough Nene Valley station to Wansford station, a return trip of 15 miles (24km); 01780 784444; www.nvr.org.uk
- Longthorpe Tower: just off the route, to the west of Peterborough; www.english-heritage.org.uk
- Flag Fen Bronze Age Centre: just off the route, near Shanks Millennium Bridge; 0844 4140646; www.english-heritage.org.uk

TRAIN STATIONS Peterborough.

BIKE HIRE Lakeside Leisure: 01733 234418;
www.lakesideleisure.com

FURTHER INFORMATION
- To view or print National Cycle Network routes, visit
  www.sustrans.org.uk
- Maps for this area are available to buy from
  www.sustransshop.co.uk
- Peterborough Tourist Information: 01733 452336;
  www.visitpeterborough.com

ROUTE DESCRIPTION
This ride runs west from the city centre on the 'spoke',
which is signed as Route 63, following the River Nene,
past the rowing lake and the Nene Valley Railway Line to
Ferry Meadows Country Park.

After following traffic-free trails up to this point, you join
the network of quiet lanes linking the pretty villages of
Marholm and Etton. The second part of the ride follows
the 'rim' of the Green Wheel as far as Glinton, then
uses another 'spoke', Route 12, through Werrington,
which is largely on urban cycle lanes, to return to the
pedestrianized heart of the city.

OTHER NEARBY CYCLE ROUTES
Peterborough is at a crossroads of the National Cycle
Network: Route 63 goes from Wisbech to Leicester;
Route 12 from London to Spalding; and Route 53 from
Kettering into the centre of Peterborough. Marked
by distinct blue and white signs, Regional Route 21
designates the Peterborough Green Wheel and overlaps
with all three National Cycle Network routes.

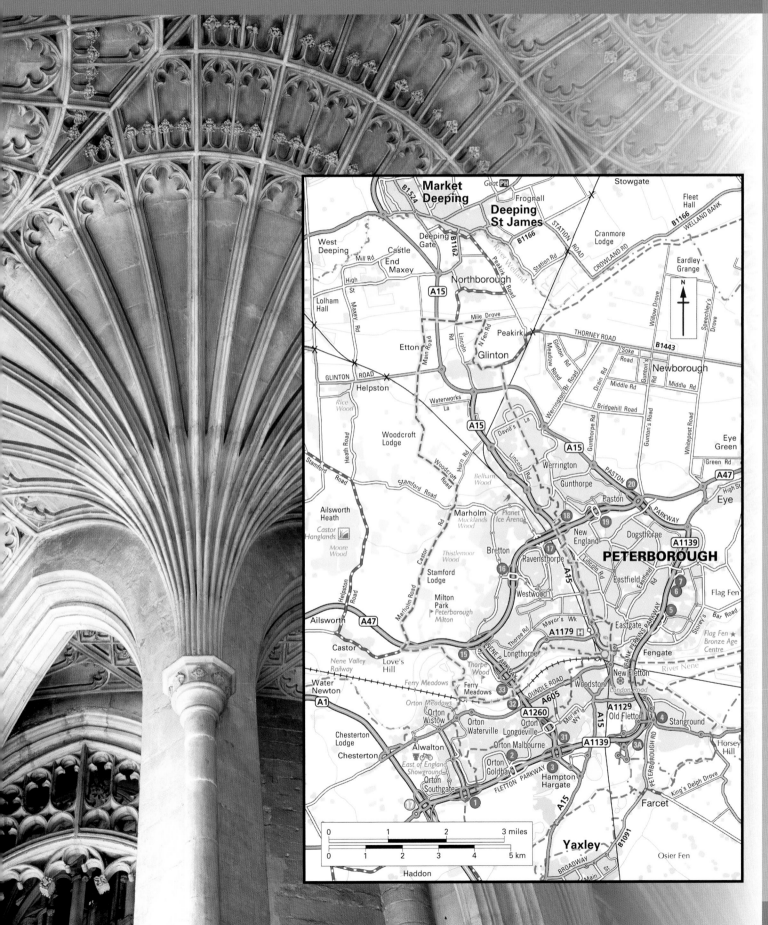

Market
Deeping
Geat PH
Frognall
Stowgate
Fleet
Hall
B1524
Deeping
St James
B1166
Cranmore
Lodge
WELLAND BANK
B1166
West
Deeping
Deeping
Gate
B1162
STATION ROAD
Eardley
Grange
Castle
End
Maxey
Station Rd
CROWLAND RD
Mill Rd
River Welland
N
Lolham
Hall
High St.
Maxey Rd
Northborough
A15
Peakirk Road
Speechley's
Willow Drove
Mile Drove
Peakirk
THORNEY ROAD
Etton
Main Road
Lincoln Rd
N Fen Rd
Glinton
B1443
GLINTON ROAD
Glinton Rd
Drain Rd
Newborough
Helpston
Meadow Road
Gunton's Rd
Middle Rd
Middle Rd
Rice
Wood
Waterworks
La
David's La
Werrington Rd Road
Bridgehill Road
Whitepost Road
Eye
Green
Woodcroft
Lodge
A15
Gunthorpe Rd
Gunton's Rd
Green Rd
Stamford Road
Hurn Rd
Lincoln Rd
A15
Werrington
PASTON
A47
Heath Road
Woodcroft Road
Belham
Wood
Gunthorpe
20
Paston
High St
Eye
Ailsworth
Heath
Stamford Road
Castor Rd
Marholm
Mucklands
Wood
Planet
Ice Arena
18
New
England
PARKWAY
Castor
Hanglands
Moore
Wood
Thistlemoor
Wood
Bretton
17
19
Dogsthorpe
A1139
PETERBOROUGH
Marholm Road
Stamford
Lodge
Ravensthorpe
16
A15
Eastfield
Eastfield Rd
7
Helpston Road
Milton
Park
Peterborough
Milton
Westwood
6
Flag Fen
5
Ailsworth
A47
Mayor's Wk
Eastgate
FRANK PERKINS PARKWAY
Storey's
Bar Road
Castor
A1179
H
Fengate
Flag Fen
Bronze Age
Centre
Nene Valley
Railway
Love's
Hill
15
NENE PARKWAY
Thorpe Rd
Longthorpe
New Fletton
River Nene
Water
Newton
Thorpe
Wood
Ferry
Meadows
33
Woodston
London Road
A1
Ferry Meadows
32
OUNDLE ROAD
A605
A1129
Old Fletton
4
Stanground
Orton Meadows
A1260
Orton
Wistow
Orton
Waterville
Morley Wy
A15
Horsey
Hill
Chesterton
Lodge
Orton
Longueville
31
A1139
3A
Alwalton
Orton Malbourne
Peterborough Rd
Chesterton
East of England
Showground
2
Orton
Goldhay
3
Farcet
Orton
Southgate
FLETTON PARKWAY
Hampton
Hargate
17
1
A15
King's Delph Drove

0   1   2   3 miles
0   1   2   3   4   5 km

Yaxley
B1091
Osier Fen

Haddon
BROADWAY
Main St.

THE MARRIOTT'S WAY

The trail provides an exit from the heart of Norwich into the countryside on one of the longest disused railways in the country. The route is signposted the Wensum Valley Walk from the centre of Norwich and becomes The Marriott's Way near Drayton. William Marriott was the chief engineer and manager of the Midland & Great Northern Joint Railway for an astonishing 41 years. The whole route is studded with a wide variety of broad-leaved trees – oak, ash, hawthorn, silver birch and sycamore. The clear, gently flowing waters of the River Wensum are crossed several times on fine old metal bridges with wooden planking. Between Lenwade and Reepham, you have the option of the full route following the Themelthorpe Loop or taking a shortcut, which saves 4 miles (6.5km) and provides a better surface.

Keep an eye open for the local flora and fauna, as the closure of the railway has been good news for the trackside vegetation and the wildlife that now inhabits it. You may well see jays, magpies, green woodpeckers and wrens. A wide range of plant life, including primroses and wild strawberries, has attracted a rich variety of insects, particularly butterflies and moths. Where the verges are wetter, marsh-marigolds, meadowsweet, Norfolk reeds and horsetail also thrive.

National Route: 1

START Norwich train station.

FINISH Reepham market place.

DISTANCE 15 miles (24km).

GRADE Easy.

SURFACE Traffic-free

HILLS None.

YOUNG & INEXPERIENCED CYCLISTS

There are some on-road sections through Norwich where care is required, otherwise the route is traffic-free and flat – great for young children just learning to ride!

REFRESHMENTS
• Lots of choice in Norwich.
• A number of options in Drayton and Reepham, including the tearooms at Reepham train station.

THINGS TO SEE & DO
NORWICH:
• Norwich Cathedral: a Norman cathedral with the second tallest spire in the country; 01603 218300; www.cathedral.org.uk
• Norwich Castle: built in the 12th century and now Norfolk's principal museum; 01603 493625; www.museums.norfolk.gov.uk
• The Lanes: a network of medieval streets, lanes and alleys with half-timbered houses.
• Cow Tower: purpose-built artillery blockhouses dating back to 1398; www.english-heritage.org.uk

• Dinosaur Natural History Park, Weston Park, Lenwade; 01603 870245; www.dinosauradventure.co.uk
• Reepham: a historic town dating back to the 13th century, although the current market dates from the 18th century, with many traditional shops.

THE MARRIOTT'S WAY

Street. In Tombland, a short detour will take you to the cathedral, which is well worth a visit.

From the centre of Norwich, follow signs for Wensum Valley Walk, to join the traffic-free path by the River Wensum, which is built on the line of the disused Midland & Great Northern Joint Railway. The path takes you through the woodlands of Mileplain Plantation, which is full of sweet chestnut trees, making the route a special treat in the autumn.

It's not all fields and woods, though, since the path also follows the River Wensum; old metal bridges carry you back and forth across it several times. On the edge of Reepham, Route 1 leaves the disused railway to follow minor roads into the centre of Reepham, where the small market square is well worth a stop. There are several pubs in the village to take a welcome break before the return journey to Norwich.

NEARBY CYCLE ROUTES

National Route 1 continues north on-road to Fakenham, or south from Norwich on-road to Beccles. It is part of the Hull to Harwich route and the 3,730-mile (6,000-km) long North Sea Cycle Route, which runs through eight different countries.

TRAIN STATIONS Norwich.

BIKE HIRE Enquire locally.

FURTHER INFORMATION
- To view or print National Cycle Network routes, visit www.sustrans.org.uk
- Maps for this area are available to buy from www.sustransshop.co.uk
- Norwich Tourist Information: www.visitnorwich.co.uk

ROUTE DESCRIPTION

From Norwich train station, turn left and cross the main road into the Riverside area, with bars, nightclubs and new housing, before crossing the river on a foot/cycle bridge. This takes you into King Street and the older part of the city.

Follow this attractive street to Tombland before following a one-way system to St George Street, Colegate and Oak

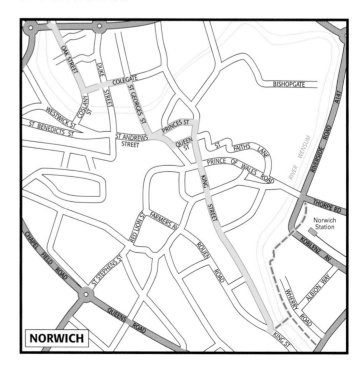

NORWICH

The Marriott's Way carries on for another 6 miles (9.5km) east from Reepham to Aylsham, although the surface is not as good as that between Norwich and Reepham. At Aylsham, you can join the Bure Valley Route (unsurfaced) to Wroxham.

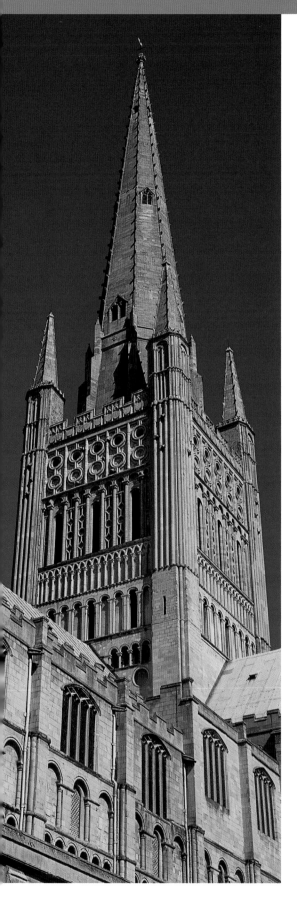

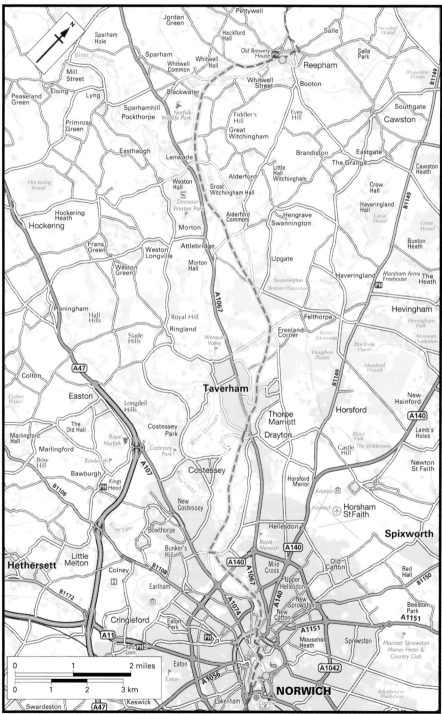

GREAT SHELFORD TO WATERBEACH VIA CAMBRIDGE

The section between Great Shelford and Addenbrooke's Hospital marks the 10,000th mile of the National Cycle Network, opened in September 2005 by Sir John Sulston, the Nobel Prize-winning British scientist behind the Human Genome Project. The artwork along this route celebrates the role of the nearby Sanger Institute in decoding the vital human gene *BRCA2*. A series of stripes in four colours, representing the 10,257 genetic letters, or bases, of *BRCA2*, has been laid on the cycle path using thermoplastic strips, heat-welded onto the tarmac. It is the sequence of the four bases, colour-coded – adenine (A) in green; cytosine (C) in blue; guanine (G) in yellow; and thymine (T) in red – that contains the code for life.

Four species of trees have also been planted at intervals along the route, to improve the local environment and to represent the colours of the four genome bases: yew (*Taxus baccata*), green; rowan (*Sorbus aucuparia* 'Sheerwater Seedling'), blue; crab apple (*Malus* 'Rudolph'), yellow; and cherry (*Prunus cerasifera* 'Nigra'), red.

The route continues from Addenbrooke's Hospital into Cambridge, with its stunning university colleges, and then follows the River Cam to Waterbeach, ending at the train station car park.

National Route: 11

START Shelford train station, Great Shelford.

FINISH Waterbeach train station.

DISTANCE 12 miles (19.5km).
Shorter option, from Great Shelford to Cambridge: 5 miles (8km).

GRADE Easy.

SURFACE Tarmac or fine crushed stone on the towpath.

HILLS None.

YOUNG & INEXPERIENCED CYCLISTS
The route is mainly traffic-free, but particular care is needed in Cambridge city centre, which is often very busy with pedestrians, cyclists and the occasional bus.

REFRESHMENTS
Lots of choice in Cambridge.

THINGS TO SEE & DO
CAMBRIDGE:
• University colleges: www.cam.ac.uk
• Fitzwilliam Museum: the collection includes paintings from the 14th century, sculpture, oriental art and antiquities from Egypt, the Ancient Near East, Greece, Rome and Cyprus; www.fitzmuseum.cam.ac.uk
• Cambridge Museum of Technology: based in the original sewage pumping station for Cambridge, the exhibits include the pumping station's original equipment and other engines; 01223 368650; www.museumoftechnology.com
• Nine Wells Nature reserve: between Shelford and Cambridge

TRAIN STATIONS
Shelford; Cambridge; Waterbeach.

BIKE HIRE
• City Cycle Hire, Cambridge: 01223 365629; www.citycyclehire.com

- Cambridge Station Cycles: 01223 307125;
  www.stationcycles.co.uk

FURTHER INFORMATION

- To view or print National Cycle Network routes, visit
  www.sustrans.org.uk
- Maps for this area are available to buy from
  www.sustransshop.co.uk
- Cambridge Tourist Information: 0871 226 8006;
  www.visitcambridge.org

ROUTE DESCRIPTION

Starting at Shelford train station, head northeast along Station Road, turning left into Chaston Road, which forms part of National Route 11. At the village edge, the route joins a path that follows the railway, with distinctive coloured stripes marking the 10,000th mile of the National Cycle Network.

At Addenbrooke's Hospital, the route joins roads and cycle paths heading to Cambridge city centre, entering from the south at Granta Place. In the summer, this area is busy with students, tourists and locals, gathered around the many punts that moor here. The route then goes along King's Parade, past King's College, through the heart of the city, where there is plenty to see and do.

From Cambridge city centre, the route follows the River Cam to Waterbeach, crossing the river at the

new Riverside bridge and then following the towpath to Waterbeach, where a path leads from the river to the station car park.

NEARBY CYCLE ROUTES

Cambridge has the highest number of cyclists in the UK, and you will soon realize that you are not alone. There are a number of signed routes around the city, with the most attractive ones being those that follow green corridors. Routes are of varying standards, and cyclists

will need to look out for motorized traffic, pedestrians and other cyclists! National Route 51 crosses route 11 in Cambridge, then follows the Cambridgeshire Guided Bus along a disused railway to St Ives. The previous route through the villages of Girton, Oakington and

Longstanton remains an option, but the opening of the guided busway in 2009 has enabled a largely traffic-free route. To the east of Cambridge, Route 51 runs along the opposite bank of the River Cam that's followed in Route 11, before heading east towards Newmarket.

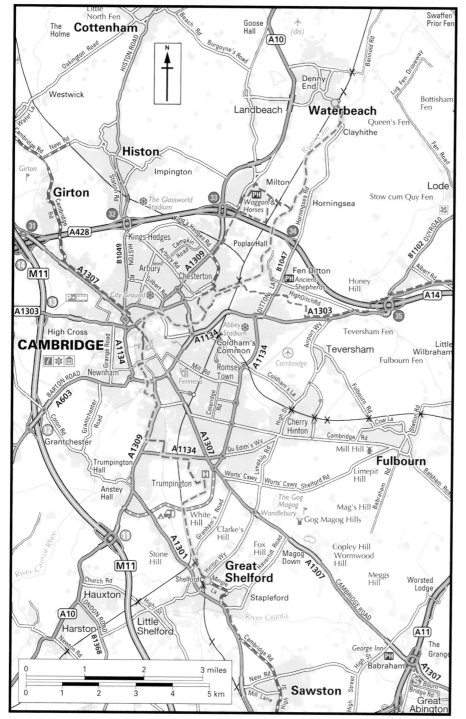

BEDFORD TO SANDY

Bedford has been a market town for the surrounding agricultural area for many centuries. Two castles were built in Norman times but were destroyed in 1224, with only a mound remaining today. Bedford's most famous son is John Bunyan, the author of *The Pilgrim's Progress*, who was imprisoned for his beliefs for 12 years in Bedford Gaol in the late 17th century. Built in 1849, the Meeting House is located on the original site of the barn where he preached, and the nearby Bunyan Museum contains personal relics. An interesting fact about Bedford is that it has one of the highest concentrations of Italian immigrants in the UK – almost 30% of the population is Italian or of Italian descent. Perhaps not surprisingly, Bedford's Little Italy has an impressive variety of Italian bars, restaurants and delicatessens.

Sandy's history dates back to Roman times: Caesar's Camp is an ancient hill fort set in the wooded hills to the south east of the town. Nowadays, Sandy is more famous as the headquarters of the Royal Society for the Protection of Birds (RSPB), which is adjacent to the Lodge Nature Reserve, a mixture of formal gardens with large specimen trees and an azalea walk, heathland and woodland, giving visitors the opportunity of seeing some 100 species of birds.

National Routes: 51 and 12

START Bedford Embankment by the town bridge.

FINISH Sandy market place.

DISTANCE 9 miles (14.5km).

GRADE Easy.

SURFACE Smooth and level route, mainly following riverside paths or a disused railway.

HILLS None.

YOUNG & INEXPERIENCED CYCLISTS
Nearly all traffic-free. Mainly quiet roads in Sandy.

REFRESHMENTS
• Lots of choice in Bedford.
• Priory Country Park.
• Visitor Centre at Danish Camp.
• Sandy market place.

THINGS TO SEE & DO
• Bedford Victorian Embankment Gardens.
• John Bunyan Museum, Bedford; 01234 213722; www.bedfordmuseum.org/johnbunyanmuseum
• Priory Country Park: a haven for wildlife, with lakes, meadows and woodland, and a visitor centre; 01234 211182; www.priorycountrypark.co.uk
• Willington Dovecote and Stables: 16th-century stable and stone dovecote now in the care of the National Trust. Viewing by appointment with the volunteer custodian on 01234 838278; www.nationaltrust.org.uk
• Danish Camp, Willington: historic monument, where the Vikings are believed to have repaired their boats. Visitor centre, refreshments, day fishing and boat rides on the river; 01234 838709; www.danishcamp.co.uk
• Blunham: pretty village dating back to Saxon times.
• Sandy: market gardening centre since the early 17th century.
• The Lodge nature reserve (RSPB), Sandy: beautiful gardens with opportunities to spot woodpeckers and other woodland birds; 01767 680551; www.rspb.org.uk

TRAIN STATIONS Bedford; Sandy.

BIKE HIRE
- Marina Cycles, Priory Country Park: 01234 340090
- Danish Camp, Willington: 01234 838709; www.danishcamp.co.uk

FURTHER INFORMATION
- To view or print National Cycle Network routes, visit www.sustrans.org.uk
- Maps for this area are available to buy from www.sustransshop.co.uk
- Bedford Tourist Information: 01234 221712; www.bedford.gov.uk/tourism

ROUTE DESCRIPTION

Beginning in the centre of Bedford by the Town Bridge, follow the embankment past the castle mound to the elegant Victorian Embankment Gardens. Follow the River Ouse Newcut to the wildlife haven of Priory Country Park. The ride then continues along the route of a former railway, crossing the A421 and passing Willington Dovecote. The route rejoins the river for a while, bringing you to the Danish Camp. From there, you ride through the pretty village of Blunham, following Station Court, turning south on to Station Road and east again to rejoin the railway line. Cross over the River Ivel and cycle into Sandy, going under the A1 before joining paths and quiet roads that lead to the centre of Sandy, where the bustling market place is a focal point. The Lodge nature reserve (home to the RSPB) is on the southeastern side of the town, and is well worth a visit.

OTHER NEARBY CYCLE ROUTES

National Route 12 heads north–south from Peterborough to beyond Hatfield, merging with Route 51 in the Sandy area. Route 12 is only partly completed, but the intention is for it to continue through St Neots and Biggleswade.

There are plans for an orbital route around Bedford, which will be known as The Bedford Green Wheel. Route 51 continues along the River Great Ouse, west from Bedford town centre through Kempston before following minor roads to the Forest Centre and Millennium Country Park at Marston Moretaine. This is a popular area for cycling and away from busy roads. There are many attractive quiet lanes and villages popular with cyclists in Bedfordshire, including The Thatcher's Way, which starts at Priory Country Park.

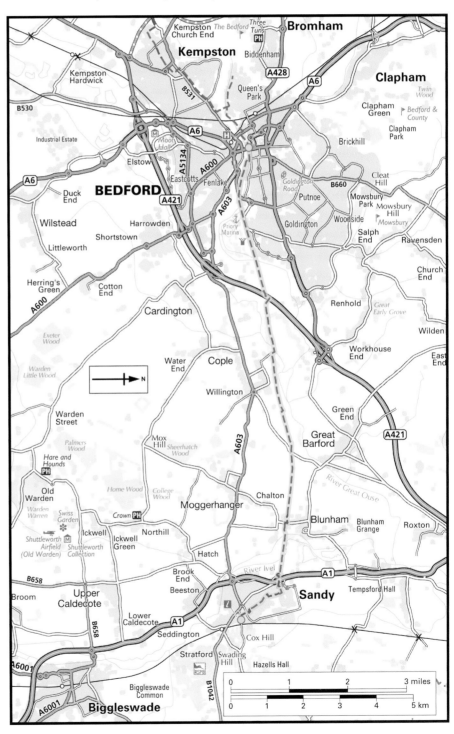

CHELMSFORD STATION TO CHELMER VILLAGE & NEWNEY GREEN

The name Chelmsford is derived from Ceolmaer's Ford, a historic crossing of the River Chelmer, situated close to where the stone bridge in the town's high street is now. The Romans built a fort here, Caesaromagus, at the junction of the River Chelmer and the River Can, on the road linking London to Colchester. By the early 13th century, it was recognized as the county town of Essex and has remained so to this day. The Cathedral Church of St Mary the Virgin was built around 1420.

These two rides connect town to country by using Chelmsford's riverside paths alongside the River Can. To the west, Writtle has one of the loveliest village greens in Essex, with a duck pond and a backdrop of Tudor and Georgian houses. Longer rides are possible on quiet lanes leading west from Writtle through delightful undulating countryside to the pretty villages of The Rodings. These are a collection of eight villages and hamlets (Abbess, Aythorpe, Beauchamp, Berners, High, Leaden, Margaret and White Roding) located in the River Roding valley, with old churches, half-timbered cottages and moated halls.

National Route: 1

START Chelmsford train station

FINISH Fox and Raven pub, Chelmer Village, or the Duck Inn, Newney Green.

DISTANCE
Chelmsford train station to Chelmer Village:
2 miles (3km).
Chelmsford train station to Newney Green:
6 miles (9.5km).

GRADE Easy.

SURFACE Tarmac paths and minor roads.

HILLS None.

YOUNG & INEXPERIENCED CYCLISTS
Easy-going, mainly traffic-free rides, leading to generally quiet minor roads, but care should still be taken.

REFRESHMENTS

- Chelmsford town centre.
- Writtle College garden centre and teashop.
- Fox and Raven pub, Chelmer Village.
- Duck Inn, Newney Green.

THINGS TO SEE & DO

- Central Park and Admiral's Park feature a lake, golf course and riverside paths.
- Old Chelmsfordians' sports field often hosts football and cricket matches.

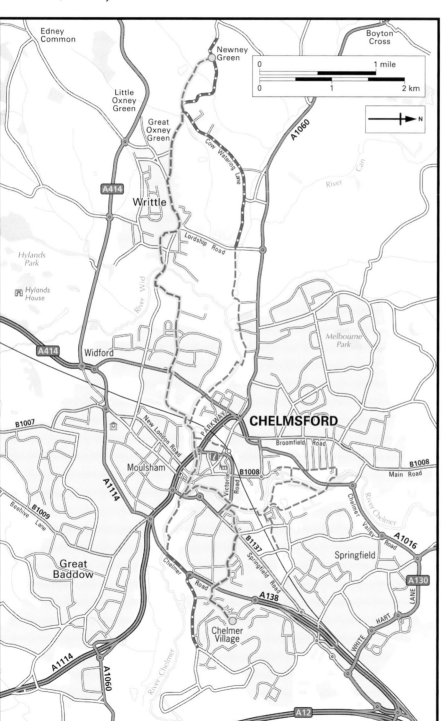

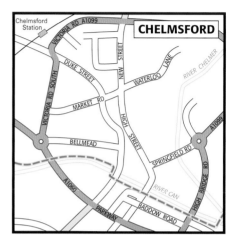

- Chelmsford Museum: 01245 605700;
www.chelmsfordbc.gov.uk/museums
- Writtle village green and duckpond.
- Hylands House and Park: best known for hosting major events and festivals but is worth a visit in its own right; can be accessed through Writtle; www.chelmsford.gov.uk/hylands

TRAIN STATIONS Chelmsford.

FURTHER INFORMATION
- To view or print National Cycle Network routes, visit www.sustrans.org.uk
- Maps for this area are available to buy from www.sustransshop.co.uk
- Chelmsford Tourist Information: 01245 283400; www.chelmsford.gov.uk

ROUTE DESCRIPTION
From Chelmsford station, cross over Duke Street and head down Park Road, turning right to cross a park and through a subway into Central Park. For those wanting to head straight out to the countryside, turn right, but to explore routes through the town centre and out to Chelmer Village, turn left in Central Park and follow Route 1, past Essex County Cricket ground on your right and across the high street. This attractive route continues along the river corridor to Chelmer Village, a relatively modern development on the edge of Chelmsford. Here, you can stop for refreshments at the Fox and Raven pub, or turn back and retrace your steps back to Central Park.

Alternatively, travelling west from Chelmsford station, follow the river through Chelmsford and out to Writtle College. Continue on Route 1 through the grounds of the college, emerging on to minor roads at the rear. The adventurous could continue on route 1 all the way to Harlow or create their own new routes using the minor roads. The small village of Newney Green, with its attractive Duck Inn, is the first village you come to.

NEARBY CYCLE ROUTES
National Route 13 is intended to link Chelmsford with the Thames Estuary routes further south, but the route is still in development, although it is signed through to the south of Chelmsford.

The Flitch Way starts at Braintree, easily reached by train from Chelmsford. This forms part of Route 16 of the National Cycle Network and follows the disused railway that used to link Braintree with Bishop's Stortford.

The Wivenhoe Trail links Colchester and Wivenhoe along the River Colne corridor. Both towns are accessible by train from Chelmsford.

ARTWORKS

On many walking and cycling routes across the UK, Sustrans has worked with artists to create artworks that add significance to and reflect the character of the passing landscape. These artworks have become navigational aides, marking off key sections along the route and increasing the enjoyment of the journey.

Communities often become involved in the commissioning process, giving an historical context and providing local anecdotes to accompany the background research. Through this participation and practical workshops organized by artists, local residents and young people can become the owners and caretakers of these new artworks.

STONE COLUMN BY JERRY ORTMANS
COLLIERS WAY, NEAR WELLOW, SOMERSET
A memorial to the 'Father of English Geology', William Smith, who lived at Tucking Mill, right on the route, 200 years ago. Smith was the surveyor and resident engineer on the Somersetshire Coal Canal, where he observed that fossils could be used to identify different rock strata, a fundamental principle of geology that is upheld to this day. He is famous for producing the first-ever geological map.

VIEWING PLATFORM BY ANDREW SABIN
WANDLE TRAIL, SOUTH WEST LONDON (See pages 83-85)
Creates an undulating path to the centre of the River Wandle at its confluence with the River Graveney. The platform offers an appreciation of the waterways from a usually hidden perspective.

SPIRALLING STEAM BY ROB WOODS
DIDCOT, OXFORDSHIRE
This artwork reflects the steam emissions from nearby Didcot power station.

SOUND POLES BY JONY EASTERBY
TREDEGAR PARK, NEWPORT, SOUTH WALES
A playful musical experience: cycling between 15 poles activates strips set into the path, which trigger sound chimes fixed to the top of each pole.

GENOME STRIPES BY KATY HALLETT
CAMBRIDGE TO GREAT SHELFORD (See pages 102-105)
Working with Sir John Sulston from nearby Sanger Institute, this installation illustrates the gene BRCA2. The 10,257 coded stripes, in exact order, celebrate the 10,000th mile of the National Cycle Network.

GATEWAYS
Gateways create a sense of entering a special place, where different values apply. Distinctive designs establish an identity for a route, assist with navigation and help locate the path in relation to other landmarks. Marking the start and finish of a route, and occasionally set at access points, gateways also define boundaries.

TWISTED ARCH BY COD STEAKS
BRISTOL & BATH RAILWAY PATH (See pages 20-23)

KEYHOLE ARCH BY JEREMY CUNNINGHAM
BATHGATE TO AIRDRIE

a seat, Sustrans has a collection of them with dozens of quite different designs. Bespoke street furniture along a route sets a precedent, a design continuum helping to punctuate a path, giving shape and rhythm to a journey. The position and orientation of each seat is critical, inviting people to sit at a particular site to enjoy a specific view.

CYCLE ARCH BY DOMINIC CLARE
GATEWAY TO PORTHMADOG

WAVE SHELTER BY GEOFF STAINTHORPE
TARKA TRAIL, DEVON

SENTINEL 1 BY JIM PAULSEN
BRISTOL & BATH RAILWAY PATH (See pages 20-23)

SEATS
Seats are frequently requested by the public who want places to rest and, despite the simplicity and function of

ARCH BENCH BY BEN MAY
TARKA TRAIL, DEVON

THRONE BY PAUL ANDERSON
TARKA TRAIL, DEVON

BIRD TRIO BY KATY HALLETT
TARKA TRAIL, DEVON

THRONE BY TONY EASTMAN
ELY, CAMBRIDGESHIRE

ROGER WITHERS MEMORIAL BENCH BY NEIL GOW
WYE VALLEY, BIBLINS BRIDGE, ROUTE 30

WINDBLOWN OAK BY JIM PARTRIDGE AND CLAIRE WALMSLEY
BRISTOL & BATH RAILWAY PATH (See pages 20-23)

SLEEPER SEAT BY JIM PARTRIDGE AND CLAIRE WALMSLEY
BRISTOL & BATH RAILWAY PATH (See pages 20-23)

EGG SEATS BY KATY HALLETT
COSSINGTON TO BAWDRIP TRAIL, SOMERSET

REFLECTIVE SPACE BY LEIGH ROBERTS
PHOENIX TRAIL, PRINCES RISBOROUGH TO THAME (See pages 56-59)

CIRCULAR BENCH BY RICHARD STUMP
PHOENIX TRAIL, PRINCES RISBOROUGH TO THAME (See pages 56-59)

1 *Twisted Arch* by Cod Steaks 2 *Keyhole Arch* by Jeremy Cunningham 3 *Cycle Arch* by Dominic Clare 4 *Sound Poles* by Jony Easterby 5 *Throne* by Tony Eastman 6 *Signal Seat* by Angus Ross 7 *Bird Trio* by Katy Hallett 8 *Irish Elks* by Sally Matthews 9 *Lincolnshire Reds* by Sally Matthews

SIMPLICITY BENCH BY YUMIKO AOYAGI
PHOENIX TRAIL, PRINCES RISBOROUGH TO THAME (See pages 56-59)

WAVY BENCH BY STEVE ELDERKIN
PHOENIX TRAIL, PRINCES RISBOROUGH TO THAME (See pages 56-59)

SIGNAL SEAT BY ANGUS ROSS
PHOENIX TRAIL, PRINCES RISBOROUGH TO THAME (See pages 56-59)

DIGGER SEAT BY JASON LANE
SPEN VALLEY, YORKSHIRE (See pages 188-191)

CYCLE SEAT BY ALUN EVANS
SPEN VALLEY, YORKSHIRE (See pages 188-191)

SALLY MATTHEWS AND SUSTRANS

The artist Sally Matthews creates beautiful, lifelike animals from bits of old scrap metal. Her work has universal appeal and is unfailingly popular. Sally has worked on six commissions with Sustrans on routes across the UK. She says:

'Everyone has their own reasons for using animals in art. For me, I always go back to the animals themselves for inspiration – my love for them, their different forms, their movement, smell and nature are the reasons for my making them. Their nature, even that of a domesticated or trained animal, is unpredictable and wild, and their presence is always enlivening. I want my work to remind people of our need for animals and of the example their nature provides us with.'

IRISH ELKS
COALVILLE, LEICESTER

BEAMISH SHORTHORN
CONSETT, COUNTY DURHAM

SHEEP
TREDEGAR PARK, NEWPORT, SOUTH WALES

LINCOLNSHIRE REDS
WATER RAIL WAY, LINCOLNSHIRE (See pages 128-131)

LINCOLNSHIRE LONG WOOLS
WATER RAIL WAY, LINCOLNSHIRE (See pages 128-131)

WE ALL WALK THE SAME PATH
SPEN VALLEY, YORKSHIRE (See pages 188-191)

MIDLANDS

Stretching from the Welsh Borders in the west to the coast of Lincolnshire in the east, the Midlands encompass the United Kingdom's industrial heartland but also some of its most popular tourist destinations, such as the Peak District National Park and Stratford-upon-Avon. In this region, too, are some of the country's best-known cycle trails, such as the Tissington and High Peak Trails near Ashbourne or the circuit of Rutland Water to the east of Leicester.

Looking to the area's industrial heritage is a good place to start for an overview of what the National Cycle Network offers in the region. Not only have many traffic-free trails been created on the course of old railways that were built in a fever of Victorian development from 1830-1880 but there are opportunities to ride through the cradle of the Industrial Revolution from Telford south to Ironbridge, and to explore Birmingham, the country's industrial powerhouse *par excellence*, via the extensive network of canals through the heart of this resurgent city. Cycle routes radiate from Gas Street Basin, the very epicentre of the canal network in Birmingham, which is a dazzling mix of the old and the new.

Several other towns in the Midlands, such as Stoke, Leicester, Derby and Lincoln, have developed a fine network of cycle trails, all of which fulfil many functions. They are useful for commuters and school children, places where young children can learn to ride, attractive there-and-back rides in themselves from town to country and also a way out of the urban areas into the wider countryside for more experienced cyclists who don't need to transport their bikes by car to get out to quieter rural destinations.

Long-distance routes in the region include a continuation of the Harwich to Hull Cycle Route (Route 1) across the flat, dark fenland of Lincolnshire and over the Lincolnshire Wolds to the Humber Bridge; the Pennine Cycleway (Route 68), that starts in Derby on its way several hundred miles north to the Scottish Border at Berwick-upon-Tweed; and two alternative routes from Oxford to Derby. One off these routes travels west via Stratford, Birmingham and Lichfield, the other goes east via Milton Keynes, Northampton and Leicester.

Traffic-free rides can also be found on the railway path known as the Brampton Valley Way from Market Harborough to Northampton, the Cloud Trail from Derby to Worthington, the Stratford-upon-Avon Greenway or the Birmingham Canal towards Wolverhampton. One of the most popular areas for family rides is in Clumber Park, close to Worksop in Nottinghamshire. Route 6 north from Mansfield takes you right through the park.

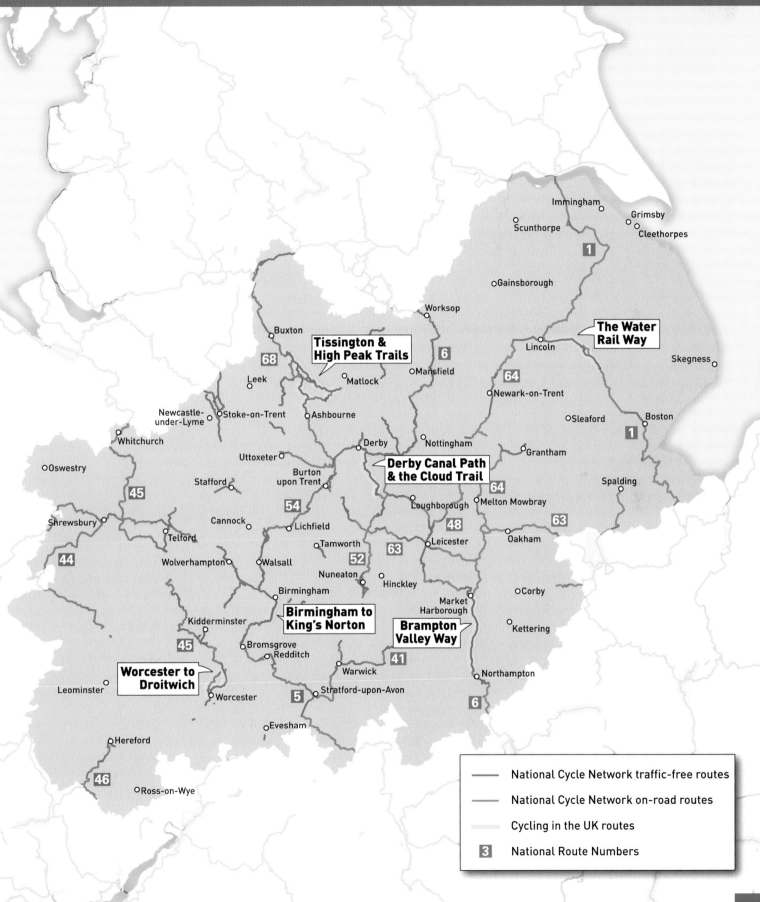

Immingham
Grimsby
Scunthorpe
Cleethorpes
1
Gainsborough
Worksop
Buxton
The Water Rail Way
Tissington & High Peak Trails
6
Lincoln
Skegness
Leek
68
Matlock
Mansfield
64
Newark-on-Trent
Newcastle-under-Lyme
Stoke-on-Trent
Ashbourne
Sleaford
Boston
Whitchurch
Derby
Nottingham
1
Oswestry
Uttoxeter
Derby Canal Path & the Cloud Trail
Grantham
Stafford
Burton upon Trent
64
Spalding
45
54
Loughborough
Melton Mowbray
Shrewsbury
Cannock
Lichfield
48
63
Telford
Tamworth
63
Leicester
Oakham
44
Wolverhampton
Walsall
52
Nuneaton
Hinckley
Corby
Birmingham
Market Harborough
Kettering
Birmingham to King's Norton
Kidderminster
Brampton Valley Way
45
Bromsgrove
Redditch
41
Worcester to Droitwich
Warwick
Northampton
Leominster
Worcester
5
Stratford-upon-Avon
6
Evesham
Hereford
46
Ross-on-Wye

—— National Cycle Network traffic-free routes

—— National Cycle Network on-road routes

—— Cycling in the UK routes

3 National Route Numbers

119

BIRMINGHAM TO KING'S NORTON

Birmingham grew impressively during the Industrial Revolution of the 18th and 19th centuries to become Britain's second largest city. Its prosperity was based on manufactured goods, produced in hundreds of small workshops and transported on an amazing network of canals, all of which allowed the city to become a world powerhouse in the production of everything from nails to steam engines. Grand Victorian public buildings stand alongside soaring structures of glass and steel in the dynamic heart of the city. This ride links Centenary Square to the delights of Cannon Hill Park, where there are always fantastic displays of flowers, shrubs and rare ornamental trees – this is the start of the Rea Valley Route. The ride then continues on to King's Norton Park.

The River Rea rises southwest of Birmingham in Waseley Country Park, and flows northeast across the city. Although a small river, it has been called the 'Mother of Birmingham', as it has played a vital role in the development of the city, particularly the Digbeth area, where there was a small settlement hundreds of years ago. Over 20 mills once flourished in the Rea Valley, many of them built for corn grinding, but during the Industrial Revolution they provided water power for Birmingham's industries.

National Route: 5

START Centenary Square, Broad Street.

FINISH King's Norton Park.

DISTANCE 7 miles (11km).

GRADE Easy.

SURFACE Mixture of road, tarmac cycle paths and stone-based tracks.

HILLS None.

YOUNG & INEXPERIENCED CYCLISTS

The ride uses some traffic-calmed streets in central Birmingham, although some streets are still busy. Once out of the centre, all the busy roads are crossed via toucan crossings. The section along the Rea Valley Route, through Cannon Hill Park and along the Worcester & Birmingham Canal, is traffic-free.

REFRESHMENTS
- Lots of choice in Birmingham city centre.
- Cafe/tea room in Cannon Hill Park.

THINGS TO SEE & DO

BIRMINGHAM:
- *Spirit of Enterprise* sculpture, Centenary Square
- The ICC conference centre; 0121 200 2000; www.theicc.co.uk
- Symphony Hall; 0121 780 3333; www.thsh.co.uk
- The NIA (National Indoor Arena); 0121 780 4141; www.thenia.co.uk
- The Rep (Birmingham Repertory Theatre); 0121 245 2000; www.birmingham-rep.co.uk
- The Mailbox shopping and entertainment complex; 0121 632 1000; www.mailboxlife.com
- Bullring shopping complex; 0121 632 1500; www.bullring.co.uk
- Birmingham Cathedral; 0121 262 1840; www.birminghamcathedral.com

- Shopping streets of New Street/Corporation Street.
- Cannon Hill Park: beautiful park with boating lake, children's playgrounds, picnic areas and tea rooms; www.birmingham.gov.uk/cannonhillpark.bcc
- Cadbury World, Bournville: famous chocolate factory, where you can find out how chocolate is made and visit the shop for refuelling; 0845 450 3599; www.cadburyworld.co.uk
- King's Norton Park: playground

FURTHER INFORMATION

- To view or print National Cycle Network routes, visit www.sustrans.org.uk
- Maps for this area are available to buy from www.sustransshop.co.uk
- Birmingham Tourist Information: 0121 202 5115; www.visitbirmingham.com

TRAIN STATIONS

Birmingham New Street; King's Norton; Bournville.

BIKE HIRE

- On Your Bike: 0121 666 6933; www.onyourbike.net
- Midland Cycle Hire; 01562 711144; www.midlandcyclehire.co.uk

ROUTE DESCRIPTION

Starting from the impressive Centenary Square, you make your way through the city centre, past Gas Street canal basin and then head off towards The Mailbox complex, Hippodrome Theatre and more built-up areas of the city. The journey to the Rea Valley Route is made much easier and more enjoyable by a series of contraflow cycle lanes and toucan crossings. A minaret at the end of Gooch Street is testimony to the number of Muslims living in this multi-cultural city and stands in contrast to

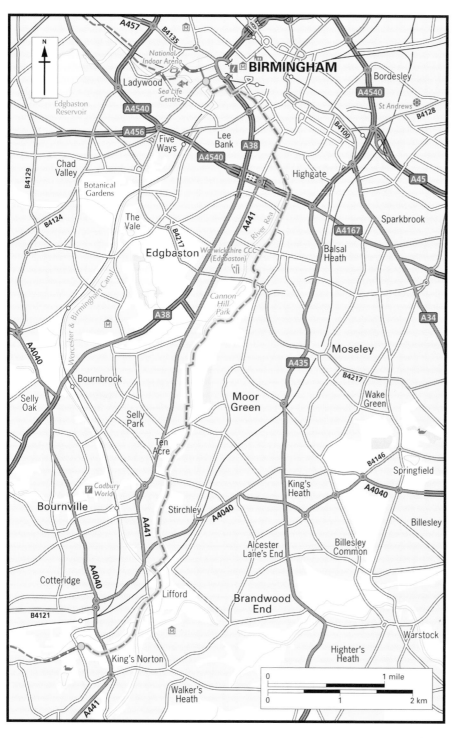

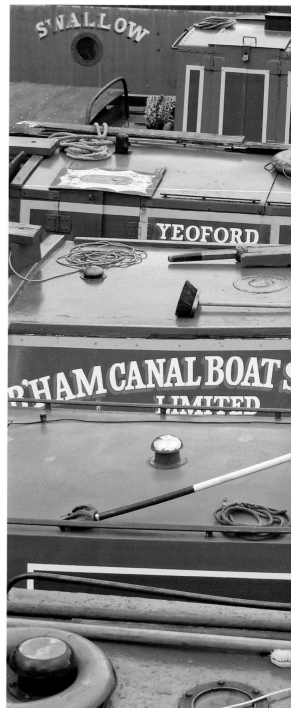

the ornate facade of Edward Road Baptist Church that is situated further along the route. Travel through the beautiful and green Cannon Hill Park, which marks the start of the traffic-free Rea Valley Route. Follow this for 4 miles (6.5km) before joining the excellent towpath of the Worcester & Birmingham Canal for one section.

For chocoholics, there's a diversion to Cadbury World at Bournville (this route also links the ride to Bournville station). The main ride continues on to King's Norton Park, where there is a playground for children.

It is possible to continue on Route 5 along the line of the river valley to Northfield, Longbridge and southwards towards Stratford-upon-Avon.

NEARBY CYCLE ROUTES

Birmingham is at a crossroads of the National Cycle Network.

- Route 5 travels north from Reading through Oxford, Banbury, Stratford and Bromsgove (and is followed in this ride into the centre of Birmingham). It continues northeast via Sandwell Valley Country Park, Walsall, Lichfield and Burton-on-Trent to Derby.
- Route 54 goes from Dudley to Stourbridge (there are plans to continue the route to Hereford).
- Route 81 follows the Main Line Canal to Wolverhampton and Shrewsbury.

Birmingham has more miles of canal than Venice, and a large stretch of the towpath network is open to cyclists. There are, though, some parts that are not due to safety considerations, such as steep lock flights and low bridges, but these are clearly signed. There is much to explore, including the Worcester & Birmingham Canal towpath, which is used for part of this route. For the most up-to-date information, contact British Waterways: 0121 200 7400; www.waterscape.com

The proposed National Route 535 will link Birmingham to Sutton Park, a large park just north of Birmingham, where motor traffic is restricted to the outskirts. A section of it is already signed as the North Birmingham Walking and Cycling Route.

The Kingswinford Railway Path runs for 10 miles (16km) from Pensnett (west of Dudley) to Wolverhampton.

DERBY CANAL PATH & THE CLOUD TRAIL

The route out of Derby to Worthington was one of the first built by Sustrans. It starts near the heart of the city and sets out on an attractive path beside the River Derwent, which would take you to Elvaston Castle if you wished. However, the Canal Path turns south away from the river and follows the course of a dry waterway to join the still navigable Trent & Mersey Canal at Swarkestone. After about 1 mile (1.6km), you leave the towpath to join The Cloud Trail, a dismantled railway path that will take you as far as the village of Worthington and up to nearby Cloud Quarry. On the way, watch out for colourful milemarkers and four enigmatic wayside figures made of Swithland slate.

The Derby Canal Path and The Cloud Trail are part of the much longer Route 6 of the National Cycle Network, which runs all the way from London to the Lake District.

Melbourne is an appealing town just off the route, with thatched, whitewashed cottages and the remains of a 14th-century castle. Just beyond Melbourne, you will see the outline of the Norman church of St Mary and St Hardulph set high on the limestone bluff above the village of Breedon on the Hill.

National Route: 6

START Derby train station or the Riverside Path in the centre of Derby (Bass's Recreation Ground).

FINISH Worthington and Cloud Quarry.

DISTANCE 13 miles (21km).

GRADE Easy.

SURFACE Traffic-free, fine-quality stone paths with short road sections.

HILLS None.

YOUNG & INEXPERIENCED CYCLISTS
Once onto the Riverside Path, the route is excellent for novices and young children. All the busy roads are crossed via bridges, subways or toucan crossings. There is a 1-mile (1.6-km) road section to visit Melbourne and a shorter, quieter road section to visit Worthington.

REFRESHMENTS
• Lots of choice in Derby.
• Lots of choice in Melbourne.
• Malt Shovel pub in Worthington.

THINGS TO SEE & DO
DERBY:
• Derby Cathedral: from the station, follow Route 6 in the other direction towards the city centre; 01332 341201; www.derbycathedral.org
• Derby Museum and Art Gallery; 01332 641901; www.derby.gov.uk
• Silk Mill: one of the first factories in the UK and part of the Derwent Valley Mills World Heritage Site; 01332 255308; www.derby.gov.uk

DERBY CANAL PATH & THE CLOUD TRAIL

- Swarkestone: village where Bonnie Prince Charlie turned his army around in 1745, making it the southernmost point reached by the army on its way to London. Swarkestone Bridge was built in the 14th century.
- Trent Viaduct, near Melbourne: Grade II listed structure, built in 1869 and repaired by Sustrans in the late 1980s.
- Melbourne: remains of a 14th-century castle.
- The Cloud Cuckoos: a pair of giant iron birds fiercely guard their only egg, close to the edge of Cloud Quarry.
- Worthington: village boasting an attractive church with a small wooden spire and an octagonal red-brick lock-up dating back to the 18th century.

FURTHER INFORMATION

- To view or print National Cycle Network routes, visit www.sustrans.org.uk
- Maps for this area are available to buy from www.sustransshop.co.uk
- Derby Tourist Information: 01332 255802; www.visitderby.co.uk

TRAIN STATIONS Derby.

ROUTE DESCRIPTION

Starting at Derby train station (Pride Park exit), use the link route to join the Derwent path. Follow this eastbound for about 1 mile (1.6km) before turning south onto Derby Canal Path, a specially built cycle path that takes you to the Trent & Mersey Canal at Swarkestone. Turn left onto the towpath then, after another mile (1.6km), turn right, leaving the towpath to join The Cloud Trail. This traffic-free path crosses the Trent Viaduct near Melbourne, then skirts the villages of King's Newton and Wilson en route to Worthington.

Watch out for a left turn, just before you reach Worthington car park. Follow this around and up to the rim of Cloud Quarry, which has dramatic viewpoints and the sardonic Cloud Cuckoos.

From the Cuckoos, it's possible to continue along quiet lanes and traffic-free sections for 10 miles (16km) to Loughborough, where there is a train station. Follow the signs for Route 6.

NEARBY CYCLE ROUTES

Derby is at a major junction of the National Cycle Network and has more than its share of associated traffic-free paths.

Derby Riverside Path follows the Derwent east to a turn-off for Elvaston Castle Country Park, with its tea room and perimeter track. Beyond Elvaston, Route 6 extends, partly off-road, via Borrowash and Breaston to Long Eaton.

To the north of Derby city centre (Exeter Bridge), National Route 54 enters the Derwent Valley Mills World Heritage

Site, brushing past the Silk Mill Industrial Museum and on to Chester Green and Darley Abbey.

About 1.5 miles (2.5km) west of the city centre, the other arm of National Route 54 joins a largely traffic-free trail that runs 6 miles (9.5km) to Hilton.

For a more ambitious ride, watch out for the National Route 68 turn at Etwall. From here, you could join the Pennine Cycleway, which would take you up-hill and down-dale, all the way to Scotland.

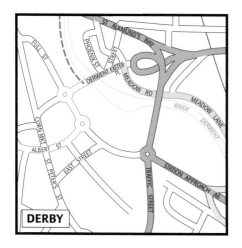

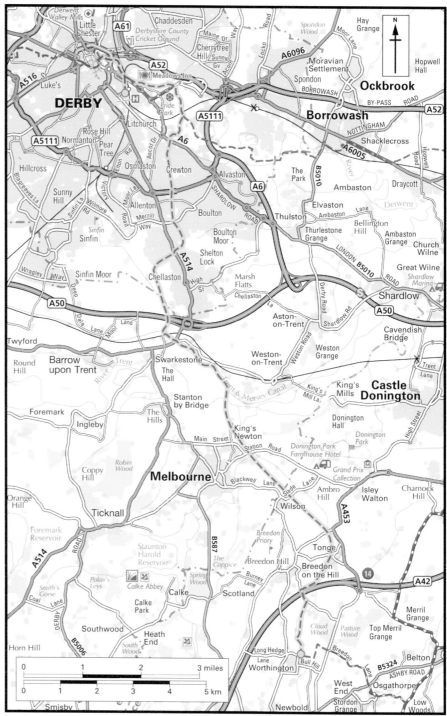

THE WATER RAIL WAY

The main traffic-free section of the route along the former Lincoln to Boston Railway line follows the River Witham from Lincoln, past Washingborough, to Bardney and onto Southrey, Stixwould and Kirkstead Bridge, close to the village of Woodhall Spa. The path features vast open fenland landscapes, with long views and expansive skies. To the north stands Lincoln Cathedral, to the south St Botolph's Church (the 'Stump'), which, on a clear day, can be seen from many miles away.

Many of the artworks commissioned for the sculpture trail along the route were inspired by the poems of Alfred, Lord Tennyson, and commemorate the 200th anniversary of his birth in Lincolnshire in 1809. Cyclists can learn about the history surrounding the trail and the wildlife it attracts from the information boards along the route, as well as enjoying the sculptures of Lincoln Red cattle, Lincoln Longwool sheep and Lincolnshire Curly-coated pigs, created by Sally Matthews and inspired by the local environment and breeds of animal (see page 117).

The spectacular triple-towered Norman and Gothic cathedral in Lincoln stands on a limestone plateau among the medieval buildings of the old city and can be seen from the Water Rail Way as far south as Stixwould.

National Route: 1

START Waterside South Bridge.

FINISH Kirkstead Bridge, near Woodhall Spa.

DISTANCE 15 miles (24km).
Shorter options, from Lincoln to Bardney: 9 miles (14.5km); Bardney to Woodhall Spa: 7 miles (11km).

GRADE Easy.

SURFACE
The bridleway section southeast of Bardney can be muddy when wet. The surface on the rest of the route is tarmac and easily accessible in all weathers.

HILLS None.

YOUNG & INEXPERIENCED CYCLISTS
This route is flat and almost entirely traffic-free. As it's a linear route, with lots of good turnaround points, you just need to assess how far you want to cycle. At Kirkstead Bridge, you can walk along the pavement on the road bridge if you feel the road is too busy.

REFRESHMENTS
- Lots of choice in Lincoln.
- Carpenter's Arms pub just off the route in Fiskerton (cross the river at Five Mile Bridge).
- Cafe at the Goods Shed, Bardney.
- Pubs in Washingborough, Bardney, Southrey and at Kirkstead Bridge and Martin Dales.
- A number of choices in Woodhall Spa.

THINGS TO SEE & DO

LINCOLN:

- Lincoln Cathedral: mostly 13th century with some parts dating back to 1072; 01522 561600; www.lincolncathedral.com
- Lincoln Castle: dating from 1068, the castle was used as a court and prison for 900 years; 01522 511068; www.lincolnshire.gov.uk
- Ellis Windmill: dating from 1798, this was one of nine windmills on the site and was working until the 1940s; 01522 528448; www.lincolnshire.gov.uk
- Fiskerton Fen Nature Reserve; 01507 526667; lincstrust.org.uk
- Bardney Abbey, just off the route in Bardney: remains of a Benedictine abbey; www.lincsheritage.org
- Bardney Heritage Centre, off the route in Bardney; 01526 397299; www.lincsheritageforum.org.uk
- Kirkstead Abbey, just off the route near Kirkstead Bridge: abbey ruins dating from 1139; www.woodhallspa.org

WOODHALL SPA:

- Cottage Museum: local photographs and memorabilia reflecting the history of the town; 01526 353775; www.woodhallspa.org
- Kinema in the Woods: Britain's only rear projection cinema, opened in 1922; also Kinema Too; 01526 352166; www.thekinemainthewoods.co.uk
- Moor Farm and Kirkby Moor Nature Reserves: heath and woodland near Woodhall Spa; www.lincstrust.org.uk

FURTHER INFORMATION

- To view or print National Cycle Network routes, visit www.sustrans.org.uk
- Maps for this area are available to buy from www.sustransshop.co.uk
- A Water Rail Arts leaflet is available to download from www.sustransshop.co.uk
- Lincolnshire Tourist Information: 01522 526450; www.visitlincolnshire.com
- Woodhall Spa Tourist Information: 01526 353775 www.woodhallspa.org

THE WATER RAIL WAY

TRAIN STATIONS Lincoln.

BIKE HIRE

Bardney Heritage Centre: adult bikes only; 01526 397299

ROUTE DESCRIPTION

From Witham Park at the east end of Waterside South in Lincoln, take the Water Rail Way path along the south side of the River Witham towards Washingborough. The route follows a tree-lined strip of land between the river and the Sincil Drain, to pass Five Mile Bridge (cross here for Fiskerton) and along to Bardney Lock. In Bardney, choose the traffic-free summer route, which may be muddy after rain, or the all-weather route on roads through the village and out along the B1190, through Southrey to join the path again just after the village. The Water Rail Way then follows the east side of the river to Kirkstead Bridge, where you can take roads into Woodhall Spa or cross over the bridge to Martin Dales. All along the route you will see wonderful sculptures. For a longer ride, continue on the Water Rail Way on minor roads to Langrick Bridge, then on a traffic-free section, again following the River Witham, into Boston (17 miles/27km).

NEARBY CYCLE ROUTES

From Woodhall Spa, the Water Rail Way follows National Route 1 on minor roads to Langrick Bridge, then a further traffic-free section by the River Witham into Boston. From Boston, Route 1 follows quiet roads into

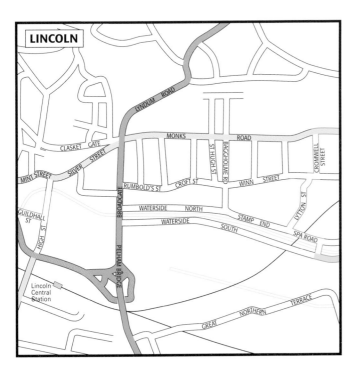

LINCOLN

LYNDUM ROAD
CLASKET GATE
MONKS ROAD
ST HUGH ST
BAGGHOLME RD
CROMWELL STREET
MINT STREET
SILVER STREET
RUMBOLD'S ST
CROFT ST
WINN STREET
BROADGATE
GUILDHALL ST
HIGH ST
WATERSIDE NORTH
WATERSIDE SOUTH
STAMP END
LYTTON ST
SPA ROAD
PELHAM BRIDGE
Lincoln Central Station
GREAT NORTHERN TERRACE

130 CYCLING IN THE UK

Cambridgeshire. Lincoln is a hub on the National Cycle Network, with both Routes 1 and 64 meeting in the city centre. Route 64 follows a traffic-free path west along the Roman Fossdyke Canal before joining the railway path to Skellingthorpe and Harby. Quiet lanes link the route to a short section of traffic-free path at Collingham and under busy main roads into Newark, where a further 5 miles (8km) of totally traffic-free path lead to Cotham. Route 64 south of Newark Northgate station gives a further 5 miles (8km) of peaceful traffic-free path.

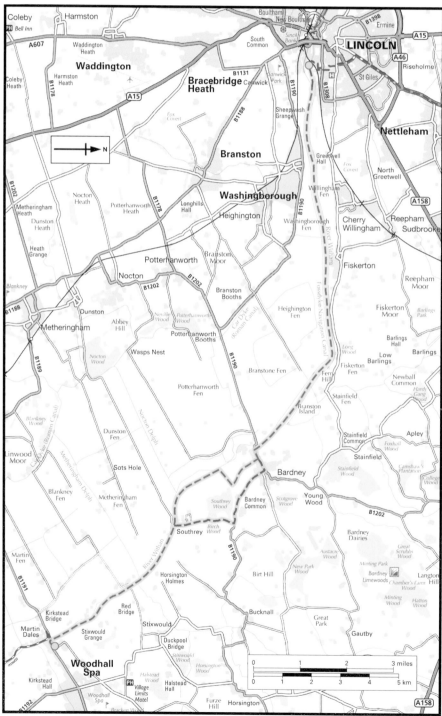

TISSINGTON & HIGH PEAK TRAILS

These two trails are the most famous railway paths in the Peak District, passing through neat pastures bounded by drystone walls and the dramatic limestone scenery of the Derbyshire Dales, including several rock cuttings. The two trails link at Parsley Hay. On the Tissington Trail, there is a steady climb of almost 213m (700ft) from Ashbourne to Parsley Hay. For this reason, it is worth starting at Ashbourne when you are fresh, going uphill towards Parsley Hay, leaving you with a downhill ride on the way back.

The High Peak trail offers a superb challenge in the heart of the Peak District, from High Peak Junction via Middleton Top and Parsley Hay to Sparklow. This ride describes the section from Middleton Top to Parsley Hay. Following it in this direction means that you have an uphill climb on the outward journey and downhill on the return. Unless you are a fit and experienced cyclist, it is suggested that you go no further east than the Middleton Top Visitor Centre, as there are two very steep sections.

National Routes: 54 (High Peak Trail) and 68 (Tissington Trail)

START
Tissington Trail: Station Road, Ashbourne, or the other side of the tunnel near Mapleton Road.
High Peak Trail: Middleton Top Visitor Centre.

FINISH Parsley Hay.

DISTANCE
Tissington Trail: 13 miles (21km).
High Peak Trail: 17 miles (27km).

GRADE Easy, provided you walk the few hills on the High Peak Trail.

SURFACE Dust surface.

HILLS Steady climb of almost 213m (700ft) from Ashbourne to Parsley Hay.

YOUNG & INEXPERIENCED CYCLISTS
Tissington Trail: You will need to take care at the occasional road crossings. In Ashbourne, the old railway tunnel has been reopened and is lit, so if you start from Station Road on the south side of town, the journey will be traffic-free all the way and have easy gradients, apart from a fairly steep incline at Mappleton.

High Peak Trail: There is a short, sharp incline at Hopton where you may need to walk. The route is traffic-free.

REFRESHMENTS
- Lots of choice in Ashbourne.
- Dog & Partridge pub, Thorpe.
- Coffees and teas at Basset Wood Farm, Tissington.
- Waterloo Inn, Biggin.
- Dawn's Refreshments at Parsley Hay Cycle Centre.
- Rising Sun Inn, Middleton.
- Cafe at Middleton Top.
- Cafe at National Stone Centre near Wirksworth.

THINGS TO SEE & DO
- Middleton Top Engine House: built in 1829 to haul wagons up the Middleton incline. It's possible to see the engine in motion on selected dates between April and October; www.derbyshire-peakdistrict.co.uk/middletontop.htm
- National Stone Centre Centre on High Peak Trail, near Wirksworth: a Site of Special Scientific Interest (SSSI),

the centre contains six former quarries, four lime kilns and over 120 disused lead mine shafts, along with rocks, minerals and wildlife treasures; 01629 824833; www.nationalstonecentre.org.uk

TRAIN STATIONS

Experienced riders only: Cromford; Buxton; Derby.

BIKE HIRE

• Ashbourne: 01335 343156.

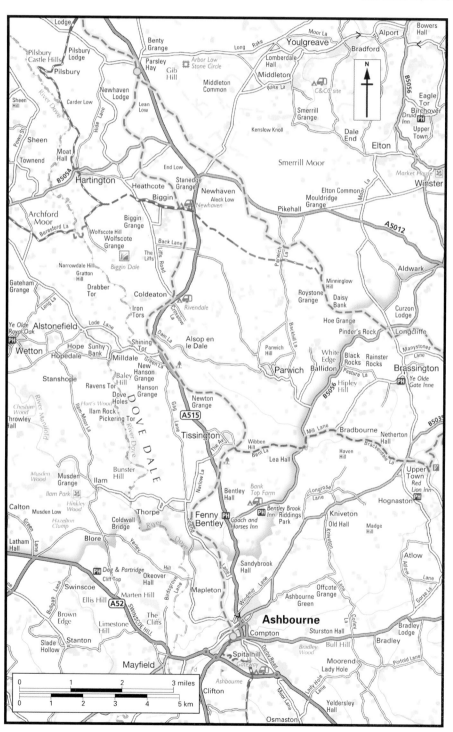

- Middleton Top Cycle Hire: 01629 823204; www.peakdistrict-tourism.gov.uk/peakdistrict/cycle
- Peak Cycle Hire, Parsley Hay: 01298 84493; www.peakdistrict.org

FURTHER INFORMATION

- To view or print National Cycle Network routes, visit www.sustrans.org.uk
- Maps for this area are available to buy from www.sustransshop.co.uk

- Dedicated information on the Tissington and High Peak Trails: www.derbyshire-peakdistrict.co.uk
- Derbyshire Tourist Information: 0800 0199 881; www.visitderbyshire.co.uk
- Ashbourne Tourist Information: 01335 343666; www.visitpeakdistrict.com

ROUTE DESCRIPTION
TISSINGTON TRAIL:
Start at Station Road in Ashbourne, then take the traffic-free path through the Ashbourne Tunnel. You then follow the railway path all the way to Parsley Hay. There is a relatively steep incline at Mappleton. En route, you'll pass through Thorpe, one of the railway stopping points on the original line, and Tissington – a perfect village, with duckpond, picturesque cottages, historic church and tearooms. The route continues through Alsop-en-le-Dale to Hartington station, just over a mile from Hartington Village, where you can see the old signal box. The Tissington Trail meets the High Peak Trail at Parsley Hay.

HIGH PEAK TRAIL:
Middleton Top is about 0.5 mile (0.8km) northwest of Wirksworth. Shortly after starting out, the trail bores through a hillside before reaching the turn-off for Carsington Water and Tissington (signed 54a – see below). The main trail continues westwards, climbing the short, sharp Hopton Incline – you may want to get

off here and walk. Next, watch out for the long, curving stone-built causeway, where the path turns through 90 degrees, just before Longcliffe. Now you're in real White Peak country, where the skilled masonry of the original railway engineers blends wonderfully with the surrounding homes, field walls and rock faces. Dramatic long views alternate with craggy cuttings along one of the most spectacular cycle paths in Britain until you reach the relative enclosure of the tea-stop at Parsley Hay.

As an alternative, there is a link on Route 54a that leaves High Peak Trail just north of Hopton village and joins the Tissington Trail at Tissington, taking in the visitor centre at Carsington Reservoir on the way. Much of this runs on-lane, some is quite steep and there are several busier road crossings, so this section is better suited to more experienced riders.

NEARBY CYCLE ROUTES
Tissington Trail forms part of the Pennine Cycleway Route 68, a 350-mile (563-km) challenge route between Derby and Berwick-upon-Tweed.

High Peak Trail is part of National Route 54, which runs from Derby to Burton-upon-Trent, Lichfield and Birmingham.

Route 6 goes from Derby to Nottingham in one direction, and Loughborough and Leicester in the other.

OTHER WAYMARKED OR TRAFFIC-FREE RIDES INCLUDE:
• Carsington Water, an 8-mile (13-km) circular ride.

• Manifold Trail, from Waterhouses to Hulme End.
• Mickleover Trail, going from Derby to Hilton.
• Derby Canal Path and The Cloud Trail, connecting Derby with Worthington (see page 124).

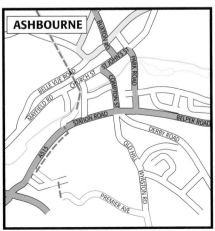

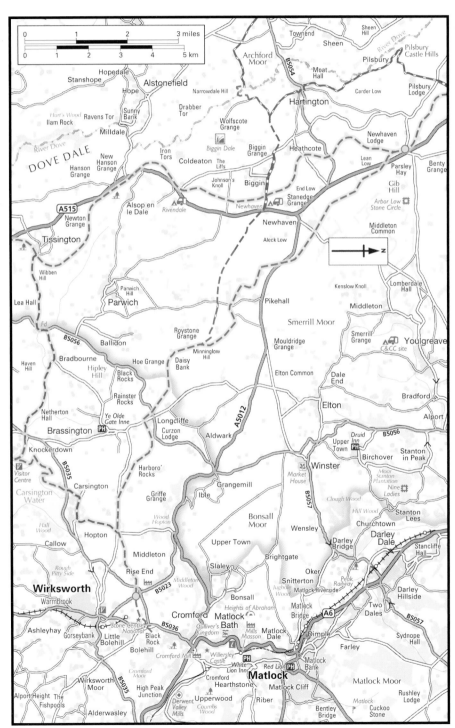

WORCESTER TO DROITWICH

These are two options for cycling from Worcester to Droitwich, using either Route 45 or 46 of the National Cycle Network. Currently, the routes do not meet up in Droitwich and negotiating the roads in town can be tricky, so the ride is not described as a singular circular one here.

Route 45 links the two towns on the eastern side, and follows a combination of quiet lanes and the towpath of the Worcester & Birmingham Canal. The canal was built in 1791–1815, connecting the River Severn at Worcester to the growing industrial city of Birmingham. Nowadays, it is primarily used for pleasure boats. The cycle route will eventually extend from Salisbury in Wiltshire to Chester in Cheshire. Route 46, meanwhile, links them on the western side. This on-road route follows a similar line to the Droitwich Canal for much of the way, leaving Worcester from the racecourse.

The 14th-century tower of Worcester Cathedral dominates the city by the banks of the River Severn. The cathedral was started in the late 11th century and has a dazzling array of fine carvings. Among Worcester's many attractive old buildings are the 15th-century Commandery, once almshouses for the aged and the poor and now a visitor centre, adjacent to Route 45.

National Routes: 46 and 45

START
National Route 46: entrance to Pitchcroft Racecourse, Worcester.
National Route 45: towpath alongside the retail park on George Street/Tallow Hill, Worcester.

FINISH
National Route 46: Droitwich Spa train station.
National Route 45: Junction of Corbett Avenue and Worcester Road, Droitwich Spa.

DISTANCE Both routes are just under 8 miles (13km).

GRADE Easy to moderate.

SURFACE
National Route 46: Tarmac.
National Route 45: Loose gravel on the canal towpath, which can get muddy when wet, and tarmac elsewhere.

HILLS Mainly flat. Short hills in the middle of both routes.

YOUNG & INEXPERIENCED CYCLISTS
There are fairly busy roads at the ends of both routes, so you may want to cross them on foot with young children.

REFRESHMENTS
• Lots of choice in Worcester, including the Cavalier Tavern, right on the canal towpath, and the Pump House Environmental Centre.
• Mughouse Pub, Claines.
• Lots of choice in Droitwich Spa.

THINGS TO SEE & DO
WORCESTER:
• Worcester Guildhall; 01905 723471

- Worcester Cathedral; 01905 732900; www.worcestercathedral.co.uk
- Worcester Porcelain Museum; 01905 21247; www.worcesterporcelainmuseum.org.uk
- The Greyfriars: 15th-century merchant's house; 01905 23571; www.nationaltrust.org.uk
- Pump House Environmental Centre: includes display of sustainable technologies; 01905 734934; www.dwt.org.uk
- Droitwich Spa: attractive spa town, with medieval churches and half-timbered buildings.

FURTHER INFORMATION
- To view or print National Cycle Network routes, visit www.sustrans.org.uk
- Maps for this area are available to buy from www.sustransshop.co.uk
- Worcester Tourist Information: 01905 726311; www.visitworcester.com
- Droitwich Spa Tourist Information: 01905 774312
- To make the route circular, starting from Worcester, obtain the 'Droitwich to Worcester Cycle Routes Map' from from Worcester hub on 01905 765 765.

TRAIN STATIONS
Worcester Foregate Street; Worcester Shrub Hill; Droitwich Spa.

BIKE HIRE
Peddlers, Worcester: 01905 24238

ROUTE DESCRIPTION
NATIONAL ROUTE 46:
Start at the entrance to Pitchcroft Racecourse in Worcester, which is opposite the junction of Severn Terrace and Castle Street. Pass through the ornate gates and turn to the right, following the side of the racecourse. On race days, this path is closed, so you will need to follow the signed diversion route (which also starts at the entrance gate) instead.

At the far end of the racecourse, leave the park through a metal gate and enter Waterworks Road. At the Pump House Environmental Centre, turn left onto the cycle path across the park. (The diversion route for race days rejoins the main route here.) Exit the park onto Tower Road, turning left. Follow the road around and bear right into Park Avenue, then left onto Sabrina Avenue. Turn left onto Northwick Road, then turn right onto Beckett Road.

Continue onto Cornmeadow Lane through Claines, taking care at the junction just by the church. Continue, taking Danes Green, then turn left on to Dilmore Lane through Fernhill Heath. At the bottom of the steep hill, there is a tight bend to the right, which can sometimes have

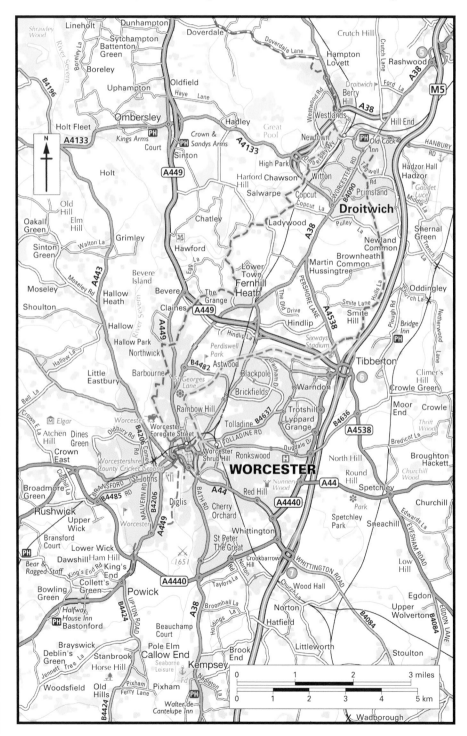

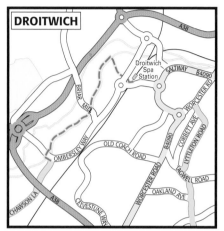

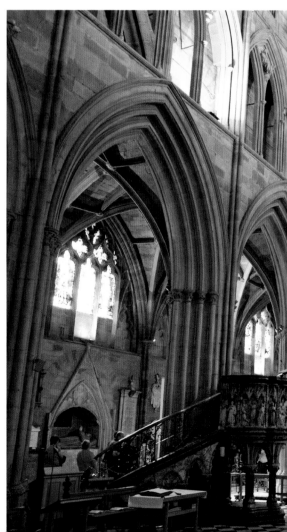

WORCESTER

gravel on it, so take care. Cross the Droitwich Canal via a narrow bridge. Take Porters Mill Lane (on the right, after the bridge), then turn right at the junction, crossing back over the canal through Ladywood, where there is another steep hill leading to a narrow bridge. Take a left turn, then a right, and bear right, after which follow the signs and local routes to Droitwich Spa train station.

NATIONAL ROUTE 45:
At the retail park on George Street/Tallow Hill in Worcester, join the towpath on the opposite side of the canal to the pizza restaurant. Follow the Worcester & Birmingham Canal towpath (signposted for Droitwich) to Offerton Bridge, crossing over wherever signposted. Just after the lock keeper's cottage, leave the towpath via a gap in the hedge. Take Offerton Lane, Hulls Lane and Newland Common Road to Oakley Wood. Continuing on Newlands Road, there is a steep section through Primsland, before continuing on to Droitwich.

NEARBY CYCLE ROUTES
National Route 45 continues from Droitwich to Bridgnorth. There are a number of signed leisure routes that loop around Worcester. Further details and maps are available from Worcestershire County Council's website: www.worcestershire.whub.org.uk (click on transport, then click on the bike symbol on the picture, then choose Cycling Routes).

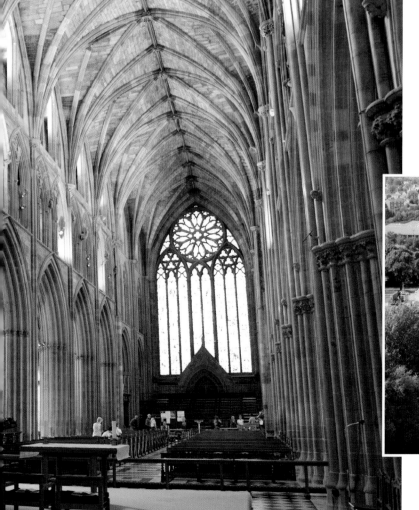

BRAMPTON VALLEY WAY

This is one of the longest dismantled railway paths in the region, connecting Market Harborough with the outskirts of Northampton near Kingsthorpe and forming part of Route 6 of the National Cycle Network. It is a wide, well-maintained trail with few barriers, making it a perfect 'conversational' ride: a chance to catch up with friends while getting some exercise. The trail includes two tunnels, where you will need lights. There are some old steam locomotives and rolling stock at Chapel Brampton. After the railway line was closed in 1981, it was purchased by Northamptonshire County Council in 1987 and opened for recreational use as the Brampton Valley Way in 1993. Named after the Brampton Arm, a tributary of the River Nene, the railway path follows the river valley for much of its length.

There are two other nearby traffic-free rides: an arm of the Grand Union Canal leads northwest from Market Harborough towards Foxton Locks; also, at the southern end of this route, there is a waymarked link on bridleways and quiet lanes to the circuit of Pitsford Water and Brixworth Country Park.

National Route: 6

START Market Harborough train station.

FINISH Broughton Crossing near Kingsthorpe, just north of Northampton.

DISTANCE 14 miles (22.5km).

GRADE Easy.

SURFACE Rolled stone paths.

HILLS Gentle railway gradients; no steep hills.

YOUNG & INEXPERIENCED CYCLISTS

Nearly all the route is off-road but with some crossings, especially at Lamport, where care is needed and children should be closely supervised.

REFRESHMENTS

- Lots of choice in Market Harborough.
- The Bulls Head pub in Arthingworth, just off the route.
- Pitsford & Brampton station.
- The Windhover family pub at Broughton Crossing.

THINGS TO SEE & DO

- Market Harborough: attractive market town with a wealth of Georgian architecture.
- Kelmarsh Hall: 18th-century historic house, set in beautiful gardens; 01604 686543; www.kelmarsh.com
- Cottesbrook Hall: Queen Anne house (1702), reputed to be Jane Austen's inspiration for *Mansfield Park*; 01604 505808; www.cottesbrookehall.co.uk
- Lamport Hall Gardens and Farm Museum: Grade I listed building, home to the Isham family for more than 400 years; 01604 686272; www.lamporthall.co.uk
- Brixworth Country Park: visitor centre, nature trails and scenic picnic sites; www.northamptonshire.gov.uk
- Northampton and Lamport Steam Railway: at Pitsford & Brampton Station; 01604 820327; www.nlr.org.uk

FURTHER INFORMATION

- To view or print National Cycle Network routes, visit www.sustrans.org.uk
- Maps for this area are available to buy from www.sustransshop.co.uk
- Northamptonshire Tourist Information: www.explorenorthamptonshire.co.uk

- Market Harborough Tourist Information: 01858 821 270
- Northampton Tourist Information: 01604 622 677; www.explorenorthamptonshire.co.uk

TRAIN STATIONS
Market Harborough.

BIKE HIRE
Pitsford Cycle Hire, Brixworth Country Park: 01604 881777; www.pitsfordcycles.co.uk

ROUTE DESCRIPTION
From Market Harborough station, head westwards on Rockingham Road (A4304) and left at the traffic lights into Kettering Road which becomes Springfield Street. Turn left and directly right into Britannia Walk. The path starts at the southern end of Britannia Walk, runs alongside Oaklands Park and crosses Scotland Road, where you need to take care. You soon reach rolling open countryside, climbing gently to the Oxenden tunnel (use your lights) before crossing the flat valley of the River Ise.

For a refreshment break, take the byway to the left just before the Ise bridge and follow it into Arthingworth, a pretty village with a good pub. Turn right onto Kelmarsh Road at the edge of the village and follow it to the picnic site, where you rejoin the railway path. Alternatively from here, cross the railway path and continue on Kelmarsh Road to meet Kelmarsh Hall.

Continuing southwards on the railway path, ride past woodlands on either side and beneath High

Northamptonshire, with the help of Kelmarsh tunnel (again, use your lights). Take care crossing the A508 south of the tunnel. Just before you reach Brixworth you have the option of taking a detour to Cottesbrooke Hall by turning right at the Brixworth–Creaton Road crossing.

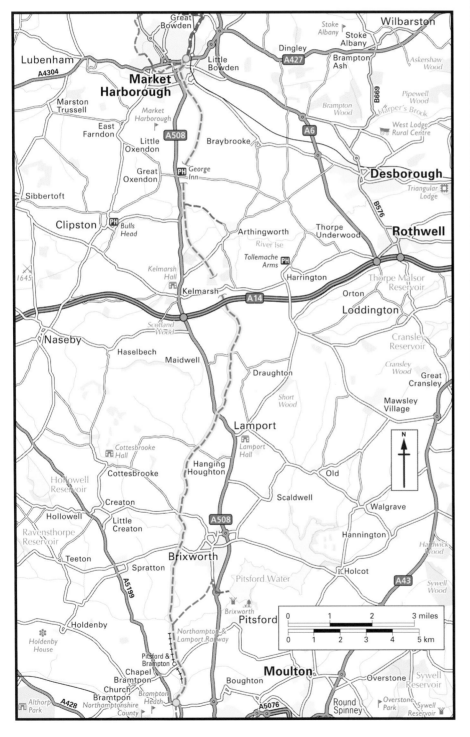

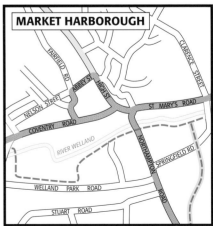

MARKET HARBOROUGH

Alternatively, turn left into Brixworth for Brixworth Country Park. Back on the railway path, you'll soon cycle alongside the Northampton and Lamport Steam Railway before reaching the end of the ride at Boughton Crossing, just north of Kingsthorpe on the A5199.

Route 6 continues southwards from Boughton Crossing into Northampton but the route requires major rebuilding at one point and is not recommended for family travel.

NEARBY CYCLE ROUTES

National Route 6 runs southwards through Northampton to Milton Keynes and Oxford. Northwards, it heads for Leicester, Loughborough and Derby. National Route 64 diverges from Route 6 in Market Harborough and follows mostly quiet lanes over High Leicestershire to Melton Mowbray, crossing the Leicester-Oakham-Rutland Water section of Route 63 en route.

OTHER WAYMARKED OR TRAFFIC-FREE ROUTES INCLUDE:
• Great Central Way, Riverside and Watermead Park, Leicester.
• Rutland Water Circuit near Oakham, off National Route 63.

INDUSTRIAL HERITAGE ROUTES

Many of the National Cycle Network routes pass close by areas that are rich in architectural reminders of our industrial heritage. Here is a selection of some of the best. For more information, visit www.sustrans.org.uk

SOUTH WEST OF ENGLAND
GRANITE WAY, OKEHAMPTON TO LYDFORD (See pages 16-19)
National Route 27
Built in 1874 and spanning 104m (114yd), Meldon Viaduct, which is made of steel, soars over an area of industrial archaeology. Meldon Dam lies to the southwest, while in the valley to the south are the remains of copper and arsenic mines and limestone quarries from the 18th and 19th centuries.

SOUTH EAST OF ENGLAND
HASTINGS FUNICULAR RAILWAYS, SUSSEX COAST
National Route 2
Opened in 1902, the East Hill Lift in Hastings is the steepest funicular railway in the United Kingdom and provides views over the Old Town and The Stade, home to the largest beach-launched fishing fleet in Europe. Whereas the East Hill Lift gives access to Hastings Country Park, the town's other funicular railway, the West Hill Lift, climbs to Hastings Castle.

LONDON
GRAND UNION CANAL, PADDINGTON TO PERIVALE
National Route 6
The difficulties of serving London from the Grand Junction Canal (opened in 1794) via the tidal Thames showed the need for a canal route into the city, hence the construction of the Paddington branch of the canal. Starting at Southall, it became by far the most important of the Grand Junction branches. In 1929, the canal was renamed the Grand Union Canal.

EAST OF ENGLAND
SHANKS MILLENNIUM BRIDGE, PETERBOROUGH
(See pages 94-97)

National Route 63
This outstanding bridge over the River Nene at Stanground Washes is constructed from weathering steel, which prevents the bridge from corroding and eliminates forever the need for painting. Manufactured partly from recycled metal, the bridge has been carefully designed to minimize any disturbance to the birds that live and breed on the Nene Washes.

MIDLANDS
IRONBRIDGE GORGE TO TELFORD, SHROPSHIRE
Silkin Way, National Route 55
Described as the birthplace of the Industrial Revolution, Ironbridge is where Abraham Darby I perfected the technique of smelting iron with coke. His grandson, Abraham Darby III, built the famous iron bridge over the River Severn to link two areas of industrial activity. The bridge opened on New Year's Day, 1781.

WALES
PENRHYN QUARRY, BANGOR
Lôn Las Ogwen, National Route 85
Large-scale commercial slate mining in north Wales began in 1782 with the opening of Cae Braich y Cafn quarry, later Penrhyn Quarry, near Bethesda in the Ogwen Valley. Welsh output far exceeded that of other areas, and by 1882, 92 per cent of Britain's slate production was from Wales, with the quarries at Penrhyn and Dinorwig producing half of this between them.

HENGOED VIADUCT, NORTHWEST OF NEWPORT, SOUTH WALES
Celtic Trail, National Route 47
Work began on Hengoed Viaduct in 1853, and it was the last major project to be completed on the Taff Vale Extension before the railway line was opened in 1858. Consisting of 16 arches, the viaduct is 260m (285yd) long, 36m (120ft) high and on a slight curve. The first arch on the eastern side was constructed at a skewed angle to accommodate the Brecon & Merthyr main line that passed under it.

1 Hewenden Viaduct, Yorkshire 2 Belfast Lough, Northern Ireland 3 The Iron Bridge, Shropshire 4 Cullen Viaduct, Scotland 5 Hastings, East Sussex 6 Hengoed Viaduct, Wales 7 Canal towpath, Little Venice, London

NORTH OF ENGLAND

HEWENDEN VIADUCT, NEAR BRADFORD
Great Northern Trail, National Route 69

Grade II listed Hewenden Viaduct is one of the tallest in Britain and has spectacular views across the wooded valley below. Constructed in 1884, it stands 37m (122ft) high, with 17 arches spanning 344m (378yd) across. Shifting sands forced the builders to dig the foundations far deeper than anticipated – it is said that the arches stood as deep in the ground as they did above ground.

LAMBLEY VIADUCT, HALTWHISTLE, NORTHUMBERLAND
South Tyne Trail, National Route 68

Lambley Viaduct is one of the most impressive structures on the River Tyne. It was built in 1852 for the Alston branch of the Newcastle & Carlisle Railway, with trains bringing lead and coal down to Haltwhistle station for transhipment. The viaduct spans a steep wooded valley, and there are excellent views from the top.

SCOTLAND

INNOCENT RAILWAY TUNNEL, EDINBURGH
National Route 1

At the foot of Holyrood Park in Edinburgh is a hidden tunnel, dividing Arthur's Seat and the crags to the east from the city to the west. Called the Innocent Railway Tunnel, it was built in the 1830s to connect Dalkeith in the south with Edinburgh. 'Innocent' refers to the fact that no workers were killed during the tunnel's construction, which was unusual for the time.

CULLEN VIADUCT, CULLEN, NORTHWEST OF ABERDEEN
National Route 1

The upper part of the town of Cullen was planned in 1832. When the railway was being built, the Countess of Seafield would not allow the track to come through the grounds of her home Cullen House, so it was carried on viaducts through the town.

NORTHERN IRELAND

HARLAND & WOLFF SHIPYARD, BELFAST (See pages 264-267)
Comber Greenway, National Route 93

Founded in the mid-19th century, Harland & Wolff was for many years one of the most important shipbuilders in the world. Between 1909 and 1914, it built *The Olympic*, *The Britannic* and, most famously, the ill-fated *Titanic*. The company is now diversifying into renewable energy development and bridges, but the Belfast skyline is still dominated by its twin gantry cranes, known as Samson and Goliath.

WALES

With the highest mountain in all of England and Wales, three National Parks (Snowdonia, Brecon Beacons and Pembrokeshire), a dazzling and spectacular coastline around its south west peninsula, the easy lanes of Anglesey in the north, lots of mountains in the middle and the rich industrial heritage of the old coal-mining areas in the south, Wales has a fantastic variety of scenery to choose from when deciding where to go for a ride.

Lôn Las Cymru, the long-distance route that runs the length of Wales, represents one of the toughest and most spectacular challenges on the whole National Cycle Network. It crosses three mountain ranges; Snowdonia, the Cambrian Mountains and the Brecon Beacons, before its final long gentle descent to Cardiff. However, even on such a tough ride there are many easier sections that will appeal to novices and families, giving a taste of what the route has to offer: Lôn Las Menai and Lôn Eifion are two railway paths starting at the foot of the mighty Caernarfon Castle with fine views over the Menai Straits and the mountains of Snowdonia; the Mawddach Trail runs along the breathtaking Mawddach Estuary from Dolgellau to the coast at Barmouth; the last 30 miles of the route, from Merthyr Tydfil to Cardiff and also known as the Taff Trail, are on a series of railway and riverside paths alongside the River Taff.

The Celtic Trail is a popular long-distance route from Fishguard on the Pembrokeshire Coast to beautiful Chepstow Castle at the mouth of the River Wye. Highlights include the stunning Atlantic coastline and the glories of the Bishop's Palace in St David's, and vary from the castles at Pembroke, Tenby and Kidwelly to the wide coastal promenade around the gentle curve of Swansea Bay. Inland options allow you to visit the stone circles in the atmospheric Preseli Hills, or the National Botanic Garden of Wales to the east of Carmarthen. Some of the best traffic-free sections run east, west and north from Llanelli, including the stupendous Millennium Coastal Park. The eastern half of the ride explores the old coal-mining valleys, with many miles of old railways converted to recreational use. The High Level Route between Neath and Pontypridd is an exhilarating climb along a forested route above the valleys.

The third (mapped) long-distance ride in Wales is two rides in one: together Lôn Cambria and Lôn Teifi cross the heart of Mid Wales from Fishguard to Shrewsbury, following the River Tefi from Cardigan Bay almost to its source at Teifi Pools. A tough crossing of the Cambrian Mountains leads to the upper end of the splendid Elan Valley Trail, running close to the reservoirs that store water for Birmingham. Between the attractive market towns of Rhayader and Llanidloes the route crosses from the upper Wye Valley to the upper Severn Valley, now followed to journey's end in the historic town of Shrewsbury.

Last but far from least, mention must be made of the wonderful open breezy promenade ride along the north coast of Wales all the way from Llandudno to Prestatyn, probably the best trail in the country to make use of the train taking you one way into the wind and allowing an exhilarating wind-propelled, one-way ride back to the start.

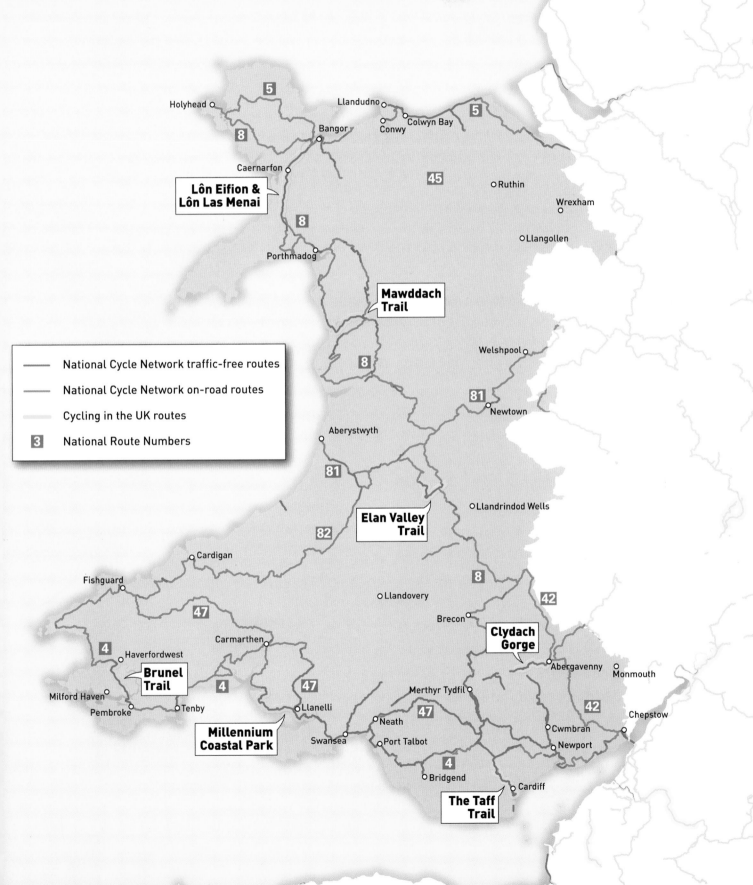

Holyhead

5

Llandudno
Conwy
Colwyn Bay

8

Bangor

5

Caernarfon

**Lôn Eifion &
Lôn Las Menai**

45

Ruthin

Wrexham

8

Llangollen

Porthmadog

**Mawddach
Trail**

Welshpool

8

81

Newtown

Aberystwyth

- National Cycle Network traffic-free routes
- National Cycle Network on-road routes
- Cycling in the UK routes

3 National Route Numbers

81

Llandrindod Wells

82

**Elan Valley
Trail**

Cardigan

Fishguard

8

Llandovery

42

Brecon

47

**Clydach
Gorge**

Abergavenny

Monmouth

4

Haverfordwest

Carmarthen

**Brunel
Trail**

4

Merthyr Tydfil

42

Milford Haven

47

Chepstow

Pembroke

Tenby

Llanelli

Neath

47

Cwmbran

**Millennium
Coastal Park**

Swansea

Port Talbot

Newport

4

Bridgend

Cardiff

**The Taff
Trail**

THE TAFF TRAIL

The entire 55-mile (88-km) long Taff Trail/Taith Tâf runs north from Cardiff to Brecon, largely traffic-free, along a mixture of riverside paths, railway paths and forestry roads. It offers a magnificent exit from the very heart of Cardiff and links together some fine traffic-free trails alongside the River Taff, passing right beneath the splendid Millennium Stadium.

Between Llandaff and Tongwynlais, you pass the Mellingriffith Water Pump – this water-powered beam engine was erected in 1807 to pump water 3m (10ft) up from the river to the Glamorganshire Canal. The pump worked for 140 years until 1948, when the canal was closed and filled in.

Castell Coch is a Grade I listed building described as 'one of the most fascinating surviving relics of Victorian Medievalism'. With its conical turrets rising above the surrounding beech woodland, it is an outstanding landmark.

National Route: 8

START Cardiff Bay.

FINISH Castell Coch.

DISTANCE 7 miles (11km).

GRADE Easy.

SURFACE Mixture of tarmac and good-quality gravel paths.

HILLS None as far as Tongwynlais. There is a short steep climb up to Castell Coch.

YOUNG & INEXPERIENCED CYCLISTS
The route is almost entirely traffic-free from Cardiff to Tongwynlais. There is a short on-road section through Tongwynlais.

REFRESHMENTS
- Lots of choice in Cardiff centre.
- A number of pubs in Tongwynlais.
- Cafe in Castell Coch (you will need to pay an entrance fee to go inside the castle).

THINGS TO SEE & DO
CARDIFF:
- Cardiff Bay Millennium Waterfront: vast freshwater lake, with a range of tourist attractions and shops, restaurants and bars at Mermaid Quay; www.cardiffbay.co.uk
- National Museum Cardiff; 029 2039 7951; www.museumwales.ac.uk
- Techniquest: science-based attraction with planetarium and exhibitions; 029 2047 5475; www.techniquest.org
- Millennium Stadium: opened in June 1999, with the first retractable roof in the UK, the stadium has hosted the Rugby World Cup, FA Cup Finals plus a wide range of concerts and motorsports events; www.millenniumstadium.com
- Cardiff Castle: with 2,000 years of history, the castle has been a Roman garrison, a Norman stronghold and lavishly developed with fairytale gothic towers in Victorian times; 029 2087 8100; www.cardiffcastle.com
- Llandaff Cathedral: stands on one of the oldest Christian sites in Britain; www.llandaffcathedral.org.uk
- Mellingriffith Water Pump, between Llandaff and Tongwynlais: 19th-century industrial monument,

considered one of the most important in Europe.

- Castell Coch: fairytale-style, Victorian Gothic castle, designed by William Burges; 029 2081 0101; www.cadw.wales.gov.uk

TRAIN STATIONS Cardiff Bay.

BIKE HIRE
Pedal Power, Cardiff Caravan Park, Bute Park: 029 2039 0713; www.cardiffpedalpower.com

FURTHER INFORMATION
- To view or print National Cycle Network routes, visit www.sustrans.org.uk
- Maps for this area are available to buy from www.sustransshop.co.uk
- For more information on routes in Wales, visit www.routes2ride.org.uk/wales
- Cardiff Tourist Information: 0870 121 1258; www.visitcardiff.com
- Wales Tourist Information: 0870 830 0306; www.visitwales.co.uk

ROUTE DESCRIPTION
From the Celtic Ring in Cardiff Bay (please walk through this very busy pedestrian section), follow Stuart Street west and turn left into Windsor Espanade. Pass through

Hamadryad, then follow the course of the River Taff, with the river on your left, until you cross it at Clarence Road Bridge. Keeping the river on your right, cycle inland, with the city centre and views of the Millennium Stadium and Cardiff Castle across the water. Continue on the traffic-free Taff Trail, signposted as 'The Taff Trail' and 'National Route 8', crossing the river again at Llandaff.

After a short road section through Tongwynlais and a very steep climb up the entrance drive, you reach the fairytale Castell Coch. If you're continuing northwards from Castell Coch, retrace your route by descending the hill to Tongwynlais, to join a traffic-free path to Taff's Well station and Pontypridd.

NEARBY CYCLE ROUTES

The Taff Trail forms part of National Route 8, which extends to Holyhead in north Wales.

Just north of Castell Coch, the Taff Trail joins the Celtic Trail/Lôn Geltaidd (National Route 4), which runs from Fishguard to Chepstow.

OTHER WAYMARKED OR TRAFFIC-FREE ROUTES INCLUDE:
• The Ely Trail, which can be joined at the southern end of the Taff Trail. It leads to St Fagans and the open-air National History Museum.

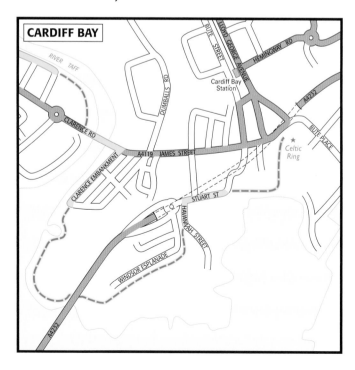

- Good-quality towpaths along the canals leading
  northwest from Newport to Crosskeys (National Route
  47) and north to Cwmbran and Pontypool (National
  Route 46).

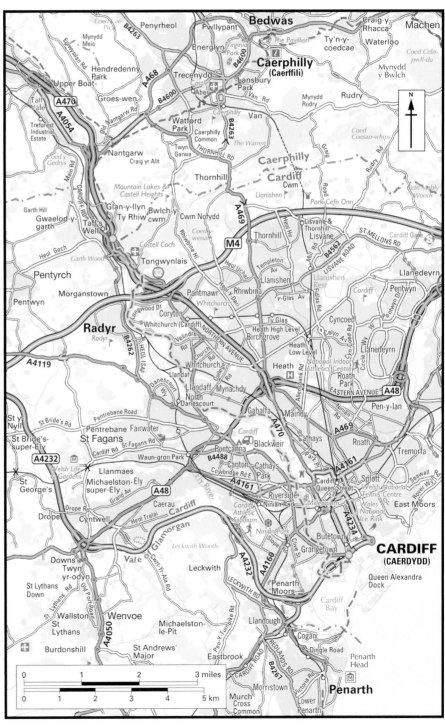

MILLENNIUM COASTAL PARK

Kidwelly is a town dominated by the massive towers of its castle, which is still in remarkably good condition. The town and castle were built by the Normans in the 12th century. Below the castle walls a bridge dating back to the 14th century spans the Gwendraeth Fach river. The 13th-century Gothic church once served as a Benedictine monastery. Kidwelly prospered during the Industrial Revolution and was the location of a large brickworks and tinworks, the history of which can be explored further in the town's Industrial Museum.

The Millennium Coastal Park/Parc Arfordirol Y Mileniwm was originally a project started by Llanelli Borough Council to turn a 12-mile (19.5-km) stretch of industrial wasteland along the coast into a green recreational corridor. It is now one of the most popular sections of the National Cycle Network in Wales, offering superb views across the Loughor estuary to the hills of the Gower peninsula. There is a series of attractions along the route, including Pembrey Country Park, which backs onto the long sandy beach of Cefn Sidan; the newly created marina at Burry Port; Sandy Water Park (with an option to explore the trail up Swiss Valley); the Discovery Centre at Llanelli's North Dock and the National Wetlands Centre at Penclacwydd.

National Route: 4

START Banc Pen-dre, Kidwelly town centre.

FINISH Bynea train station.

DISTANCE 18 miles (29km).
Shorter options, from Burry Port to Pembrey Country Park: 3.5 miles (5.5km); Kidwelly to Pembrey Country Park: 6 miles (9.5km); Penclacwydd to Llanelli: 4.5 miles (7km); Penclacwydd to Burry Port: 7 miles (11km).

GRADE Easy.

SURFACE Mixture of tarmac and gravel paths.

HILLS None.

YOUNG & INEXPERIENCED CYCLISTS
There is a short on-road section at the start in Kidwelly, where care should be taken. This is an excellent route for young children, provided you take account of the wind!

REFRESHMENTS
- Lots of choice in Kidwelly, Burry Port and Llanelli.
- Cafe at North Dock, Llanelli.
- Cafe at Pembrey Country Park (just off the route).
- Cafe at Discovery Centre in Coastal Park, near Llanelli.
- Cafe at the Wildfowl & Wetlands Centre in Penclacwydd at the end of the ride.

THINGS TO SEE & DO
KIDWELLY:
- Kidwelly Industrial Museum: 01554 891078; www.kidwellyindustrialmuseum.co.uk
- Kidwelly Castle: impressive remains dating back to the 12th century; 01554 890104; www.cadw.wales.gov.uk.
- Pembrey Country Park: attractions include a dry ski slope, 9-hole pitch and putt course, miniature railway, large adventure playground and an 8-mile (13-km) long beach; 01554 833913; www.onebiggarden.com
- National Wetland Centre Wales, Llanelli: includes the Millennium Wetland complex, home to wildlife as diverse as dragonfly and little egret; 01554 741087;

www.wwt.org.uk
- Discovery Centre: located in the heart of the Millennium Coastal Park, with an information centre, children's play area, exhibitions and refreshments; 01554 777744; www.onebiggarden.com
- Views of Gower Peninsula: spectacular coastline and the first place in Britain designated an Area of Outstanding Natural Beauty (AONB).

TRAIN STATIONS
Kidwelly; Burry Port; Llanelli; Bynea.

BIKE HIRE
- Pembrey Country Park: 01554 834443
- Discovery Centre, North Dock, Llanelli: 01554 756603

FURTHER INFORMATION
- To view or print National Cycle Network routes, visit www.sustrans.org.uk
- Maps for this area are available to buy from www.sustransshop.co.uk
- For more information on routes in Wales, visit www.routes2ride.org.uk/wales
- Wales Tourist Information: 0870 830 0306; www.visitwales.co.uk

ROUTE DESCRIPTION
Starting from Kidwelly, you quickly join a traffic-free path that continues more or less unbroken to Bynea, to the east of Llanelli. You soon enter the sandy woodlands of Pembrey Forest, where there are many tracks based around the visitor centre.

Beyond Pembrey Forest, the route follows long sections of cycle paths with wonderful views. Between Burry Port and Llanelli, you cross the railway line twice via huge land bridges covered with earth and grass.

Towards the end of the ride, you could visit The Wildfowl & Wetlands Centre in Llanelli before continuing on to Bynea, where you can catch a train back to Kidwelly via Llanelli, though services are limited from this station. Alternatively, you can press on to Swansea, from where there are regular train services.

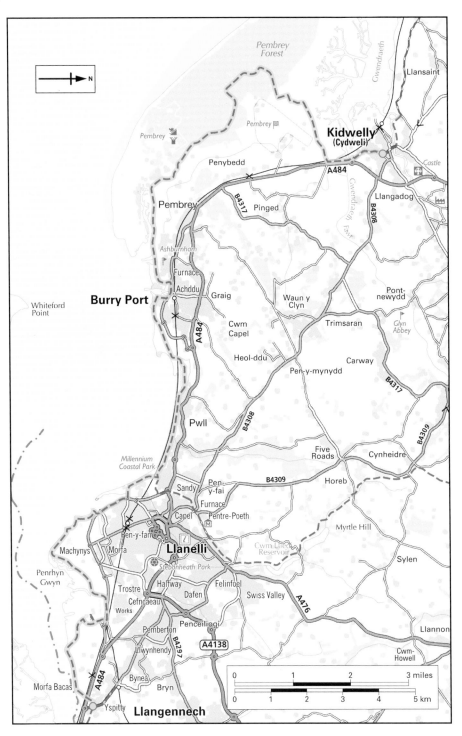

NEARBY CYCLE ROUTES

The ride described here is part of National Route 4, the Celtic Trail/Lôn Geltaidd, which runs from Fishguard to the old Severn Bridge near Chepstow.

National Route 47 runs north from Llanelli via Swiss Valley to Cross Hands, with a traffic-free section for 13 miles (21km). National Route 43 will eventually link Swansea to Builth Wells, where it joins Lôn Las Cymru from Cardiff to Anglesey (National Route 8).

There are many more tracks to explore in Pembrey Forest, around the Country Park.

LÔN EIFION & LÔN LAS MENAI

Caernarfon is dominated by the towers and battlements of its mighty castle, built for Edward I in the 13th century, to command the entrance to the Menai Strait. Its unique polygonal towers, intimidating battlements and colour-banded walls were designed to echo Constantinople, the imperial power of Rome and the dream castle of Welsh myth and legend. Inside the walled town, there are narrow streets lined with ancient houses, shops and inns. On the higher ground on the east side of the town is the site of the old Roman fort of Segontium. The investiture of Charles, the Prince of Wales, was held in the castle on 1 July 1969. Ironically, Caernarfon is a focus for the cause of Welsh nationalism and has the highest proportion (86 per cent) of Welsh speakers in all of Wales.

Two railway paths start near the castle in Caernarfon. The longer of the two, Lôn Eifion, climbs south to Bryncir, with views out over Caernarfon Bay and inland towards Snowdonia; The shorter Lôn Las Menai runs north east along the coast, linking Caernarfon with the old slate harbour of Y Felinheli.

National Route: 8

START
Travelling south on Lôn Eifion: Caernarfon Castle.
Travelling north east on Lôn Las Menai: Victoria Dock, Caernarfon.

FINISH
Travelling south on Lôn Eifion: Bryncir.
Travelling north east on Lôn Las Menai: Garddfon Inn, Y Felinheli.

DISTANCE
Lôn Eifion: 12.5 miles (20km).
Lôn Las Menai: 4 miles (6.5km).

GRADE
Easy/moderate from Caernarfon to Bryncir; easy from Caernarfon to Y Felinheli.

SURFACE Tarmac.

HILLS
Lôn Eifion: there is a long steady climb of 152m (500ft) over approximately 10 miles (16km) from Caernarfon to the radio mast, 2 miles (3km) south of Penygroes.
Lôn Menai: no hills, although there is a short climb on the edge of Y Felinheli.

YOUNG & INEXPERIENCED CYCLISTS
Lôn Eifion: all traffic-free but there are short road sections to reach the centre of Caernarfon.
Lôn Las Menai: traffic-free but there are short road sections to reach the centres of Caernarfon and Y Felinheli.

REFRESHMENTS
• Lots of choice in Caernarfon.
• Pubs and small shops in communities along the route.
• Cafe at Inigo Jones Slateworks, Groeslon.
• Pubs and cafes in Penygroes.
• Pub and a garden centre cafe in Bryncir.
• Pubs and small shops in Y Felinheli.

CAERNARFON

CHURCH ST
MARKET ST
CASTLE ST
SHIREHAL ST
PEN DEITSH
TAN Y BONT
BALACLAFA
STRYD BANGOR (BANGOR STREET)
A4086 PENLLYN
A487
B4366
TANRALT
A4086
A4085
FFORDD CWSTENIN
A487
FFORDD SANTES HELEN (ST HELEN'S ROAD)

Caernarfon Castle

THINGS TO SEE & DO

- Caernarfon Castle: well-preserved medieval castle; 01286 677617; www.cadw.wales.gov.uk
- Welsh Highland Railway: mountain railway line, which closed in the 1930s and is now being reopened, with the section from Caernarfon to Hafod y Llyn already open; 01286 677018; www.whr.bangor.ac.uk/whr.htm
- Dramatic views of Snowdonia.
- Inigo Jones Slate Works, Groeslon: workshops and showrooms, where you can see craftsmen cut, shape and polish raw slate slabs into practical products such as kitchen worktops and different craft items; 01286 830242; www.inigojones.co.uk
- Menai Strait: channel separating the island of Anglesey from the mainland.
- Menai Suspension Bridge: opened in 1826, this bridge over the Menai Strait was designed by Thomas Telford to help reduce the travel time from London to Holyhead; www.anglesey-history.co.uk
- Britannia Bridge: rail bridge across the Menai Strait designed by Robert Stephenson, son of the locomotive pioneer George Stephenson; www.anglesey-history.co.uk
- Superb views of the island of Anglesey.

TRAIN STATIONS

BANGOR.
There are also narrow gauge steam railway stations at Caernarfon and Dinas Junction.

BIKE HIRE

Beics Menai Cycles, Caernarfon: 01286 676804; www.beicsmenai.co.uk

FURTHER INFORMATION

- To view or print National Cycle Network routes, visit www.sustrans.org.uk
- Maps for this area are available to buy from www.sustransshop.co.uk
- Caernarfon Tourist Information: 01286 672232; www.visitcaernarfon.com
- Wales Tourist Information: 0870 830 0306; www.visitwales.co.uk

ROUTE DESCRIPTION

LÔN EIFION
Join National Route 8 as it passes between the castle and the town square and then turns south into St Helens Road, passing the dock buildings. After 366m (402 yards), you will see the Welsh Highland Railway, and immediately after the station turn left onto the Lôn Eifion cycle path. As you ride along the path, don't be surprised to see a steam locomotive alongside you.

Pass under the Lôn Eifion signs to climb gradually through delightful woods. After 2 miles (3km) you approach the station at Dinas. Here, the railway peels off east, while the cycle route continues south. In another couple of miles you pass the Inigo Jones Slate Works.

You soon reach the village of Penygroes, 7 miles (11km) from Caernarfon. Lôn Eifion continues and climbs into wilder scenery, with excellent views of Snowdonia and the hills of the Lleyn Peninsula, and after 9 miles (14.5km) you reach the highest point, close to some gravel pits. Now you can enjoy a gentle downhill stretch until the cycleway ends at the village of Bryncir. Route 8 joins a minor road and turns right. However, at this point, you can also turn left into Bryncir.

If you would like to extend your ride, you can press on to Criccieth, and although the route is mainly on-road from Bryncir, it's a very enjoyable ride on country lanes and through villages. After turning right, follow the signs for Route 8 through a farmyard and then on quiet lanes to the village of Llanystumdwy, which was home to the famous Welsh politician David Lloyd George. The route crosses over the bridge and turns left, passing the Lloyd George memorial. From here, it is just a couple of miles to the pretty seaside town of Criccieth, with its excellent views over Cardigan Bay.

LÔN LAS MENAI
From Victoria Dock in Caernarfon, follow the 4-mile (6-km) railway path through broad-leaf woodland to the old slate harbour of Y Felinheli (Port Dinorwig). There are views of the Menai Strait and across the water to the

island of Anglesey. You'll also see two famous bridges: the Menai Suspension Bridge and the Britannia Bridge.

NEARBY CYCLE ROUTES

The Lôn Eifion and Lôn Las Menai form part of National Route 8, Lôn Las Cymru, which links Holyhead to Cardiff. Regional Route 61 (Lôn Gwyrfai) joins Route 8 (Lôn Eifion) just south of Caernarfon and goes to Waunfawr.

National Route 5 runs along the north Wales coast, while National Route 82 (Lôn Las Ogwen) runs south of Bangor.

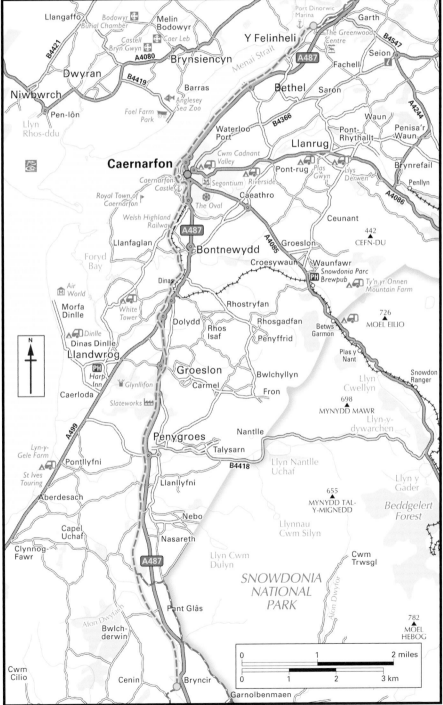

CLYDACH GORGE

Abergavenny's narrow streets are testimony to the town's long history, linked to the fortunes of its ruined 11th-century castle. The town is surrounded by mountains, most notably Blorenge, Ysgyryd Fawr (the Skirrid) and the Sugar Loaf, the latter rising to almost 610m (2,000ft) to the northwest of the town. The Usk Valley represents a real dividing line between the Brecon Beacons National Park and the lush green pastures grazed by sheep to the north and the old industrial heritage of the Welsh Valleys to the south, dominated by rows of terraced houses rising in ranks above the valley floors where the old coal mines were once worked by local men. Passing high above Clydach Gorge/Ceunant Clydach, and following the line of the former Merthyr, Tredegar and Abergavenny Railway, the almost entirely traffic-free route runs between Llanfoist, just to the south of Abergavenny, and Brynmawr. The Clydach Gorge route has taken more than two decades to complete and marks the beginning of the Heads of Valleys route from Abergavenny to Neath. It also forms a key part of the Valleys Cycle Network, which will be developed over the coming years.

National Route: 4

START Llanfoist, south of Abergavenny.

FINISH East side of Brynmawr, at the roundabout at the junction of the A465 and the A4047.

DISTANCE 8 miles (13km).

GRADE Moderate.

SURFACE Tarmac or gravel.

HILLS Steady climbs with a short steep climb after Gilwern train station.

YOUNG & INEXPERIENCED CYCLISTS
Traffic-free route, with one short, quiet lane section. There is a busy road crossing to get to the centre of Brynmawr.

REFRESHMENTS None.

THINGS TO SEE & DO
• Views of beautiful Clydach Gorge lined with stately beech trees.

• Monmouthshire & Brecon Canal: 35-mile (56-km) canal, which winds through peaceful countryside from Brecon, south to Cwmbran; www.waterscape.com
• Blaenavon Industrial Landscape: a World Heritage Site, conserving the area that, from the mid-18th century, was instrumental in the development of the iron and coal industries in the UK; www.world-heritage-blaenavon.org.uk
• Big Pit: National Coal Museum; 01495 790311; www.museumwales.ac.uk

TRAIN STATIONS
Abergavenny.

BUSES
Beacons BikeBus runs on Sundays and Bank Holidays (summer only), from Cardiff to the Brecon Beacons National Park; www.cyclebreconbeacons.com

BIKE HIRE
Bike Base Wales, Abergavenny: 01873 855999; www.bikebasewales.com

FURTHER INFORMATION

- To view or print National Cycle Network routes, visit www.sustrans.org.uk
- Maps for this area are available to buy from www.sustransshop.co.uk

- For more information on routes in Wales, visit www.routes2ride.org.uk/wales
- Abergavenny Tourist Information: 01873 853254; www.visitabergavenny.co.uk
- Wales Tourist Information: 0870 830 0306; www.visitwales.co.uk

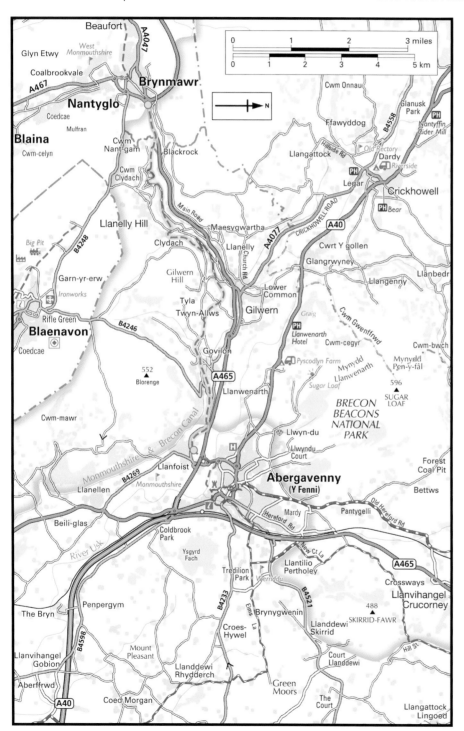

ROUTE DESCRIPTION

The railway path starts at the car park on the west edge of Llanfoist, on the B4269, and from here you simply follow the signs for National Route 46 up the hill. Sustrans volunteer rangers have also signed an excellent link from Abergavenny train station, so if you are arriving by train, turn right on exiting the station and follow Route 46 to Llanfoist.

On leaving the car park, the route climbs steadily and crosses the B4246 via the ingenious bridge designed by Christopher Wallis; his father was Barnes Wallis, the famous scientist, engineer and inventor of the bouncing bomb, as used in the 'Dambusters' raid of the Second World War. The route then crosses over the Monmouthshire and Brecon Canal, another great feat of engineering, and on to Govilon, where it crosses the road

at the old train station. The next section passes though railway cuttings and woodland, and has good views out over the Usk Valley.

On arriving at Gilwern train station, where the old platform still exists, the route leaves the railway for a short time and follows quiet lanes. Care should be taken on this section because it includes a very steep short climb. However, your effort is rewarded by a spectacular traffic-free route of 3 miles (5km). Once back on the old railway, carry on up to Clydach, where the route passes over a stone viaduct, and the industrial past of the area is in evidence. Cross the road again in Clydach village, and enter the Cwm Clydach Site of Special Scientific Interest (SSSI), where there are rare orchids and other plants of national significance. After coming out of this woodland section, take time to stop and enjoy the fantastic views of Clydach Gorge and the Black Mountains.

The next section looks unfinished because the route is on a grass-covered railway track bed; it contains grassland fungi of rare international importance, so the route has been left untouched to preserve it. The route winds on, passing through a series of railway tunnels and eventually arrives on the outskirts of Brynmawr. Sustrans plans to link the end of the route to the town centre but this has not yet been achieved, so if you are heading into Brynmawr, please take care when crossing the very busy road. The joy of the return journey is that almost no pedalling is needed, so you can sit back and take in the fantastic views.

NEARBY CYCLE ROUTES

National Route 46 links Abergavenny to Hereford. National Route 42 goes south to Chepstow and north to Usk and Hay on Wye via Gospel Pass. At Hay on Wye, Route 42 links to National Route 8 and together they form the long-distance route Lôn Las Cymru. National Route 492 and then National Route 49 go via lanes and B roads from Blaenavon to Newport.

Cycling is permitted on sections of the Monmouthshire & Brecon Canal, which runs from Brecon to Cwmbran (see www.waterscape.com for details).

BRUNEL TRAIL

Neyland was no more than a small fishing village until 1856, when Isambard Kingdom Brunel decided it should become the western terminus of his Great Western Railway, bringing passengers from London to ships bound for southern Ireland or even across the Atlantic. The passenger trade ceased at the end of the 19th century but Neyland continued to flourish as a fishing port until 1964, when operations closed down. The economic decline that followed was halted in the late 1980s with the building of the new marina. The Cleddau Bridge, a crucial road link between the south and north banks of the waterway, was opened in 1975, replacing the ferry that used to run between Neyland and Hobb's Point.

The Brunel Trail/Llwybr Brunel climbs along the old railway path, linking Neyland Marina with Haverfordwest, the headquarters of the county and the market town for most of Pembrokeshire, with its important location at the tidal limit of the Western Cleddau river.

National Route: 4

START Pembroke Dock train station or Brunel Quay, Neyland Marina, near Pembroke.

FINISH Haverfordwest town centre.

DISTANCE 10 miles (16km).

GRADE Easy.

SURFACE Tarmac or gravel.

HILLS Some short climbs; moderate gradients.

YOUNG & INEXPERIENCED CYCLISTS
Traffic-free, with a few minor roads to cross.

REFRESHMENTS
• Cafe at Brunel Quay.
• Choices in Neyland.
• Lots of choice in Haverfordwest.

THINGS TO SEE & DO
• Westfield Pill Nature Reserve

• Cleddau estuary
• Neyland Marina: picturesque and sheltered yachting marina.
• Haverfordwest Priory: recently excavated remains of an early 13th-century Augustinian priory, with the only surviving ecclesiastical medieval garden in Britain; www.cadw.wales.gov.uk
• Haverfordwest Castle: founded by Gilbert de Clare in the early 12th century; 01437 763087; www.haverfordwest-town-museum.org.uk
• Haverfordwest Town Museum: 01437 763087; www.haverfordwest-town-museum.org.uk

TRAIN STATIONS
Johnston; Pembroke Dock; Haverfordwest.

BIKE HIRE
Mike's Bikes, Haverfordwest: 01437 760068; www.mikes-bikes.co.uk

FURTHER INFORMATION
• To view or print National Cycle Network routes, visit www.sustrans.org.uk
• Maps for this area are available to buy from www.sustransshop.co.uk

- For more information on routes in Wales, visit www.routes2ride.org.uk/wales
- Haverfordwest Tourist Information: 01437 763110; www.visitwales.co.uk
- Wales Tourist Information: 0870 830 0306; www.visitwales.co.uk

ROUTE DESCRIPTION
From Pembroke Dock train station, follow National

Route 4 signs over the Cleddau Bridge. Either cycle to Honeyborough Roundabout, then turn left off the route onto the road into Neyland, or follow signs after the second bridge, which involves crossing the busy road, then heading down a very steep shale footpath alongside the bridge and into Westfield Pill.

At Neyland, the route starts at Brunel Quay, and initially shares a traffic-calmed road through the Marina before

linking up with a path through Westfield Pill Nature Reserve, where you may need to dismount to get through the A-frame barriers. There is car parking available at the Marina, and a cafe serving meals and hot drinks – you might want to make the most of this opportunity for refreshments, as there is only a small shop in Johnston.

Once you reach the railway path, the route is self-contained, mostly tarmac and well signposted. The route crosses three narrow lanes, which are clearly visible and without much traffic. The route rises gently from Neyland to Johnston through woodland and farmland. At Johnston, the route continues north to Haverfordwest, via a purpose-built wooden cycleway alongside the existing railway line. Leave Route 4 at Merlin's Bridge and follow the cycle lanes into Haverfordwest town centre and to the train station, or continue on Route 4 on-road to Broad Haven and then north to St Davids, enjoying the stunning views of the Pembrokeshire coastline.

NEARBY CYCLE ROUTES

The Brunel Trail is part of National Route 4 and the Celtic Trail, which goes from Chepstow to Fishguard via Swansea. The nearest traffic-free trail is from Pembrey Country Park (Kidwelly) to Llanelli (see pages 154-157).

HAVERFORDWEST

ELAN VALLEY TRAIL

The Elan Valley reservoirs were built in the early 20th century to supply the growing city of Birmingham with water. Until then, many of the city's inhabitants drew their water from polluted wells, and this, combined with the crowded and unsanitary conditions in the slum districts, often led to epidemics of typhoid and cholera. With the building of the new dams and reservoirs, clean, fresh water was carried from Mid Wales to Birmingham via a 73-mile (117-km) viaduct.

The reservoirs are truly spectacular, set among the mountains of Mid Wales, surrounded by mixed woodland and boasting some of the most beautiful dams in the whole of the country. The Elan Valley Trail/Llwybr Cwm Elan follows the line of the old Birmingham Corporation Railway, which was used to carry materials for building the dams. At the dam at the southern end of Craig Goch Reservoir, you will probably choose to turn around and head downhill back to Rhayader. However, if you are feeling fit, you could complete a challenging loop by following the lane north, then dropping back to Rhayader via the Aberystwyth Mountain Road. The trail forms part of Lôn Cambria (National Route 81), which runs east from Aberystwyth through Rhayader to Shrewsbury.

National Route: 81

START West side of Rhayader.

FINISH Craig Goch Reservoir.

DISTANCE 9 miles (14.5km).

GRADE Moderate.

SURFACE Tarmac or gravel.

HILLS
There is a long climb up to Rhayader Visitor Centre, but this makes an excellent descent on the return journey.

YOUNG & INEXPERIENCED CYCLISTS
The ride is essentially traffic-free along an old railway line, although there are a few short on-road sections.

REFRESHMENTS
- Pubs, cafes and shops in Rhayader.
- Cafe in Elan Valley Visitor Centre.

THINGS TO SEE & DO
- Elan Valley reservoirs and visitor centre: learn more about the construction of the reservoirs; 01597 810898; www.elanvalley.org.uk
- Carngafallt: RSPB nature reserve, where you can see a wide variety of birds and possibly badgers and hares as well; 01654 700222; www.rspb.org.uk

TRAIN STATIONS
Llandrindod Wells.

It is 15 miles (24 km) from Llandrindod Wells to the route start at Rhayader. If you want to hire a bike, you can use the bus service from Llandrindod Wells to Rhayader. If you want to arrive by train with your bike, you can follow the Radnor Ring on-road from the station to Newbridge-on-Wye and then pick up National Route 8 northwards to Rhayader (about 13.5 miles/22km each way).

BIKE HIRE
Clive Powell Mountain Bike Centre, Rhayader: 01597 811343; www.clivepowell-mtb.co.uk

FURTHER INFORMATION
- To view or print National Cycle Network routes, visit www.sustrans.org.uk
- Maps for this area are available to buy from www.sustransshop.co.uk
- For more information on routes in Wales, visit www.routes2ride.org.uk/wales
- Wales Tourist Information: 0870 830 0306; www.visitwales.co.uk

ROUTE DESCRIPTION
National Route 81, to the west of Rhayader, follows the former trackbed of the railway built by the Birmingham Corporation to carry materials and workers for building the reservoir system at the turn of the 20th century. The project was conducted with unusual sensitivity: the Elan Valley has retained some wildness and natural beauty, and the reservoirs do resemble natural lakes.

ELAN VALLEY TRAIL

The stylish gateway to the railway path marks the beginning of your ride through this beautiful wooded valley. The Visitor Centre (with toilets, information, cafe and play area) is halfway up the trail, making it an ideal resting place, although there is a long descent to the visitor centre from the main trail. Ride along the north bank of Caban-Coch Reservoir and then up the eastern edge of Garreg-ddu and Penygarreg reservoirs. The beauty of this ride is the landscape, with waterfalls tumbling down hills topped by ancient cairns.

The trail ends at the car park at the southern end of Craig Goch Reservoir, where there are also toilets. National Route 81 continues northwards on-road towards Aberystwyth. To get back to Rhayader, turn around and retrace your outward route. Alternatively, if you're on a mountain bike, you have the option of heading eastwards on a (hilly) bridleway via a Roman camp to the lane that will take you back into Rhayader.

NEARBY CYCLE ROUTES

National Route 8, known as Lôn Las Cymru, which links Holyhead to Cardiff, runs through Rhayader and uses a section of the Elan Trail.

Regional Route 25, known as the Radnor Ring, is a delightful circular ride linking Rhayader with Llandrindod Wells. There are other quiet lanes and bridleways around Rhayader, which make it such an ideal base for a weekend's cycling.

MAWDDACH TRAIL

Starting right in the heart of the handsome grey stone town of Dolgellau, the Mawddach Trail/ Lôn Mawddach runs alongside the estuary of Afon Mawddach, below the foothill of Cadair Idris, which rises to a height of over 610m (2,000ft), with views across to the hills to the north. There are two atmospheric wooden bridges on the trail: the toll bridge at Penmaenpool for road traffic and the bridge at the mouth of the estuary, which carries the railway line, pedestrians and cyclists into the seaside town of Barmouth. The area around the whole route is abundant in birdlife and, if you are lucky, you may even spot a seal. If you choose to go into the heart of Barmouth, with its sandy beaches and a wide choice of refreshments, you will need to cycle for about 0.75 mile (1.2km) on-road.

Dolgellau has become a cycling hub principally because of its proximity to the mountain bike trails in Coed y Brenin Forest, a few miles to the north, but also because of its location on Lôn Las Cymru (National Route 8). On this trail, there are two options north to Porthmadog and two options south to Machynlleth.

National Route: 8

START Main car park in Dolgellau.

FINISH Barmouth Promenade.

DISTANCE 9 miles (14.5km).

GRADE Easy.

SURFACE Tarmac or gravel.

HILLS None.

YOUNG & INEXPERIENCED CYCLISTS
Traffic-free from Dolgellau as far as the wooden railway bridge near Barmouth, then on-road into town.

REFRESHMENTS
• Pubs, cafes and shops in Dolgellau.
• George III pub at Penmaenpool: on the water's edge with good food; very popular with cyclists.
• Pubs, cafes and shops in Barmouth.

THINGS TO SEE & DO
• Dolgellau: a handsome town with 17th- and 18th-century grey stone buildings.
• Cadair Idris: 892-m (2,927-ft) high mountain.
• Arthog Bog: small wetland, with more than 130 species of plants recorded; www.rspb.org.uk
• Mawddach estuary: once a shipbuilding centre where between 1770 and 1827 over 100 boats were made from the local oak to be found along the estuary.
• Barmouth: picturesque seaside resort.

TRAIN STATIONS
Barmouth.

BIKE HIRE
Dolgellau Cycles, Dolgellau: 01341 423332; www.dolgellaucycles.co.uk

FURTHER INFORMATION
• To view or print National Cycle Network routes, visit www.sustrans.org.uk
• Maps for this area are available to buy from www.sustransshop.co.uk

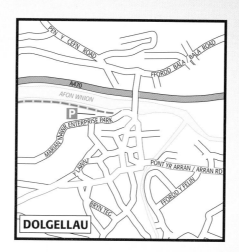

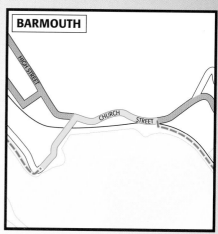

MAWDDACH TRAIL

- For more information on routes in Wales, visit www.routes2ride.org.uk/wales
- Barmouth Tourist Information: 01341 280787; www.barmouth-wales.co.uk
- Dolgellau Tourist Information: 01341 422888

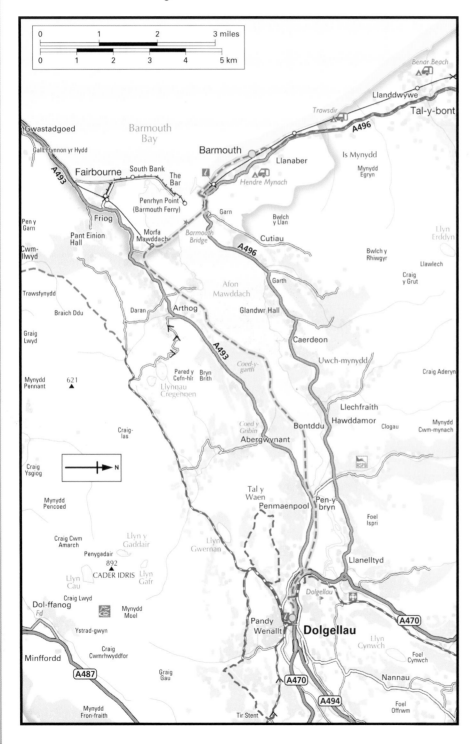

- Wales Tourist Information: 0870 830 0306; www.visitwales.co.uk

ROUTE DESCRIPTION

The trail starts right at the heart of Dolgellau, from the corner of the main car park by the bridge over the River Wnion. It follows the river out of Dolgellau and continues along the south side of the Mawddach estuary on the course of the old railway line from Barmouth to Ruabon – the line opened in 1869 and became popular with Victorian holidaymakers, particularly those from northwest England who were visiting the fashionable resort of Barmouth. It was closed in 1965. At the mouth of the estuary, use Barmouth Bridge to cross into Barmouth.

NEARBY CYCLE ROUTES

Lôn Mawddach is on National Route 8, south to Cardiff via Machynlleth, Rhayader and Builth Wells, and north to Bangor.

There are lots of mountain bike trails in Coed y Brenin Forest, to the north of Dolgellau.

THE BEST COASTAL ROUTES

Coastal paths are often magnificent cycleways, giving a tremendous sense of freedom and energy, along with breathtaking views of the coastline. Here is a selection of some of the best coastal routes the National Cycle Network has to offer. For more information, visit www.sustrans.org.uk

SOUTH WEST OF ENGLAND

MOUNTS BAY (ST MICHAEL'S MOUNT)

National Route 3

Curving in a graceful arc around Mounts Bay, the cyclepath starts at Penzance train station and heads east towards the striking outline of St Michael's Mount, a 14th-century castle set atop a small granite island and linked by a low-tide causeway to Marazion.

LYMPSTONE TO BUDLEIGH SALTERTON VIA EXMOUTH

National Route 2

From Lympstone, head south alongside the River Exe to the seaside town of Exmouth. The route then heads east along the railway path towards Budleigh Salterton, climbing gradually up through woodland on a good-quality path, then dropping down towards Knowle. Follow signs for National Route 2 on quiet streets to visit the attractive seaside town of Budleigh Salterton.

SOUTH EAST OF ENGLAND

CHALK & CHANNEL WAY (DOVER TO FOLKESTONE)
(SEE PAGES 60-63)

National Route 2

The Chalk & Channel Way runs along the top of the

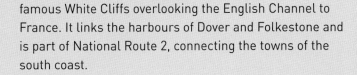

famous White Cliffs overlooking the English Channel to France. It links the harbours of Dover and Folkestone and is part of National Route 2, connecting the towns of the south coast.

ROTTINGDEAN COASTAL CYCLE ROUTE TO SHOREHAM HARBOUR & WORTHING
National Route 2
Starting on a clifftop path in Rottingdean, with amazing views out to sea, drop down to Brighton Marina and into the cosmopolitan town of Brighton. Continue along the upper promenade, past the architectural fireworks of the Royal Pavilion and on to the more leisurely atmosphere of Hove, with its beach huts and seafront lawns. After Hove Lagoon, cross the lock gates to finish in Shoreham.

THE VIKING COASTAL TRAIL (CLIFF'S END TO BIRCHINGTON ON SEA AROUND COAST)
Regional Route 15
The Romans landed at Richborough in AD 43 and from there began their conquest of Britain. Nowadays, the coastal resorts of Margate, Broadstairs and Ramsgate, and the seven pretty villages that make up the Isle of Thanet, attract visitors in their thousands to the sandy beaches and magnificent chalk cliffs.

WALES
MILLENNIUM COASTAL PATH (KIDWELLY TO LLANELLI)
(See pages 154-157)
National Route 4
Huge earthworks including two award-winning earth bridges over the mainline railway have created this magnificent coastal park. This ride is one of the most popular sections of the National Cycle Network in Wales. Enjoy the wonderful views across to the Gower Peninsula. (See pages 154-157)

LLANDUDNO TO PRESTATYN
National Route 5
A breezy open ride along the seafront between Llandudno in the west and Prestatyn in the east, with fine views of wooded hills rising steeply away from the coast. As there is normally a westerly wind blowing, it is worth catching a train one way so you are blown back to the start.

SWANSEA BIKE PATH
National Route 4
The wide curving sweep of Swansea Bay is the perfect setting for a bike path, running from the award-winning Maritime Quarter in the centre of the city round to Mumbles along the route of the former Mumbles railway. The route has stunning views across to Mumbles Head, the start of the Gower Peninsula.

THE DRAMWAY (SAUNDERSFOOT TO STEPASIDE)
National Route 4
A series of short tunnels that cut through the rocky cliffs allows you to cycle from the centre of the bustling seaside resort of Saundersfoot along the coast directly above the crashing waves of Carmarthen Bay. At Wiseman's Bridge, the trail turns inland through woodland to Stepaside. Another short section of traffic-free path continues alongside the coast, east from Wiseman's Bridge towards Amroth and Amroth Castle.

NORTH OF ENGLAND
SCARBOROUGH TO WHITBY
National Route 1
Connecting the attractive towns of Scarborough and Whitby, this long railway path lies within the North York Moors National Park and offers fine views out over the North Sea. It is a challenging route, with two long climbs, reaching a highpoint of 190m (623ft) at Ravenscar.

ALNMOUTH TO CRASTER OR DRURIDGE BAY
National Route 1
This ride gives you two options: north from the handsome town of Alnmouth to the small fishing port of Craster, with an adventurous beach section north of Boulmer, or south past the mighty Warkworth Castle and the marina at Amble to the wide sandy sweep of Druridge Bay.

BERWICK TO HOLY ISLAND
National Route 1
The Northumberland Coast offers long sandy beaches and magnificent castles. Berwick's town walls date from Elizabethan times and are perfectly preserved. Heading south along the clifftop, views open up towards the Holy Island of Lindisfarne, connected to the mainland by a causeway that is covered twice a day at high tide.

1 Lympstone to Budleigh Salterton via Exmouth 2 Mounts Bay 3 Chalk & Channel Way 4 Rottingdean Coastal Route 5 The Viking Coastal Trail 6 Millennium Coastal Path 7 Swansea Bike Path 8 The Dramway 9 Berwick to Holy Island 10 Llandudno to Prestatyn 11 Berwick to Holy Island 12 Scarborough to Whitby 13 Alnmouth to Druridge Bay 14 & 15 Arbroath to Stonehaven 16 North Down Coastal Path

16

SCOTLAND

CULLEN TO GARMOUTH (MORAY)
National Route 1

Enjoy the dramatic coastal scenery along this 14-mile (22.5-km) section of National Route 1 on a mix of traffic-free coastal paths and minor roads. There are also several opportunities for shorter trips, such as the old railway viaduct high above Cullen, the coastal path between the fishing villages of Portknockie and Findochty (pronounced 'Finechty') or the railway path into Buckie.

AYR TO ARDROSSAN
National Routes 7 and 73

This 19-mile route (30.5-km) route takes in long stretches of the Ayrshire coastline between Irvine, Troon, Prestwick and Ayr, and has spectacular views across to the Isle of Arran. Passing through two Scottish Wildlife reserves, Gailes Marsh and Shewalton Wood, it offers the opportunity to experience the varied landscapes of this part of Scotland. (See pages 238-241)

ARBROATH TO STONEHAVEN
National Route 1

Lunan Bay, halfway between Arbroath and Montrose, is one of the finest sandy beaches in the whole of the UK. Only ruins remain of the nearby 15th-century Red Castle. North of Montrose, many of the villages are tucked on the shoreline around small, naturally occurring harbours like Johnshaven.

NORTHERN IRELAND & REPUBLIC OF IRELAND

CASTLEROCK TO GIANT'S CAUSEWAY (See pages 256-259)
National Route 93

This stunning cycle route runs along the North Atlantic coast from Castlerock to the Giant's Causeway, via Coleraine. Passing through the resort towns of Portrush and Portstewart, the route is well signed, with traffic-free cycling for much of the way.

NORTH DOWN COASTAL PATH
National Route 93

Running for 16 miles (26km) along the southern shore of Belfast Lough from Holywood to Portavoe by way of Crawfordsburn Country Park, the North Down Coastal Path offers much for the visitor: geological features dating back 500 million years, a great variety of wildflowers, birdlife and even glimpses of grey seals.

NORTH OF ENGLAND

Vast open spaces, four National Parks and seven Areas of Outstanding Natural Beauty (AONBs) support the view that the North of England offers some of the best cycling experiences in the country. From the world-renowned scenery of the Lake District and the World Heritage Site of Hadrian's Wall to the magnificent castles and wide, white sandy beaches of the Northumberland Coast, from the picturesque Yorkshire Dales villages nestling among green fields bounded by dry-stone walls to the heather-clad uplands of the North York Moors, the North of England has been bewitching people with its scenic grandeur from the time of Wordsworth and Coleridge onwards.

The southern third of the region is the most populated, dominated by the old mill towns of Lancashire and Yorkshire and the great northern cities of Liverpool, Manchester, Sheffield and Leeds. All these cities are linked by the predominantly traffic-free Trans Pennine Trail and its spurs, crossing the country coast to coast from Southport on Liverpool Bay to the North Sea at Hornsea. All have a growing network of traffic-free paths and of these urban trails in the big cities, arguably the best are the Otterspool Promenade in Liverpool, with fine views of the Liver Buildings, the regenerated Albert Dock (with the Beatles Museum and the famous Mersey ferry) and the linked towpaths of the Leeds & Liverpool Canal and the Aire & Calder Navigation, passing right through the heart of Leeds.

Between the River Tyne and the River Tees on the east coast is the densely populated area encompassing Newcastle, Sunderland and Middlesbrough. The area has the most extensive network of traffic-free trails in the country and several of them are used as the finishing sections for three coast to coast routes: Hadrian's Cycleway, the Walney to Wear Cycle Route and the Sea to Sea (C2C). Linking the West Cumbrian coast and the Lake District National Park to the North Sea by way of a challenging crossing of the Pennines, the Sea to Sea (C2C) Cycle Route is by far the most popular long-distance cycle route in the country, with over 14,000 people cycling from coast to coast each year. Hadrian's Cycleway takes a more northerly course, following the old Roman frontier from the Solway Coast to Tynemouth. Walney to Wear starts in southwest Cumbria, passing to the south of the Lakes, north of the Howgills and after crossing the Pennines, exploring the glories of Durham on its way to Sunderland.

The Pennine Cycleway is the longest of England's multi-day cycle routes, starting in Derby and heading north for 355 miles, skirting the western edge of the Yorkshire Dales and the Howgill Fells before dropping down into the Eden Valley and the lovely red sandstone buildings of Appleby. The Pennines are crossed at Hartside, southwest of Alston, on the way to the South Tyne Valley. North of Haltwhistle and Hadrian's Wall the big empty spaces of Wark Forest and the foothills of the Cheviots in Northumberland National Park are crossed on the way to the River Tweed and the walled ramparts of Berwick. The Coast & Castles Cycle Route threads its way north along the sublime coastline of Northumberland with its wide, white sandy beaches guarded by the magnificent castles at Warkworth, Bamburgh and Lindisfarne.

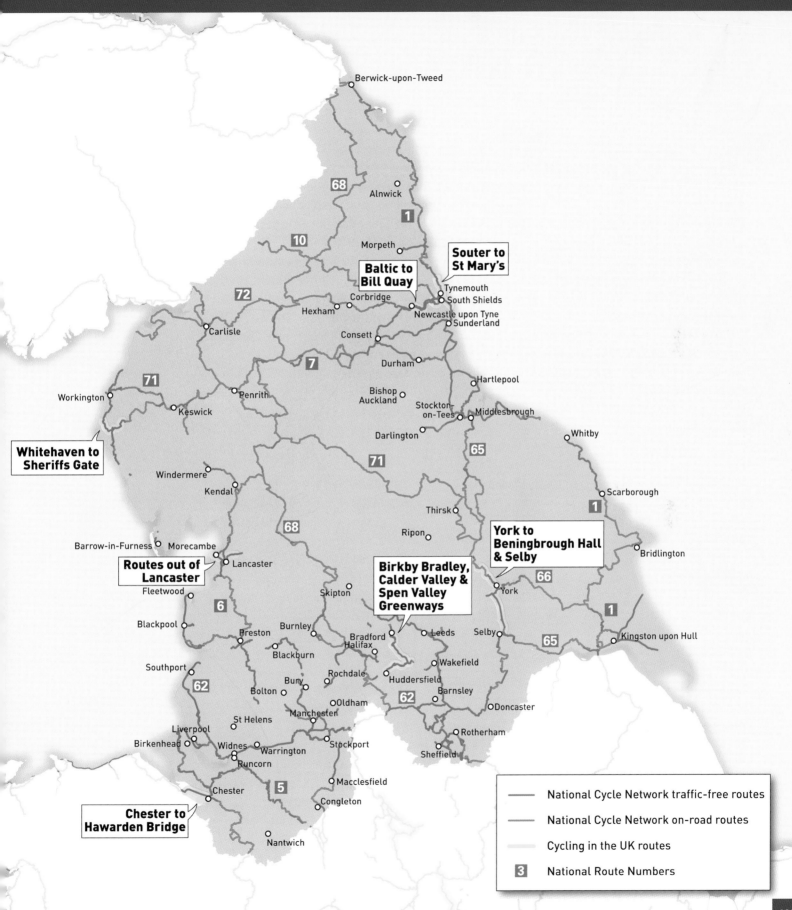

Baltic to
Bill Quay

Souter to
St Mary's

Whitehaven to
Sheriffs Gate

Routes out of
Lancaster

Birkby Bradley,
Calder Valley &
Spen Valley
Greenways

York to
Beningbrough Hall
& Selby

Chester to
Hawarden Bridge

Berwick-upon-Tweed
Alnwick
Morpeth
Tynemouth
Corbridge
South Shields
Hexham
Newcastle upon Tyne
Sunderland
Carlisle
Consett
Durham
Hartlepool
Bishop
Auckland
Stockton-
on-Tees
Middlesbrough
Darlington
Whitby
Workington
Penrith
Keswick
Windermere
Scarborough
Kendal
Thirsk
Ripon
Bridlington
Barrow-in-Furness
Morecambe
Lancaster
York
Fleetwood
Skipton
Blackpool
Burnley
Bradford
Halifax
Leeds
Selby
Kingston upon Hull
Preston
Blackburn
Rochdale
Wakefield
Southport
Bury
Huddersfield
Barnsley
Bolton
Oldham
Doncaster
Liverpool
St Helens
Manchester
Birkenhead
Widnes
Warrington
Stockport
Rotherham
Runcorn
Sheffield
Macclesfield
Chester
Congleton
Nantwich

68
1
10
72
7
71
71
65
1
68
66
6
62
62
1
65
1
5

National Cycle Network traffic-free routes

National Cycle Network on-road routes

Cycling in the UK routes

3 National Route Numbers

CHESTER TO HAWARDEN BRIDGE

Chester is a town ringed by medieval walls, with fragments dating back to Saxon and even Roman times – on the south side of the city centre is the site of the Roman amphitheatre. It is the only city in England to have preserved its walls in their entirety, and they offer a 2-mile (3-km) perimeter walk, with fine views of the city and the surrounding countryside. The medieval town flourished as a port until the silting of the River Dee in the 15th century.

Cycling is permitted along the towpath of the Shopshire Union Canal, which links the centre of town to the railway path, an attractive open ride out into the surrounding farmland, planted with potatoes, maize and grain. The Mickle Trafford to Dee Marsh railway line once carried steel to and from the steelworks on the banks of the Dee at Hawarden Bridge. The ride crosses the tidal River Dee via the bridge and ends on the south bank of the river at Connah's Quay. At Hawarden Bridge, you may wish to try the alternative return route to Chester by following the excellent trail on the north bank of the River Dee (Regional Route 89) back into the centre of town.

National Route: 5

START
Shropshire Union Canal basin, off South View Road, or Chester train station.

FINISH Hawarden Bridge.

DISTANCE 8 miles (13km).

GRADE Easy.

SURFACE Tarmac.

HILLS None.

YOUNG & INEXPERIENCED CYCLISTS
Traffic-free, although you will need to negotiate roads if you go in search of refreshments in Connah's Quay, beyond Hawarden Bridge.

REFRESHMENTS
Lots of choice just off the route on the waymarked link to the city centre, including Telford's Warehouse pub at the end of the canal towpath.

THINGS TO SEE & DO
CHESTER:
- Chester Cathedral: dating from the 13th century; 01244 324756; www.chestercathedral.com
- Grosvenor Museum: Roman archaeological finds, as well as displays on local history; 01244 402033; www.grosvenormuseum.co.uk
- Chester Castle (Agricola Tower and castle walls); www.english-heritage.org.uk
- Roman amphitheatre: www.english-heritage.org.uk

TRAIN STATIONS
Chester; Hawarden Bridge; Shotton.

BIKE HIRE
Enquire locally.

FURTHER INFORMATION
- To view or print National Cycle Network routes, visit www.sustrans.org.uk
- Maps for this area are available to buy from www.sustransshop.co.uk

The route for cyclists (and walkers) crosses the Dee at Hawarden Bridge on a new cantilevered structure funded by the local authorities. At the railway triangle at Dee Marsh, the northern leg leads to the Deeside employment zone. From here, you could get the train back from Shotton, or for a return journey, retrace the route back to Hawarden Bridge and take the riverside route alongside the River Dee back into Chester.

NEARBY CYCLE ROUTES

National Route 5 continues from Connah's Quay to the eastern outskirts of Flint, then resumes on-road to Prestatyn, where it continues traffic-free to the outskirts of Llandudno. The railway path is being extended eastwards from Hoole to Mickle Trafford.

OTHER WAYMARKED OR TRAFFIC-FREE RIDES INCLUDE:
- Woodland paths in Delamere Forest Park, to the east of Chester.
- The Whitegate Way, a railway path just a little further east from Delamere.
- A section of the Shropshire Union Canal between Chester and the boat museum at Ellesmere Port.

- Chester Tourist Information: 01244 351609; www.visitchester.com

ROUTE DESCRIPTION

Starting at the Shropshire Union Canal basin off South View Road, follow the canal towpath northwards towards the converted railway path. If you are starting from Chester train station, you can reach this by crossing Station Road, turning right into Crewe Street, then left into Egerton Street and right onto the canal towpath. The railway path and the canal towpath meet near the water meadow at Abbot's Meads, and the ride continues along the railway path (National Route 5) through Blacon, crossing the English/Welsh border and out into farmland, with the Clwyd Hills as a backdrop.

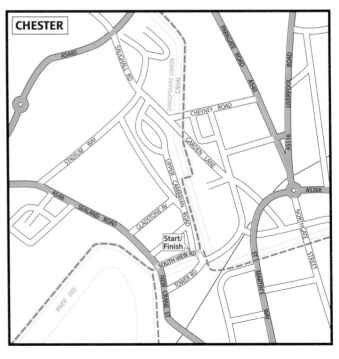

CHESTER

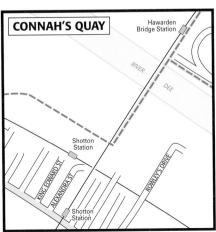

CONNAH'S QUAY

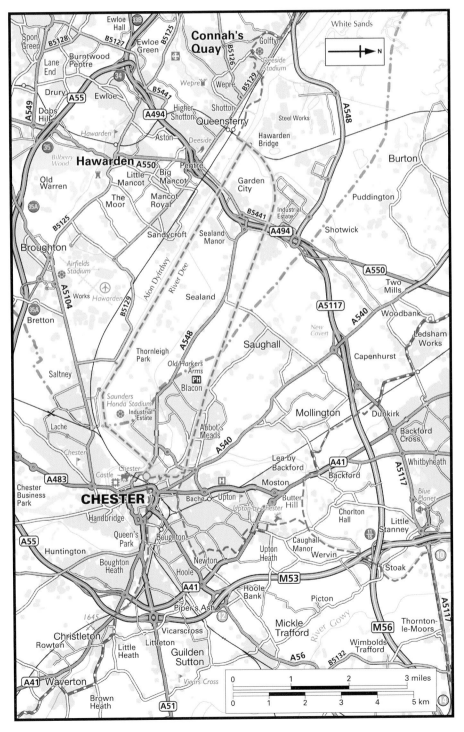

BIRKBY BRADLEY, CALDER VALLEY & SPEN VALLEY GREENWAYS

Linking Huddersfield and Bradford city centres and Dewsbury town centre, this mainly traffic-free route is ideal for family leisure cycling. Much of it is surprisingly rural, passing through a pleasant wooded and agricultural landscape. Most of the path is built on the former rail corridor of the Midland Railway, with the section from Dewsbury Moor to the town centre on a riverside path. It comprises the Birkby Bradley Greenway (National Route 69) and Calder Valley Greenway (National Route 66). At Dewsbury Moor, the Calder Valley Greenway joins the Spen Valley, which runs north through Heckmondwike, Liversedge and Cleckheaton.

There are many scenic views along the way, including those from Riddings woodland across Huddersfield to Huddersfield Football Stadium and Dalton Bank, and from Lower Spen up the Spen Valley to Norristhorpe and Roberttown. Other points of interest include Bradley Viaduct, which carries you over the River Colne and Huddersfield Broad Canal, and the River Calder bridge across the Dewsbury flood alleviation channel, with an excellent view of the river and weir. There are also local nature reserves at Dalton Bank and Lower Spen.

National Routes: 69 and 66

START Huddersfield train station.

FINISH Bradford Centenary Square.
For a shorter option, finish the ride at Mill Street West, Dewsbury town centre.

DISTANCE
Huddersfield to Bradford: 18 miles (29km).
Huddersfield to Dewsbury: 9 miles (14.5km).

GRADE Easy to moderate.

SURFACE Tarmac.

HILLS
Some moderate inclines on the Birkby Bradley and Calder Valley Greenways; a gentle climb from Dewsbury to Oakenshaw; and a few moderate climbs from the Spen Valley Greenway into Bradford.

YOUNG & INEXPERIENCED CYCLISTS
Birkby Bradley and Calder Valley Greenways: there are some short on-road sections, mostly on quiet roads. You will need to cross the busy A62 Leeds Road at Bradley using the central refuge islands provided on the route. There is also a short but busy road section with cycle lanes out of Mirfield.

Spen Valley Greenway: there is one busy road with a signalized crossing at the southern end as you arrive in the centre of Dewsbury. Best for novices and families is the 7-mile (11-km) section from the Calder & Hebble Navigation north to Oakenshaw. There are several roads to negotiate between the end of the Spen Valley Greenway in Oakenshaw and Bradford centre but the route into the city mainly follows off-road sections and on-road cycle lanes.

REFRESHMENTS
Lots of choice in Huddersfield, Mirfield, Dewsbury, Heckmondwike, Cleckheaton and Bradford, although these will require a short detour from the route.

THINGS TO SEE & DO
HUDDERSFIELD:
• Castle Hill and Victoria Tower: built to commemorate

Queen Victoria's Diamond Jubilee; 01484 223830; www.kirklees.gov.uk
- Tolson Museum: Victorian mansion house with a varied collection; 01484 223830; www.kirklees.gov.uk
- Bradley Viaduct: spectacular blue brick viaduct, with 15 high arches, over the River Colne and Huddersfield Broad Canal.

DEWSBURY:
- Victorian buildings, many connected with the once-thriving textiles trade.
- Oakwell Hall: Elizabethan house, which Charlotte Brontë visited in the 19th century and featured in her novel *Shirley*; 01924 326240; www.kirklees.gov.uk
- Red House Museum: elegant Georgian home of the Taylor family, friends of Charlotte Brontë; 01274 335100; www.kirklees.gov.uk
- Dewsbury Bus Museum: vintage buses, with open days twice a year and other visits by arrangement; www.dewsburybusmuseum.co.uk
- Dewsbury Museum: exhibits focusing on childhood; 01924 325100; www.kirklees.gov.uk
- The Minster: Dewsbury's historic parish church dating from AD 627; www.dewsburyminster.org.uk

BRADFORD:
- Bradford Cathedral: dating from the 15th century; www.bradfordcathedral.co.uk
- National Media Museum: focusing on film, photography, television, radio and the web; 0870 701 0200; www.nationalmediamuseum.org.uk
- Bradford Industrial Museum: permanent displays of textile machinery, steam power, engineering and motor vehicles; 01274 435900; www.bradfordmuseums.org
- Cartwright Hall Art Gallery: civic art gallery with contemporary exhibitions and permanent collections; 01274 431212; www.bradfordmuseums.org
- Saltaire World Heritage Site: well-preserved example of a mid-19th century industrial town; 01274 433678; www.visitbradford.com.
- Spen Valley: public artworks line the route, including Sally Matthews' flock of Swaledale sheep, sculpted from recycled engineering scrap (see page 117).

TRAIN STATIONS

Huddersfield; Deighton; Mirfield; Ravensthorpe; Dewsbury; Bradford.

BIKE HIRE Enquire locally.

FURTHER INFORMATION

- To view or print National Cycle Network routes, visit www.sustrans.org.uk
- Maps for this area are available to buy from www.sustransshop.co.uk
- Huddersfield Tourist Information: 01484 223200
- Bradford Tourist Information: 01274 433678; www.visitbradford.com

ROUTE DESCRIPTION

From the new civic square in Huddersfield, outside the magnificent porticoed train station, follow, on-road, the National Route 69 signs to the railway path. Continue on the greenway through the Colne Valley, following the course of the Huddersfield Broad Canal. Cross the busy Leeds Road to join National Route 66 and the Calder Valley Greenway. You will go over the splendid Bradley Viaduct, crossing the canal and River Colne. Between Colne Bridge and Mirfield train station, there are quiet roads with traffic-free sections. From Mirfield station, cross over the canal and take the short busy road section with cycle lanes towards Ravensthorpe. There is a traffic-free section on the outskirts of the town before the route follows Sackville Street and a traffic-free link to join the Spen Valley Greenway.

Here you have a choice: either cycle southwards on traffic-free paths that, for a short distance, go alongside the River Calder before taking you into Dewsbury, or take the path northwards, on a gentle traffic-free ascent seemingly over the top of Heckmondwicke, Liversedge and Cleckheaton before passing through a rolling golf course to the Spen Valley's end at Oakenshaw. From Oakenshaw, take the signposted route along cycle lanes and paths under the M606 to Bierley, through Bowling Park and on to Bradford Centenary Square.

En route, you will pass some stunning sculptures, including Sally Matthews' *Swaledale Flock*, *Rotate* by Trudi Entwistle, *Giant Pedal & Cycle Seats* by Alan Evans, *Lines of Desire* by Richard Harris, and poetry signs by Pauline Monkham. See also Artworks feature on pages 114–117.

NEARBY CYCLE ROUTES

National Route 66 runs from Leeds, northwest to Shipley, then south through Bradford to Dewsbury before turning west again along the Calder Valley. There are two long traffic-free trails either side of Leeds: the Leeds & Liverpool Canal northwest to Shipley, Bingley and Keighley, and the Aire & Calder Navigation southeast to Woodlesford. Further south, there are many traffic-free sections of the Trans Pennine Trail close to Barnsley.

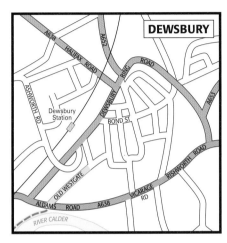

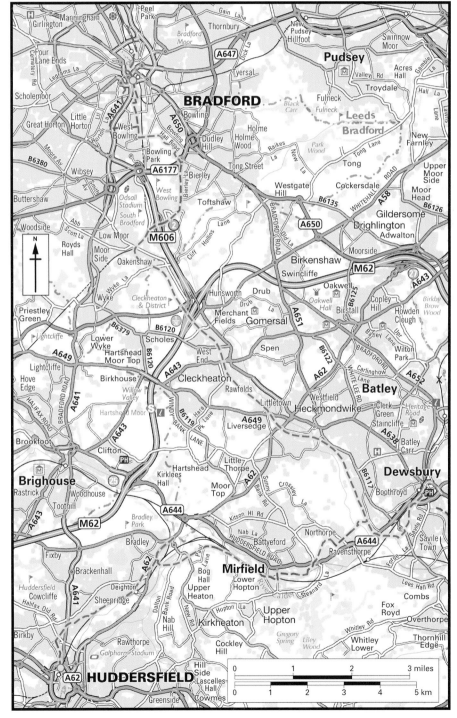

ROUTES OUT OF LANCASTER

Throughout the 18th century, Lancaster was England's principal port for trade with America. Myriad Georgian houses around the centre of the town date back to this era of prosperity. Going further back in time, the keep of Lancaster Castle is Norman, standing 24m (79ft) high with walls 3m (10ft) thick. The castle also served as the county jail; among the many notable prisoners was the Quaker leader George Fox, who was imprisoned in the 17th century. There are superb views of the surrounding countryside from the Ashton Memorial, built in 1909.

Reflecting the city's maritime heritage, the Millennium Bridge in the heart of Lancaster is the centrepiece of the city's cycle network and stands on the location of the first bridge over the River Lune. One route leads to Morecambe and its curving 4-mile (6.5-km) promenade, with views across Morecambe Bay to the mountains of the Lake District.

A second option follows the lovely majestic River Lune north to the Crook O'Lune, with views north to the hills of the Yorkshire Dales.

Lastly, to the south, you can cycle to Glasson Dock along the railway path. The canal link to Glasson was built in 1826 in response to the demands from Lancaster merchants for a larger port, so that they could increase their imports of sugar, cotton and other commodities from Africa, America and the West Indies.

National Route: 6

START Millennium Bridge, Lancaster.

FINISH Morecambe train station, or Crook O'Lune picnic site, or Glasson Dock.

DISTANCE
Lancaster to Morecambe Promenade train station:
3 miles (5km).
Lancaster to Crook O'Lune: 5 miles (8km).
Lancaster to Glasson Dock: 5 miles (8km).

GRADE Easy.

SURFACE Tarmac or fine gravel path.

HILLS None.

YOUNG & INEXPERIENCED CYCLISTS
Ideal for novices and children, mostly traffic-free with no dangerous road crossings.

REFRESHMENTS
• Lots of choice in Morecambe and Lancaster.
• Pubs just off the route in Halton and Caton.
• Pubs and other choices in Glasson.

THINGS TO SEE & DO
MORECAMBE:
• Morecambe Promenade: a vast collection of public artworks forms part of the promenade and sea defences; www.visitnorthwest.com
• Winter Gardens: Grade II listed and built in 1897; www.thewintergardensmorecambe.co.uk
• Eric Morecambe statue: tribute in bronze to Morecambe's most famous son.

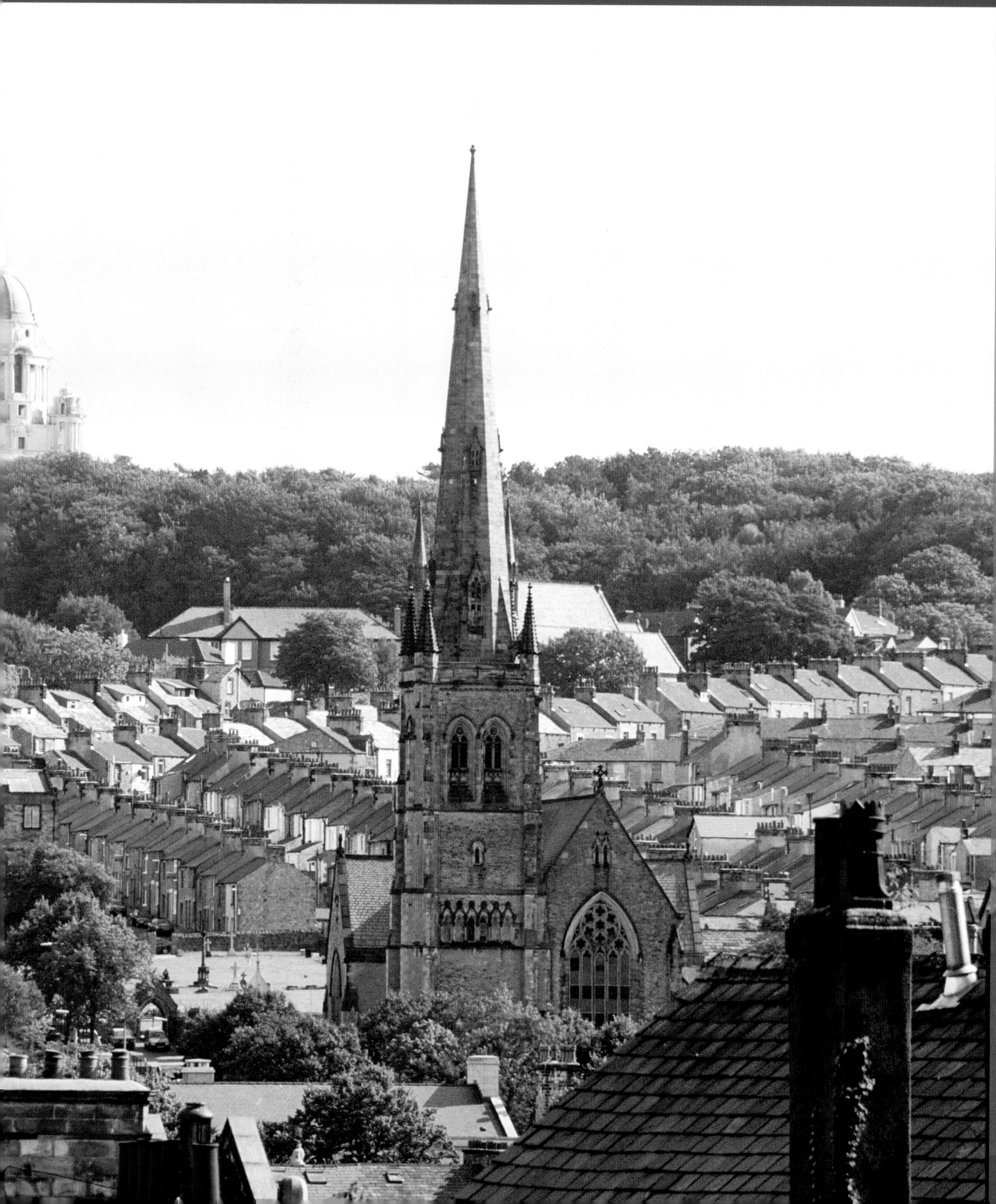

LANCASTER:

- Lancaster Castle: Grade I listed building, with parts dating back to the 12th century; 01524 64998; www.lancastercastle.com
- City Museum: covers Lancaster's history from Roman

times to the present day; 01524 64637; www.lancashire.gov.uk

- Tropical Butterfly House: situated in Williamson Park; 01524 33318; www.citycoastcountryside.co.uk
- Maritime Museum: award-winning museum housed in

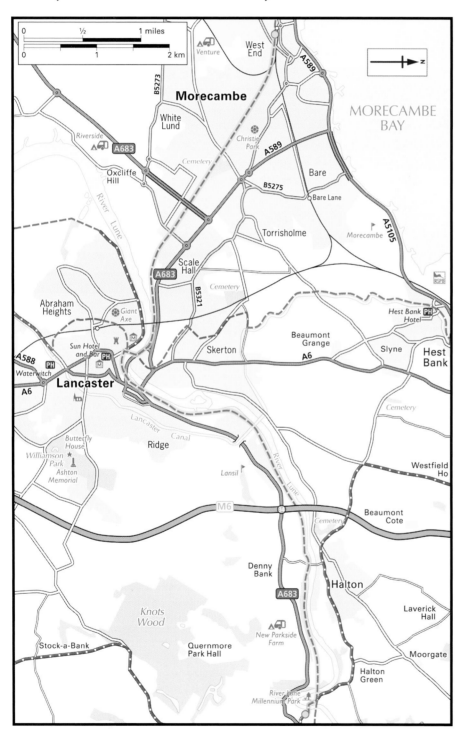

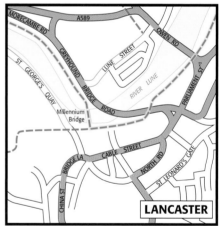

LANCASTER

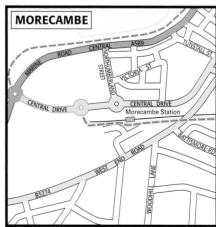

MORECAMBE

the former Port of Lancaster Custom House; 01524 382264; www.lancashire.gov.uk

TRAIN STATIONS
Morecambe; Lancaster.

BIKE HIRE
- Cycle Adventure, Lancaster: 07518 373007; www.cycle-adventure.co.uk
- Leisure Lakes Bikes, Lancaster: 01524 844389; www.leisurelakesbikes.co.uk
- Sunshine Cycles Morecambe: 01524 414709; www.sunshinecyclehire.co.uk

FURTHER INFORMATION
- To view or print National Cycle Network routes, visit www.sustrans.org.uk
- Maps for this area are available to buy from www.sustransshop.co.uk
- Morecambe Tourist Information: 01524 582808; www.citycoastcountryside.co.uk
- Lancaster Tourist Information: 01524 582394; www.citycoastcountryside.co.uk

ROUTE DESCRIPTION
For the route to Morecambe, cross the Millennium Bridge, and take the path on the north side of the River Lune. This leads to the railway path, which takes you through a largely urban area all the way to the train station in Morecambe. From here, it is just a short ride on quiet streets to the seafront.

To cycle to the Crook O'Lune picnic site, keep on the south side of the Millennium Bridge and follow the traffic-free path alongside the River Lune. You'll travel through mixed woodland before going under the mighty stone aqueduct carrying the canal, then beneath the M6 motorway bridge, and twice crossing the river at the Crook O'Lune, where the river describes a U-shaped bend between Halton and Caton. Along the way are interpretation boards with details of birds you may see along the river.

For the ride to Glasson Dock, start at the southern end of the Millennium Bridge and ride on roads through the St George's Quay area, following the signs to Glasson. When the road ends, continue on a narrower, surfaced track through open countryside to join the disused railway line alongside the Lune estuary and salt marshes. Continue by Conder Green – a good picnic site – and beside the sea wall to reach Glasson Dock.

NEARBY CYCLE ROUTES
National Route 6 passes through Lancaster on its way from Preston to Kendal. National Route 62 will eventually run close to the coast southwest of Glasson Dock to Fleetwood and Blackpool. National Route 72 explores South Lakeland on its way to Barrow. Further east, the Pennine Cycleway links Settle to Appleby-in-Westmorland.

OTHER WAYMARKED OR TRAFFIC-FREE RIDES INCLUDE:
- The towpath of the Lancaster Canal, which can be followed through Lancaster and north to Carnforth (National Route 6).
- The Lancashire Cycleway, which uses Regional Routes 90 and 91 to link Carnforth, Lancaster and Blackpool, and circle the Forest of Bowland on a 260-mile (418-km) ride.

WHITEHAVEN TO SHERIFFS GATE, ROWRAH

Whitehaven was once no more than a small fishing village but it developed as a port in the 17th century, with the discovery of coal and very high-grade iron ore. Many Georgian and Victorian buildings reflect the prosperity from this era. There are connections to George Washington – the Washingtons were a Lancastrian family who emigrated to America, and his grandmother was buried in St Nicholas's Church. The whole of the west coast of Cumbria is criss-crossed with old mineral railways, many of which have been converted to recreational use. The C2C (Sea-to-Sea), the most famous of all the long-distance cycle routes on the National Cycle Network, has two starting points on this coast: Workington and Whitehaven. This ride runs from Whitehaven, southeast towards the edge of the fells of the Lake District National Park at Cleator Moor. The ride is decorated with many sculptures and artworks, including lots of small, blue metal 'train' signposts and bizarre figures on top of tall metal posts. Beyond Kirkland, you can continue northeast on a mixture of quiet lanes and wide stone tracks, to explore the stunning scenery alongside Ennerdale Water.

National Route: 71

START Whitehaven harbour.

FINISH Sheriffs Gate, Rowrah.

DISTANCE 9 miles (14.5km).

GRADE Easy.

SURFACE Tarmac.

HILLS Uphill gradient on the outward trip but nothing too severe.

YOUNG & INEXPERIENCED CYCLISTS
Apart from a very short section on-road at the start of the route in Whitehaven, the ride is traffic-free on a railway path with a gentle climb.

REFRESHMENTS
• Choices in Whitehaven.
• Pubs at Rowrah and Ennerdale.

THINGS TO SEE & DO
• The Rum Story, Whitehaven: visitor attraction depicting the story of the British rum trade; 01946 592933; www.rumstory.co.uk
• The Beacon, Whitehaven: home to the town's museum collection, situated on the harbourside; the Met. Office Weather Gallery on the top floor offers panoramic views of the town, the coast, and across the Solway Firth to Scotland; 01946 592302; www.thebeacon-whitehaven.co.uk
• Haig Colliery Mining Museum: the site of Cumbria's last deep coal mine, situated on cliffs above Whitehaven; steam winding engine operates daily; 01946 599949; www.haigpit.com
• Michael Moon's Bookshop: large selection of second-hand books; 01946 599010

TRAIN STATIONS
Whitehaven.

BIKE HIRE
Haven Cycles, Whitehaven: 01946 63263; www.c2c-guide.co.uk

IVY
2.99

MINI ROSE
2·20

ALL NOW
£1·25

FURTHER INFORMATION

- To view or print National Cycle Network routes, visit www.sustrans.org.uk
- Maps for this area are available to buy from www.sustransshop.co.uk

- Dedicated information on whole of C2C route at www.c2c-guide.co.uk
- Cumbria Tourist Information: 01946 852939; www.visitcumbria.com

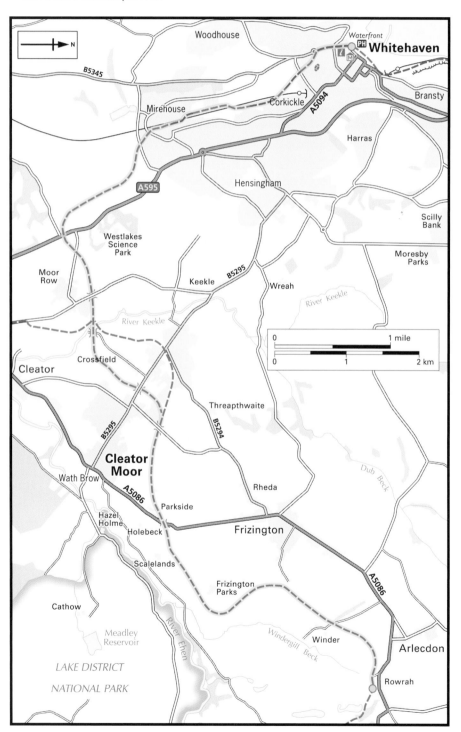

ROUTE DESCRIPTION

From Whitehaven harbour, make your way through the town towards Preston Street, from where you join the traffic-free path. There is a short section along Esk Avenue before you rejoin the path. The route then passes under the railway twice before continuing past Moor Row and through Cleator Moor. You then simply follow the path all the way to Rowrah and Sheriffs Gate at the Lake District National Park, where you will get ever-better views of the mountains ahead. The ride is decorated with many sculptures and artworks.

From Sheriffs Gate, you could continue on minor roads to Kirkland, then cycle northeast on a mixture of quiet lanes and wide stone tracks to explore the stunning scenery alongside Ennerdale Water.

NEARBY CYCLE ROUTES

This route forms part of the long-distance C2C (Sea to Sea) route (National Routes 7, 14 and 71) to Sunderland or Newcastle. An alternative start point for the C2C is Workington on Route 7. Route 7 from Workington and Route 71 from Whitehaven join 1 mile (1.6km) before Braithwaite.

National Route 72 links Whitehaven and Workington via a coastal route. It also forms part of Hadrian's Cycleway, which stretches the length of Hadrian's Wall World Heritage Site, from Glannaventa Roman Bath House in Ravenglass to Arbeia Roman Fort and Museum in South Shields.

An alternative traffic-free option to the ride described here starts from near the railway station in Whitehaven and runs northwest on Route 72 to Distington and through Workington to Camerton. Cross the river at Camerton and head for Great Clifton and along the cycleway to the roundabout to pick up A595 back towards Workington. There is a cycleway all the way to Lillyhall, and from here you can loop back towards Workington Moorclose, via new links to Lillyhall College. This is a pleasant ride of about 15 miles (24km) through rolling open landscape.

OTHER WAYMARKED OR TRAFFIC-FREE RIDES INCLUDE:
• Traffic-free trails along the shores of Ennerdale Water.
• Waymarked woodland routes in Whinlatter Forest.
• The Keswick Railway Path to Threlkeld, a 3.5-mile (5.5-km) linear path, with lots of picnic and paddling opportunities.

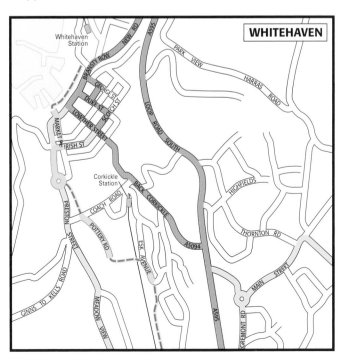

YORK TO BENINGBROUGH HALL & SELBY

This ride is made up of two traffic-free trails running north and south from the beautiful walled city of York, famous for its Roman and Viking history. The ride to the north takes a riverside path along the Ouse, passing through grazed meadowland and attractive woodland. There are several curious sculptures by Andy Hazell: seats looking like horse-drawn carriages and farm implements, a weather vane with a bicycle and dog, and a metalwork globe with depictions of York Cathedral and the walled city. Near Skelton, the route continues on quiet lanes for a further 5 miles (8km), ending at the magnificent National Trust-owned Beningbrough Hall.

To the south, a traffic-free path follows the disused railway across the flat, arable landscape of the Vale of York to Riccall and then on-lane to Selby. The ride uses the former East Coast main line, which was threatened with subsidence by the development of the huge Selby coalfield in the 1970s. A new stretch of main line was paid for by the National Coal Board and opened in 1983. The old route was then converted to recreational use by Sustrans, one of its earliest projects. On the way, look out for the famous scale model of the solar system by Peter Thompson and Willy Hoerdeman, the *Fisher of Dreams* at Naburn Bridge by Peter Rogers, and *Cassini*, the scale-model satellite probe by David Coulthard and Peter Thompson.

National Route: 65

START York train station.

FINISH Beningbrough Hall or Selby train station.

DISTANCE
York to Beningbrough Hall: 9 miles (14.5km).
York to Selby: 15 miles (24km).

GRADE Easy.

SURFACE Tarmac.

HILLS None.

YOUNG & INEXPERIENCED CYCLISTS
On the route to Beningbrough, the last 5 miles (8km) follow quiet country lanes. Mainly traffic-free, with short sections on quiet lanes in Ricall and Barlby. The cycle facilities throughout York are excellent.

REFRESHMENTS
- Lots of choice in York and Selby; also try Riccall and Bishopthorpe.
- The Sidings Hotel & Restaurant, Shipton.
- Cafe at Beningbrough Hall, open from Easter to October.
- Downay Arms pub and Blacksmith Arms pub, Newton-on-Ouse (just beyond Beningbrough).

THINGS TO SEE & DO
YORK:
- The Minster: stunning Minster built between the 1220s and the 1470s; 01904 557200; www.yorkminster.org,
- National Railway Museum: covers 300 years of railway history; includes a replica of Stephenson's Rocket and a model railway; 0844 815 3139; www.nrm.org.uk
- York Castle Museum: museum of everyday life, with re-created rooms, shops and streets showing how people used to live in the past; 01904 650335; www.yorkcastlemuseum.org.uk

YORK TO BENINGBROUGH HALL & SELBY

- Jorvik Viking Centre: explore Viking history on the very site where archaeologists discovered remains of Viking York; 01904 543400; www.jorvik-viking.centre.co.uk
- Clifford's Tower: part of York Castle, originally built by William the Conqueror in the 11th century; www.english-heritage.org.uk
- Treasurer's House: 17th and 18th-century house in the heart of historic York; 01904 624247; www.nationaltrust.org.uk
- Fairfax House: one of England's finest Georgian townhouses; 01904 655543; www.fairfaxhouse.co.uk
- Merchant Adventurer's Hall: medieval guild hall dating from 1357; 01904 654818; www.theyorkcompany.co.uk

- Selby Abbey: dating from 1069; 01757 703123; www.selbyabbey.org.uk
- Beningbrough Hall & Gardens: 18th-century mansion, with interactive galleries and paintings from the National Portrait Gallery, as well as a working walled garden; 01904 472027; www.nationaltrust.org.uk

TRAIN STATIONS
York; Selby.

BIKE HIRE
Bob Trotter Cycles, York: 01904 622868; www.bobtrottercycles.com

FURTHER INFORMATION
- To view or print National Cycle Network routes, visit www.sustrans.org.uk

- Maps for this area are available to buy from www.sustransshop.co.uk
- York Tourist Information: 01904 550099; www.visityork.org

ROUTE DESCRIPTION
From York train station, travelling northwards towards Beningbrough, cross the River Ouse alongside the railway before taking the path on the east bank of the river. Follow the course of the river to Skelton, where you join minor roads, crossing the grazed Rawcliffe Meadows to Shipton and on to Beningbrough Hall.

Travelling south, leave York station and make your way towards the River Ouse, to join the riverside path. Follow this southwards through the city and out through York's famous Knavesmire racecourse, then follow the popular railway path the rest of the way to Ricall. Take quiet roads through Ricall and again through Barlby before rejoining the path alongside the river that takes you into the market town of Selby.

NEARBY CYCLE ROUTES
York is at a crossroads of the National Cycle Network. The north–south section from Middlesbrough to Selby

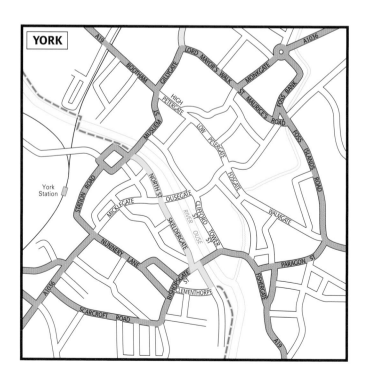

and Doncaster is signed and mapped (National Route 65), as is the route from Beverley and Pocklington to the east (National Route 66), on the Yorkshire Moors. The western section of the route to Harrogate and Leeds is still to be completed.

You can also cross the Millennium Bridge for a traffic-free route, signed as National Route 66, through Walmgate Stray, past the university to the Foss Island Railway Path and on to Stamford Bridge. There are also plenty of local cycling links through York.

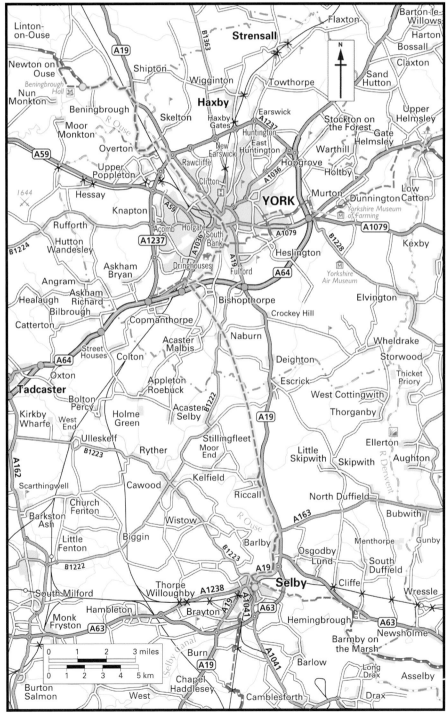

SOUTER TO ST MARY'S

This ride visits two North Sea lighthouses, one to the south and one to the north of the River Tyne estuary. They are linked via the Shields Ferry, which sails between South Shields and North Shields, and a route past Tynemouth Priory and Castle.

Souter Lighthouse, on the coastline between South Shields and Sunderland, is the world's first electric lighthouse, with fantastic views over Marsden Bay. Look out for the nesting seabirds on cliffs and stacks, and visit the tea-room serving delicious local specialities. The lighthouse is located on Lizard Point at Marsden, but takes its name from Souter Point, 1 mile (1.6km) to the south. Opened in 1871, the lighthouse was built due to the dangerous reefs in the surrounding area.

St Mary's Lighthouse is on St Mary's Island, just north of Whitley Bay, a small island linked to the mainland by a short concrete causeway that is submerged at high tide. While it no longer functions as a lighthouse, it is easily accessible (when the tide is out) and is open to visitors. It has a small museum, a visitor's centre and a cafe. Both the lighthouse and the adjacent keepers' cottages were built in 1898.

National Routes: 1 and 72

START
Souter Lighthouse, but do check which way the wind is blowing – a headwind can ruin this ride!

FINISH St Mary's Lighthouse.

DISTANCE 11 miles (17.5km).

GRADE Fairly easy with no strenuous climbs.

SURFACE Tarmac.

HILLS Very few; some short, steep banks.

YOUNG & INEXPERIENCED CYCLISTS
A mixture of traffic-free paths and quiet roads makes this a good choice for families and novices.

REFRESHMENTS
- Cafe at Souter Lighthouse.
- Marsden Grotto pub.
- Kopper Kettle cafe (Westoe Road), South Shields.
- Cafe in Tynemouth Priory.
- North Shields Fish Quay and market, selling fresh fish as well as fish and chips.
- Lots of choice in Tynemouth, Cullercoats and Whitley Bay.

THINGS TO SEE & DO
- Tynemouth Priory: medieval Benedictine priory; www.english-heritage.org.uk
- Souter Lighthouse; www.nationaltrust.org.uk
- Blue Reef Aquarium: includes seahorses, sharks, giant octopus, frogs and otters; 0191 2581031; www.bluereefaquarium.co.uk
- St Mary's Lighthouse, St Mary's Island; 0191 200 8650; www.friendsofstmarysisland.co.uk

TRAIN STATIONS

Sunderland; Newcastle.

METRO STATIONS

Folding bikes can be taken on the Metro. Tyne Dock (green line) is the nearest station to Souter Lighthouse; Whitley Bay (yellow line) to St Mary's Lighthouse.

BIKE HIRE

- South Tyneside Cycle Hire: 0191 455 6313; www.visitnortheastengland.com
- Cyclops, North Shields: adapted bikes for the disabled; 07974 720002; www.cyclopsnt.org

FURTHER INFORMATION

- To view or print National Cycle Network routes, visit www.sustrans.org.uk
- Maps for this area are available to buy from www.sustransshop.co.uk
- Northeast England Tourist Information: 0844 249 5090; www.visitnortheastengland.com
- For information about the Shields Ferry, visit www.nexus.org.uk/wps/wcm/connect/Nexus/Ferry

ROUTE DESCRIPTION

From Souter Lighthouse, ride north on National Route 1 using the cycle lane on the shared-use footway. You will shortly pass the Marsden Rock. Cross over the roundabout in front of the New Crown pub to the playing field. Follow signs for National Route 1 and the pedestrian ferry.

After a yellow gate, turn right (using road or footway) and then immediately left up Sea Way. Cross over Salisbury Place and use the traffic-free Route 1 path adjacent to Erskine Road. Cross Westoe Road and continue on Route 1, passing under the Metro and road bridges and bearing to the right past Wickes DIY store. Continue until you reach the Shields Ferry terminal. There is a bike rack on the rear lower deck.

Leave the North Shields ferry terminal and turn right along Clive Street, following signs for National Route 72 and Tynemouth/Whitley Bay. Bear right down Liddell

Street towards the North Shields Fish Quay and market. After the New Dolphin pub, turn right following signs on street lights for Route 1. You then reach the *Old Buoys* artwork, which celebrates the confluence of three National Routes: 1, 10 and 72.

Go through the car park and onto the promenade, turning left. In peak season, the promenade may be busy, so take care and warn pedestrians of your approach. Turn left up a short but steep bank for stunning views of Tynemouth Priory. At the Gibraltar Rock pub, you may decide to use the footway for the next couple of miles. Cycle alongside the Whitley Bay promenade, from where there are amazing views. Pass the Queen's Head pub and turn right down Norma Crescent after the tractors and boats in Dry Dock. There are excellent views of Tynemouth to the right, and on a clear day you can see Souter Lighthouse.

Turn left and rejoin the promenade route. Take care at a couple of road crossings that lead to the beach. Turn right off the promenade route onto the shared-use footway leading to St Mary's Lighthouse.

NEARBY CYCLE ROUTES

This route follows National Routes 72 and 1. Route 72 forms Hadrian's Cycle Way, which stretches the length of Hadrian's Wall World Heritage Site from Glannaventa Roman Bath House in Ravenglass to Arbeia Roman Fort and Museum in South Shields. Route 72 also links with National Route 7, which forms part of the C2C, running from Workington and Whitehaven to Newcastle and Sunderland. The section of the ride that uses Route 1 is part of the Coast & Castles route from Newcastle to Edinburgh.

Other traffic-free or waymarked routes include The Wylam Loop, a 20-mile (32-km) ride from Newcastle to Gateshead via Wylam, with a shorter option of Newburn to Wylam.

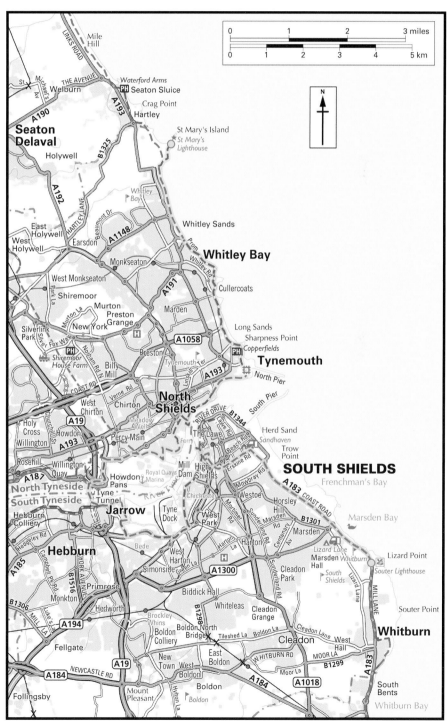

BALTIC TO BILL QUAY

Housed in a landmark industrial building on the south bank of the River Tyne in Gateshead, BALTIC is the biggest gallery of its kind in the world, presenting a dynamic, diverse and international programme of contemporary visual art. This ranges from blockbuster world-class exhibitions to innovative new work and projects created by artists working within the local community.

This route uses National Route 14 to link BALTIC with a visit to Bill Quay Community Farm, tucked away in the east of Gateshead, on the banks of the River Tyne. A rural haven and home to a variety of livestock, the farm was set up in the mid-1980s to educate and entertain the local community. It has since developed into a rare breeds centre, with such animals as cows, goats, pigs, sheep, chickens and rabbits.

The farm is host to a new arts trail. Created by local artists, the trail is made up of 25 exhibits all with a farm life theme, as well as a special piece created by local children during the summer holidays. The Green Fleece Cafe offers a hearty selection of snacks and drinks.

National Route: 14

START BALTIC gallery, Gateshead.

FINISH Bill Quay Community Farm, Gateshead.

DISTANCE 3.5 miles (5.5km).

GRADE Very easy.

SURFACE Mostly tarmac.

HILLS
A few hills with short climbs – steep but quick!

YOUNG & INEXPERIENCED CYCLISTS
There are two short on-road sections after leaving BALTIC and around the AkzoNobel factory. However, at weekends and during school holidays they will be very quiet.

REFRESHMENTS
• Cafe at BALTIC.
• Elephant on the Tyne hotel.
• Green Fleece Cafe at Bill Quay Community Farm.
• The Albion Inn and The Cricketers pub in Bill Quay.

THINGS TO SEE & DO
• BALTIC: centre for contemporary art; 0191 478 1810; www.balticmill.com
• Bill Quay Community Farm: 0191 433 5780; www.gateshead.gov.uk

TRAIN STATIONS
Newcastle Central.

BIKE HIRE
Whickham Thorns Outdoor Activity Centre, Gateshead: 0191 433 5767; www.gateshead.gov.uk

FURTHER INFORMATION
• To view or print National Cycle Network routes, visit www.sustrans.org.uk
• Maps for this area are available to buy from

www.sustransshop.co.uk
- Northeast England Tourist Information: 0844 249 5090; www.visitnortheastengland.com

ROUTE DESCRIPTION

From the front of BALTIC, head east on the path alongside the Tyne, turning right through the car park. At the junction, turn left and follow the signs for 'The Keelman's Way' (National Route 14).

After 0.5 mile (0.8km), turn right, then immediately left, past the CEMEX factory along South Shore Road. Bear left onto the trail signed National Route 14, then right up the steep bank, past the Elephant on the Tyne hotel.

Turn left in front of the Budgreen shop, following Route 14 signs. Turn left, then bear right in front of the AkzoNobel factory. Take care on this road – families may prefer to use the footway.

Follow Route 14 signs in front of the storage depot – use the shared-use footway if you wish. Bear left, continuing to follow signs for Route 14 and South Shields, then bear right down a steep, short bank.

Turn right up the steep road past the Cricketers' Arms pub and onto Hainingwood Terrace, to reach Bill Quay Community Farm.

NEARBY CYCLE ROUTES

National Route 14 links with Route 7, which forms part of the C2C route from Whitehaven or Workington to Newcastle or Sunderland. It also links with National

Route 72, Hadrian's Cycleway from Glannaventa Roman Bath House in Ravenglass to Arbeia Roman Fort and Museum in South Shields. The Coast & Castles ride on National Route 1 goes from Newcastle to Edinburgh, and the nearby Reivers Route takes National Route 10

between Tynemouth and Whitehaven via Kielder Forest and Carlisle. Other traffic-free or waymarked routes include The Wylam Loop, a 20-mile (32-km) ride from Newcastle to Gateshead via Wylam, with a shorter option of Newburn to Wylam.

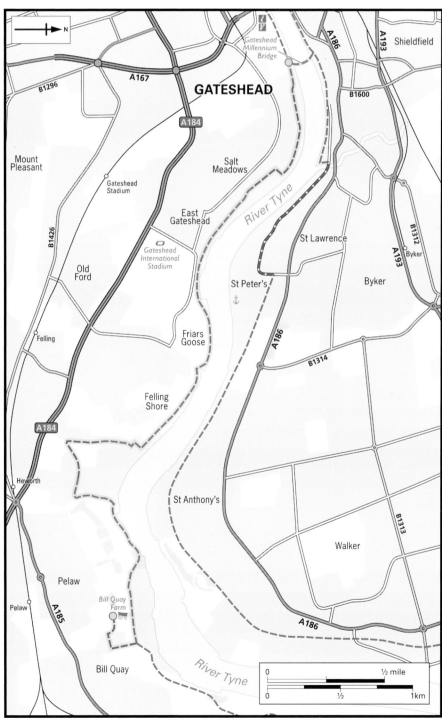

HOLIDAY & CHALLENGE ROUTES

Although the majority of the cycle rides within this book are ideal for families to enjoy, more experienced cyclists may want to try some of the long-distance and/or more challenging routes. Here we publish a small selection. For more information and to buy maps for these routes and other long-distance rides, visit www.sustrans.org.uk

HOLIDAY ROUTES

COAST & CASTLES
National Route 1
Leave the dramatic bridges over the Tyne in the centre of Newcastle and follow the Northumberland coastline northwards. On your way to the fortified town of Berwick on the north banks of the River Tweed, you will pass a series of wide, sandy beaches and dramatic castles, such as Warkworth, Bamburgh and Lindisfarne.

CORNISH WAY
National Routes 3 and 32
Explore the southwestern tip of mainland Britain from Land's End to Bude, along the sweep of Mounts Bay and past the old tin mining areas. Beyond Truro, one option uses the Clay Trails around the lunar landscape of St Austell, whereas the other takes in the famous Camel Trail. The two options rejoin in Bodmin and skirt Bodmin Moor on the way to Bude.

DEVON COAST TO COAST
National Route 27
Crossing this vast and varied county from south to north, the route starts in Plymouth and climbs on the wooded Plym Valley Trail to the edge of Dartmoor, which is followed around its western fringe. Two more railway paths, the Granite Way and the Tarka Trail, lead east then north, to drop gently down to the coast at Bideford. The coast is followed to Ilfracombe.

HADRIAN'S CYCLEWAY
National Route 72
Follow the line of the Roman frontier, from Ravenglass in West Cumbria along the Solway Coast, through the Northumberland National Park and alongside the River Tyne through Newcastle. Experience the fascinating history of Hadrian's Wall by visiting the many Roman forts and museums along the way.

HULL TO FAKENHAM
National Route 1
Cross the Humber Bridge south from Hull and make your way through the rolling open countryside of the Lincolnshire Wolds towards the splendour of Lincoln Cathedral. Largely traffic-free trails link Lincoln to Boston. The attractive towns of Wisbech, King's Lynn and Burnham Market are stepping stones on your way to journey's end at Fakenham.

CELTIC TRAIL
National Routes 4, 8 and 47
The magnificent cathedral of St David's and spectacular Chepstow Castle lie at either end of this ride across Wales at its widest point. In between lies the stunning Pembrokeshire coast, the popular Millennium Coastal Park near Llanelli and the rich industrial heritage of the South Wales valleys.

LOUGHSHORE TRAIL
National Routes 94 and 96
This is an easy, low-level ride around the shores of Lough Neagh, the largest freshwater lake in the UK and Ireland, on a mixture of quiet roads and short stretches of off-road track. Highlights include Clotworthy House, the Celtic High Cross at Ardboe, Mountjoy Castle and several nature reserves.

NORTH WEST TRAIL
National Routes 91 and 92
Criss-crossing the border between Northern Ireland and the Republic of Ireland, the trail meanders through Yeats country in County Sligo, enjoys dramatic views of the Atlantic in County Donegal and makes its way through

1

the Mourne and Strule River valleys in the heart of the Sperrins to the spectacular Fermanagh Lakelands.

CHALLENGE ROUTES

SEA TO SEA (C2C)
National Routes 7, 14 and 71

The most popular long-distance route in the UK, the C2C crosses England from the Irish Sea to the North Sea. It passes through the scenic grandeur of the Lake District, climbing up over the Pennines, then descends gently on traffic-free paths to Tynemouth or Sunderland.

LÔN LAS CYMRU
National Routes 8 and 42

Running the length of Wales from Holyhead to Cardiff, Lôn Las Cymru crosses three mountain ranges on its way through the principality. This tough challenge takes in many attractive market towns in Mid Wales before passing through South Wales, from Merthyr Tydfil to Cardiff, with its rich industrial heritage.

LOCHS & GLENS
National Route 7

This 430-mile (692-km) route links Carlisle, near the Scottish border, to Inverness in the far north of Scotland. It passes through a variety of stunning scenery, from the awe-inspiring forests and coast of southwest Scotland

1 Porth Moina, Land's End 2 & 3 Hadrian's Cycleway 4 Sea-to-Sea (C2C) 5 Highest millennium milepost, Lôn Las Cymru 6 Coast & Castles route 7 Stone sign on the Cornish Way 8 The Granite Way railway path 9 Land's End on the Cornish Way

to the dramatic mountain ranges between the Trossachs and the Cairngorms.

PENNINE CYCLEWAY
National Routes 6, 62, 67 and 68

The Pennine Cycleway offers a tough exploration of the spine of England. The route starts in Derby and passes through the Peak District and the Yorkshire Dales and Northumberland National Parks, finishing at the historic walled town of Berwick-upon-Tweed near the border between England and Scotland.

WAY OF THE ROSES
National Routes 1, 66, 67, 68, 69, 636 and 688

Another coast-to-coast route across northern England, from the sands of Morecambe Bay, through the southern fringes of the Yorkshire Dales National Park and across the rolling Yorkshire Wolds to the traditional seaside resort of Bridlington and the bracing waters of the North Sea coast.

NEW YORK 3147

JOHN O'GROATS 874

ISLES OF SCILLY 28
LONGSHIPS LIGHTHOUSE 1½

SYDNEY 10937
20TH OCTOBER

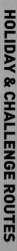

SCOTLAND

Castles, mountains, islands and an enormously long jagged coastline: if you like your cycling rugged, remote and spectacular then Scotland has it all. Most of the population lives in the Central Belt, around Glasgow, Edinburgh and the area between the two cities, so the rest of the country is lightly populated with big open spaces and low traffic levels. Long-distance routes criss-cross the country and there are plenty of family-friendly rides in and around the cities, in the Trossachs, the Great Glen and around Aviemore. For what is essentially an urban area, the Central Belt is very well served with traffic-free trails. Cycle paths run east and west from central Glasgow along the River Clyde, west past shipyards and Dumbarton Castle to the banks of Loch Lomond and east to Flemington. To the southwest a railway path heads for Paisley and Johnstone, with branches continuing either to Kilbirnie past a series of lochs or to the ferry terminal at Gourock, with vast views over the Firth of Clyde towards Helensburgh. Between Glasgow and Edinburgh you have the choice of the Airdrie to Bathgate railway path, with its series of dramatic sculptures, or the towpath of the Forth & Clyde and Union Canals. The towpaths of the Union Canal and the Water of Leith join at Kingsknowe and lead right into the heart of Edinburgh. A network of urban railway paths and longer paths lead out of the city, east to the coast at Musselburgh or west to Queensferry and the extraordinary cyclepath over the Forth Road Bridge with its bird's eye view of the Forth Estuary beneath.

The Lochs & Glens Cycle Route (Route 7) starts in Carlisle and follows the coast of the Solway Firth to Dumfries. After touching the coast again at Kirkcudbright and Creetown the route turns inland across the forested expanse of Dumfries & Galloway. A brief run along the Ayrshire coast takes you to the start of the railway paths from Kilbirnie that lead through Glasgow to Loch Lomond. The scenery becomes more mountainous along the series of traffic-free trails and quiet lanes that cross the Trossachs National Park, passing along the shores of Loch Venachar, Loch Lubnaig and Loch Tay. North west from Pitlochry the route crosses the Grampians, dropping down into Strathspey and the tourist centre of Aviemore at the foot of the Cairngorms. A final climb over Slochd summit leads to a gentle descent into Inverness.

Scotland's other main long-distance trail is Route 1, which starts its long journey in Dover. From Berwick to Edinburgh the route turns inland to sample the delights of the Scottish Borders: the majestic River Tweed, the castles at Norham and Kelso and the abbeys at Dryburgh and Melrose. After crossing the heather-clad Moorfoot Hills north of Innerleithen the route descends to Edinburgh. Across Fife and the splendid cyclepath over the Tay Road Bridge to reach Dundee, the route north to Aberdeen hugs the coast, visiting the fishing port of Arbroath. Route 1 continues north to the Moray Firth and Inverness, reaches the north coast at Tongue and turns east to John o' Groats. Ferries north to Orkney and Shetland offer options to explore the wonderful Northern Isles. Finally, running southwest from Inverness along the Great Glen all the way to the Campbeltown on the Mull of Kintyre, Route 78 explores some of the rugged west coast of Scotland taking in Fort William, the adventure capital of the Highlands and the port of Oban, where myriad ferries connect the mainland to the islands.

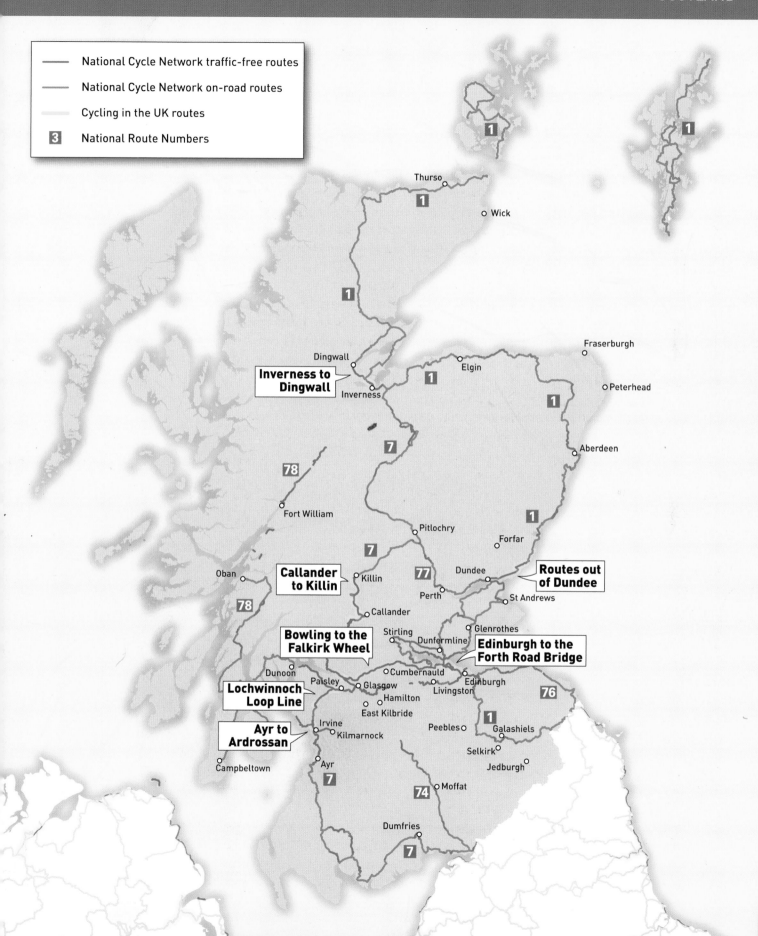

National Cycle Network traffic-free routes

National Cycle Network on-road routes

Cycling in the UK routes

3 National Route Numbers

1

Thurso

1

Wick

1

Dingwall

Inverness to Dingwall

Inverness

Elgin

1

Fraserburgh

Peterhead

7

78

1

Aberdeen

Fort William

Pitlochry

Forfar

1

7

77

Dundee

Routes out of Dundee

Oban

Callander to Killin

Killin

Perth

St Andrews

78

Callander

Glenrothes

Stirling

Dunfermline

Bowling to the Falkirk Wheel

Edinburgh to the Forth Road Bridge

Dunoon

Cumbernauld

Edinburgh

Paisley

Glasgow

Livingston

Lochwinnoch Loop Line

Hamilton

East Kilbride

76

Irvine

Ayr to Ardrossan

Kilmarnock

Peebles

Galashiels

1

Selkirk

Campbeltown

Ayr

Jedburgh

7

Moffat

74

Dumfries

7

EDINBURGH TO THE FORTH ROAD BRIDGE

Edinburgh's architectural delights are far too numerous to list here but, from a cycling perspective, riding across the Forth Road Bridge is one of the most extraordinary experiences to be had in Scotland. You cross from South Queensferry to North Queensferry in complete traffic-free safety along the cycle lanes that run either side of the bridge, hundreds of feet above the waters of the Firth of Forth, with views to the east of the magnificent Forth Rail Bridge (the one where, as the saying goes, they start painting at one end the moment they have stopped at the other!)

The route starts from Haymarket in central Edinburgh, using a railway path to leave the city to the northwest, passing close by 16th-century Lauriston Castle. Just beyond Cramond Brig, you have a choice of taking roads to Dalmeny or a more leisurely ride along the coastline of the Firth of Forth, which passes Dalmeny House, built in 1817 by the Earl of Rosebery in the Gothic Revival style.

Queensferry was named after Queen Margaret, who used the ferry to cross the Forth in the 11th century.

National Route: 1

START Haymarket train station, Edinburgh.

FINISH North end of the Forth Road Bridge, North Queensferry.

DISTANCE
11 miles (17.5km).
Alternative coastal route: 13 miles (21km).

GRADE Easy to moderate.

SURFACE Tarmac.

HILLS Rolling.

YOUNG & INEXPERIENCED CYCLISTS
At the time of writing, there are proposed changes to National Route 1 in the Haymarket area of Edinburgh, and the route will use either quiet residential streets or a busy road from Haymarket train station until the start of the railway path at Roseburn. Care should be taken on the roads and crossings in Dalmeny. There are road sections in South Queensferry and from the bridge to North Queensferry. The most exciting section for children is the crossing of the Forth Road Bridge itself, with its traffic-free cycle lanes.

REFRESHMENTS
• Cramond Brig pub, Cramond.
• Tearoom in Dalmeny House, open Sunday, Monday and Tuesday afternoons in July and August.
• The Forth Bridges Hotel, South Queensferry.
• Various choices in South Queensferry village.
• North Queensferry: Albert Hotel; Ferrybridge Hotel; Post Office Cafe.

THINGS TO SEE & DO
EDINBURGH:
• Edinburgh Castle: iconic feature of Edinburgh, perched on an extinct volcano; 0131 225 9846; www.edinburghcastle.gov.uk
• National Gallery of Scotland; 0131 624 6336;

www.nationalgalleries.org
- Scottish National Gallery of Modern Art; 0131 624 6336; www.nationalgalleries.org
- Scottish National Portrait Gallery; 0131 624 6336; www.nationalgalleries.org
- Royal Botanic Gardens: established in 1670, 70 acres of landscaped gardens, 1 mile (1.6km) from the city centre; 0131 552 7171; www.rbge.org.uk
- Palace of Holyrood: official residence in Scotland of Her Majesty The Queen, situated at the end of the Royal Mile; 0131 556 5100; www.royalcollection.org.uk
- Georgian House: restored Edinburgh town house filled with Georgian artefacts; 0844 493 2118; www.nts.org.uk

- Lauriston Castle: 16th-century tower house with 19th-century Jacobean-style additions; 0131 336 2060; www.museumsgalleriesscotland.org.uk
- Cramond Fort: site of Roman fort; www.undiscoveredscotland.co.uk
- Deep Sea World, North Queensferry: includes the UK's longest underwater viewing tunnel, coral reefs, sharks and seal sanctuary; 01383 411880; www.deepseaworld.com

TRAIN STATIONS

Edinburgh Waverley; Edinburgh Haymarket; South Gyle; Dalmeny; North Queensferry.

BIKE HIRE

- Bike Trax, Edinburgh: 0131 228 6633;
  www.biketrax.co.uk
- Cycle Scotland, Edinburgh: 0131 556 5560;
  www.cyclescotland.co.uk
- Leith Cycles, Leith: 0131 467 7775;
  www.leithcycleco.com

FURTHER INFORMATION

- To view or print National Cycle Network routes, visit
  www.sustrans.org.uk
- Maps for this area are available to buy from
  www.sustransshop.co.uk
- For more information on routes in Scotland, visit
  www.routes2ride.org.uk/scotland
- Edinburgh Tourist Information: 0845 225 5121;
  www.edinburgh.org
- Scotland Tourist Information: 0845 225 5121;
  www.visitscotland.com

ROUTE DESCRIPTION

The ride out from Haymarket train station in central Edinburgh uses a mixture of cycle paths, railway paths and quiet roads through Davidson's Mains, Barnton and across the River Almond on the lovely old Cramond Brig. Just past here, you come to the junction of National Routes 1 and 76.

Route 1 uses cycle tracks alongside roads and a quiet road to Dalmeny. It then takes quiet streets and cycle paths through South Queensferry, to cross the Forth Road Bridge (Route 1 uses the east cycle lane).

Alternatively, Route 76 takes a longer route along the coastline of the Firth of Forth, past Dalmeny House and along the high street of historic South Queensferry, before a short climb from Hopetoun Road up to the bridge, where you rejoin Route 1.

After crossing the bridge, you have the option of going into North Queensferry using a road section from the cycle path down to the village for refreshments, visiting Deep Sea World and taking a train back to Edinburgh across the Forth Rail Bridge. (From the centre of the old

village of North Queensferry, there's a steep climb back up to the station.)

If you decide to cycle back to Edinburgh, follow the signs for Route 1 from the south side of the Forth Road Bridge or take the ramp down from the bridge to follow Route 76 through South Queensferry and around the Dalmeny Estate. You rejoin Route 1 back to Edinburgh at Cramond Bridge.

NEARBY CYCLE ROUTES

National Route 75, the Clyde to Forth Cycle Route, runs across Scotland, from Gourock to Leith. National Route 754 uses the towpaths of the Union and Forth and Clyde canals, from Bowling on the Clyde to Fountainbridge in Edinburgh.

National Route 1 northbound (Coast & Castles North) connects Edinburgh with St Andrews and Dundee, and continues along the coast to Aberdeen and Inverness, eventually ending in Shetland. National Route 1 southbound is the Coast & Castles South Route, which runs from Edinburgh to Dalkeith, then south through the Scottish Borders to Berwick-upon-Tweed, following the coast to Newcastle upon Tyne.

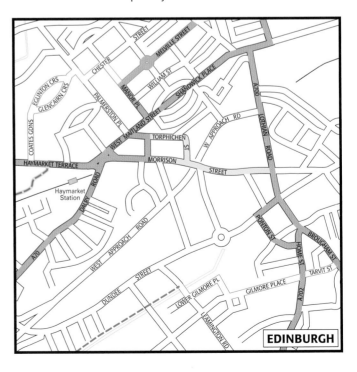

National Route 76 runs from Edinburgh to Stirling around both sides of the Forth estuary, and to Berwick-upon-Tweed via Dunbar.

There are many traffic-free trails in or near Edinburgh, such as the Innocent Railway Path, the Water of Leith, the Union Canal, and the North Edinburgh Railway Paths.

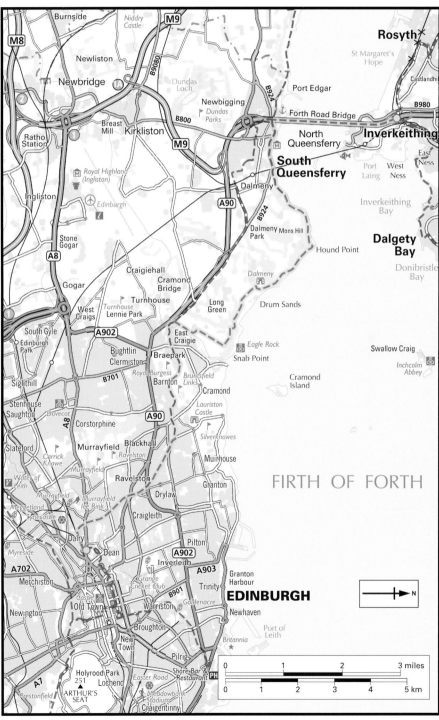

LOCHWINNOCH LOOP LINE

This route uses two dismantled railways running west from Johnstone: one heads northwest to Port Glasgow, parallel with the coast to Greenock and Gourock; the other, the Lochwinnoch Loop Line, takes a more southerly direction, passing Castle Semple Loch, Barr Loch and Kilbirnie Loch.

The colour-washed houses in Lochwinnoch date from the early 19th century, when the village was a centre for cask and barrel making. The trail is part of the Lochs & Glens Cycle Route (National Route 7), which runs from Glasgow to Carlisle. There are long-term plans to extend the traffic-free section along the River Garnock valley, from Kilbirnie to Kilwinning, thus bringing the dream of creating a traffic-free path all the way from Glasgow to the Ayrshire Coast one step closer.

Castle Semple Loch is a nationally recognized site for wild birds and a Site of Special Scientific Interest (SSSI). The visitor centre is an excellent location for water sports, walks, cycling and picnics. Boats and mountain bikes are available for hire. Near Kilbirnie, the route passes close to Glengarnock station, giving the option of taking the train for one leg of the trip to make best use of the prevailing wind.

National Routes: 7 and 75

START Paisley Canal train station, southwest of Glasgow.

FINISH End of the railway path in Glengarnock.

DISTANCE 14 miles (22.5km).

GRADE Easy.

SURFACE Tarmac.

HILLS
There is a gentle climb south from Lochwinnoch to a highpoint about halfway towards Kilbirnie.

YOUNG & INEXPERIENCED CYCLISTS
There is one short section through Elderslie where care should be taken on the busy B789 (you may prefer to walk along the pavement). You will need to use short stretches of road if you visit Kilbirnie for refreshments.

REFRESHMENTS
- Lochwinnoch: Garthland Arms pub; Brown Bull pub; Junction Cafe.
- Kilbirnie: basic cafe; fish and chip shop; Bowery pub.

THINGS TO SEE & DO
- Paisley Abbey: dating from 1163; www.paisleyabbey.org.uk
- Paisley Art Gallery and Museum: 19th-century museum and art gallery housing a world-famous collection of Paisley shawls; 0141 889 3151; www.museumsgalleriesscotland.org.uk
- Sma' Shot Cottages, Kilbarchan: 18th-century weaver's cottage, which includes exhibition room, the weaver's living area and loom room, all furnished in the style of that era; 0141 889 1708; www.museumsgalleriesscotland.org.uk

CASTLE SEMPLE:
- Castle Semple Country Park, Loch and Visitor Centre:

Part of the Clyde Muirshiel Regional Park, an excellent location for water sports, walks, cycling and picnics. The Loch is a nationally recognized site for wild birds and a Site of Special Scientific Interest (SSSI). Boats and mountain bikes are available for hire; 01505 842882; www.clydemuirshiel.co.uk

- Castle Semple Collegiate Church: late Gothic church located next to Castle Semple and Barr lochs; www.historic-scotland.gov.uk
- Lochwinnoch Nature Reserve: one of the few wetlands in west Scotland with swans, geese, ducks and great crested grebes; 01505 842663; www.rspb.org.uk

TRAIN STATIONS

Paisley Canal; Johnstone; Howwood; Lochwinnoch; Glengarnock; and many more.

BIKE HIRE

- Castle Semple Visitor Centre: 01505 842882; www.clydemuirshiel.co.uk
- RT Cycles and Fishing, Glengarnock: 01505 682191; www.cyclerepairman.co.uk

FURTHER INFORMATION

- To view or print National Cycle Network routes, visit www.sustrans.org.uk
- Maps for this area are available to buy from www.sustransshop.co.uk
- For more information on routes in Scotland, visit www.routes2ride.org.uk/scotland
- Paisley Tourist Information: 0141 889 0711
- Scotland Tourist Information: 0845 225 5121; www.visitscotland.com

ROUTE DESCRIPTION

After a safe, traffic-free section running west from Paisley Canal train station, there is a short stretch through Elderslie on the B789. A one-way system operates on the cycle route through Elderslie – follow the signs for National Route 7. You soon rejoin the course of the old railway, passing the dramatic Aurora Borealis sculpture at the junction of Routes 7 and 75. There are historic attractions along the way, including Lochwinnoch Temple and Castle Semple Collegiate Church.

The railway path continues along the glittering expanse of Castle Semple Loch and Barr Loch, passing the villages of Lochwinnoch and Kilbirnie, and finishes on the edge of Glengarnock.

A short detour on a cycle track from Route 7 in Lochwinnoch (head towards the train station) takes you to the RSPB visitor centre, where there are viewing hides. The best, most easily accessed, refreshments are either in the village of Lochwinnoch or in Castle Semple Country Park Visitor Centre.

You can catch the train back at several points along the route – Kilbirnie is served by Glengarnock station.

NEARBY CYCLE ROUTES

National Route 7 (the Lochs & Glens Cycle Route) continues southwest beyond Kilbirnie to the Ayrshire Coast. To the north, beyond Paisley, Route 7 continues into the centre of Glasgow, crosses Bell's Bridge and then follows the Firth of Clyde and the River Leven to Loch Lomond on its way to the Highlands.

National Route 75 (the Clyde to Forth Cycle Route) goes west from Paisley to Johnstone, then continues south of the Firth of Clyde to Greenock and Gourock. To the east, it passes through the centre of Glasgow and links with the Airdrie to Bathgate Railway Path. (This path is closed until late 2010 to allow the reconstruction of the railway line, but a replacement cycle path is being built.)

OTHER WAYMARKED OR TRAFFIC-FREE RIDES INCLUDE:

- The Forth & Clyde Canal towpath.
- The Clyde and Loch Lomond Cycleway through Dumbarton to Loch Lomond.
- Paisley and Clyde Railway Path.
- The Clyde Corridor Cycle Route east of Glasgow Green.

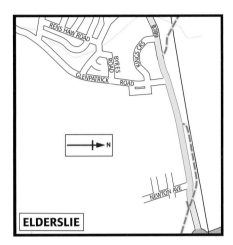

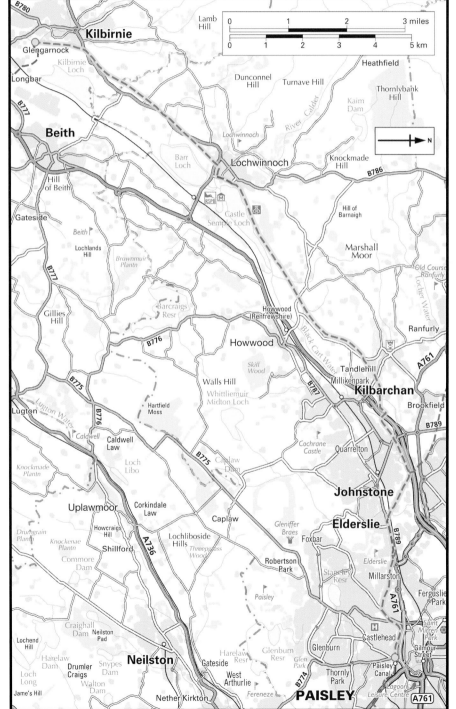

ROUTES OUT OF DUNDEE

Dundee is Scotland's fourth largest city, with a proud history of seafaring. The town grew rapidly during the Industrial Revolution as a trading centre for the British Empire and a manufacturing centre for flax and jute. The latter was imported from India and the whale oil needed for its processing came from the city's large whaling industry. Next to the award-winning Discovery Point Visitor Centre, you can visit RRS Discovery, Captain Scott's Antarctic expedition ship, which was built in Dundee. Also worth a visit are the Sensation Science Centre, and the Verdant Works, a restored jute mill and museum.

Broughty Castle, dating from the 15th century and restored in 1860, is situated on an outcrop of rock above Broughty Ferry harbour. It now houses a museum with displays on the life and times of Broughty Ferry, its people, the local environment and wildlife.

To the southeast of Tayport, Tentsmuir Forest is an open mature pine forest next to a vast expanse of sandy beaches and the Tentsmuir Point National Nature Reserve. The area is criss-crossed with easy, waymarked, off-road cycle routes. The Tay estuary forms an important feeding and roosting area for seabirds, as well as a haul-out area for common and grey seals.

National Route: 1

START
Cycle lane access point at the northern end of the Tay Road Bridge, Dundee.

FINISH
Tayport, Carnoustie or Arbroath.

DISTANCE
Dundee to Tayport: 3.5 miles (6km).
Dundee to Carnoustie: 11 miles (18km).
Dundee to Arbroath: 19 miles (30km).

GRADE Easy.

SURFACE Tarmac.

HILLS
A noticeable climb from Tayport up to the southern end of the Tay Bridge. At the northern end of the bridge, a lift takes you from street level up to the central cycle lane.

YOUNG & INEXPERIENCED CYCLISTS
Dundee to Tayport: Excellent traffic-free path running along the middle of the bridge, followed by shared-use route and railway path. No busy roads but care should be taken at crossings and at points with minimal traffic.

Dundee to Arbroath via Carnoustie: a combination of segregated cyclepaths through Dundee docks, quiet roads, traffic-free cycle routes.

REFRESHMENTS
- Lots of choice in Dundee.
- Cafe/kiosk in the car park at the southern end of the Tay Road Bridge.
- Tayport: Jane's Harbour Tearoom; Bell Rock Tavern.
- Ship Inn, Broughty Ferry.

THINGS TO SEE & DO
DUNDEE:
- Firth of Tay.
- Tay Road Bridge.

- Discovery Point, Discovery Quay: home of RRS *Discovery*, the ship that took Captain Scott on his first expedition to Antarctica, and Verdant Works, a restored jute mill; 01382 309060; www.rrsdiscovery.com
- HM Frigate *Unicorn*, Victoria Dock: wooden warship launched in 1824; 01382 200900; www.frigateunicorn.org
- Sensation Science Centre: pioneering science museum for adults and children; 01382 228800; www.sensation.org.uk

- Claypotts Castle, near Dundee: well-preserved 16th-century castle; external viewing only; 01786 431324; www.historic-scotland.gov.uk
- Broughty Castle and Museum: originally built in the late 15th century, with stunning views over the Tay; the museum tells the story of the Broughty ferry and the local area; 01382 436916; www.historic-scotland.gov.uk
- Signal Tower Museum, Arbroath: covers the history of the Bell Rock lighthouse and shore station, and houses the massive lens of the last manually operated lamp; 01241 875598; www.angus.gov.uk/history/museums

- Arbroath Abbey: beautiful ruin, founded in 1178; 01241 878756; www.historic-scotland.gov.uk

TRAIN STATIONS

Dundee; Broughty Ferry; Balmossie; Monifieth; Barry Links; Carnoustie; Arbroath.

BIKE HIRE

Cycle World Bike Hire Centre, Arbroath: 01241 876034; www.cycle-world.co.uk

FURTHER INFORMATION

- To view or print National Cycle Network routes, visit www.sustrans.org.uk
- Maps for this area are available to buy from www.sustransshop.co.uk
- For more information on routes in Scotland, visit www.routes2ride.org.uk/scotland
- Dundee Tourist Information: 01382 527527; www.angusanddundee.co.uk
- Scotland Tourist Information: 0845 225 5121; www.visitscotland.com

ROUTE DESCRIPTION

Heading towards Tayport from the Dundee side of the Tay Road Bridge, you access the bridge by lift. Cross the bridge on a central elevated cycle path, which gives great views in both directions along the Firth of Tay. There is a descent from the bridge before joining a railway path that runs along the southern shore of the Firth of Tay to the harbourside in Tayport. If you are feeling particularly energetic, you can continue on Route 1 into Tentsmuir Forest and explore the delightful waymarked woodland

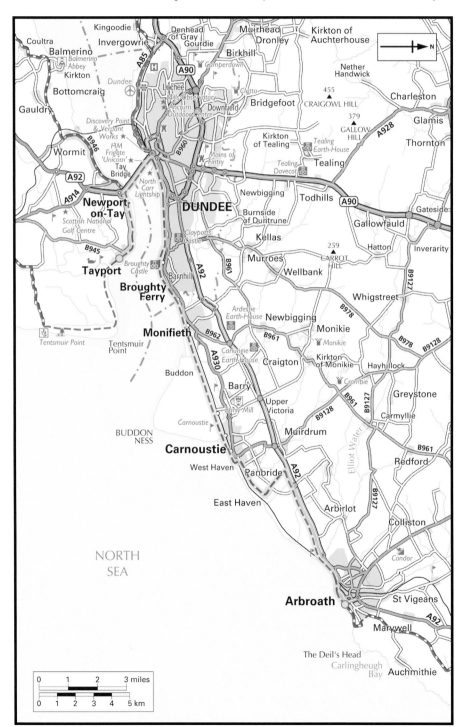

tracks that form part of the Kingdom of Fife Millennium Cycle Routes.

Heading towards Carnoustie and Arbroath, go through the Dundee port area – you will be asked for photo ID. To date, there is no access for pedestrians through the port. If you are not granted access, there is an alternative route on public roads; see map. Along busy roads you may want to push your bike along the pavement.

Beyond the docks, the route follows the shoreline on a fine promenade path and Broughty Castle comes into view. It then runs close to the sea to Monifieth, from where a well-maintained cycle path heads over Barry Links. Carnoustie offers opportunities for refreshments and a view of the famous championship golf course. The route continues on the cycle path to East Haven, where it heads inland on a farm road and then turns towards Arbroath on a cycleway alongside the A92. You can ride the route in either direction and make your return journey by bike or train. For a shorter ride, you can catch a train from one of the railway stations along the route.

NEARBY CYCLE ROUTES
The ride forms part of National Route 1, which crosses

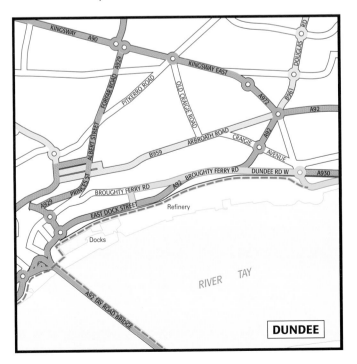

Fife from Edinburgh, then passes through Dundee on its way up the east coast to Aberdeen, Inverness and John O'Groats.

National Route 77 heads west from Dundee to Perth and north to Pitlochry.

There are easy, waymarked traffic-free trails in Tentsmuir Forest, to the southeast of Tayport, which can be accessed by following Route 1 beyond the end of this ride towards Leuchars and St Andrews.

There are three other forests in Fife with waymarked trails: Pitmedden, Devilla and Blairadam.

CALLANDER TO KILLIN

Callander lies just south of Highland Perthshire. It was created as a 'new town' in the 1730s by the Duke of Perth, and in the late 18th century it was a thriving centre for weaving. In Victorian times, it became a popular spa town due to its location close to the Trossachs and its association with the novels of Sir Walter Scott. A railway branch line from Dunblane was built in 1858, and the line was later extended to Crianlarich and Oban. The town featured in the 1960s television series *Dr Finlay's Casebook* as Tannochbrae.

You should enjoy spectacular views of Ben Ledi (879m/2,884ft) and Loch Lubnaig along the course of the dismantled railway linking Callander with Strathyre via the Falls of Leny and the west side of Loch Lubnaig. It is said that 2,000 years ago the Druids lit fires at the top of Ben Ledi to celebrate the changing of the seasons.

Rob Roy MacGregor (1671–1734) was an outlaw and Scottish folk hero, sometimes known as the Scottish Robin Hood. Celebrated in the novel *Rob Roy* by Sir Walter Scott, he lived his last years in Balquhidder. He and other members of the MacGregor clan are buried in the churchyard; his grave is marked by a slate slab carved with a kilted figure.

National Route: 7

START Callander Meadows, centre of Callander.

FINISH Killin, Balquhidder or Brig O'Turk.

DISTANCE
Callander Meadows to Killin: 25 miles (40km).
Callander Meadows to Balquhidder: 13 miles (21 km).
Callander Meadows to Brig O'Turk: 8 miles (13km).

GRADE Moderate to difficult.

SURFACE
Mixture of tarmac and stone-based tracks. There are rougher sections at the north end of Loch Lubnaig and going into Killin.

HILLS
The route has a number of hills, including:
- a steady 61-m (200-ft) climb from Callander, past the Falls of Leny, up to Loch Lubnaig.
- a steep hill at the north end of Loch Lubnaig (fantastic views!).
- a very steep climb from Lochearnhead to Glenogle.
- a steep descent from Glenoglehead towards Killin.

YOUNG & INEXPERIENCED CYCLISTS
CALLANDER TO KILLIN:
The route is mainly made up of traffic-free paths and quiet roads. There can be considerable holiday traffic between Balquhidder and Kinghouse. Take extreme care crossing the trunk road at Glenoglehead.

CALLANDER TO BRIG O'TURK:
There is a short section (0.25 mile/0.4km) on the A81 south from the centre of Callander, where care should be taken. The rest of the route is on minor roads and cycle paths.

REFRESHMENTS
- Lots of choice in Callander.
- Cafe and pubs in Strathyre.
- Teashop at the museum in Stronvar, just south of Balquhidder.
- Lots of choice in Lochearnhead.
- Lots of choice in Killin.

THINGS TO SEE & DO
CALLANDER:
- The Hamilton Toy Collection: a celebration of toys from the last hundred years; 01877 330004; www.thehamiltontoycollection.co.uk
- Kilmahog & Trossachs Mills: traditional Scottish knitwear, plus country and outdoor clothing; 01877 330178; www.trossachswoollenmill.com

- Falls of Leny and Pass of Leny: beautiful waterfalls surrounded by woodland; www.visitscotland.com
- Loch Lubnaig: small loch near Callander.
- Glen Ogle: spectacular pass with views of Loch Earn.
- Rob Roy's grave, Balquidder: grave of the famous Scottish folk hero of the early 18th century, Rob Roy MacGregor, situated in Balquhidder's parish church; www.undiscoveredscotland.co.uk
- Falls of Dochart, Killin: series of rapids that carry the River Dochart through the village.

TRAIN STATIONS
Dunblane.
From here you will need to follow roads, some busy, to Callander, approximately 11 miles (17.5km).

BUSES
Trossachs Trundler Bus can take up to two bikes from Stirling bus station to Callander (summer only); 01786 442707.

BIKE HIRE
- Mounter Bikes (Cycle Hire), Callander: 01877 331052; www.callandercyclehire.co.uk
- Killin Outdoor Centre: 01567 820652; www.killinoutdoor.co.uk

FURTHER INFORMATION
- To view or print National Cycle Network routes, visit www.sustrans.org.uk
- Maps for this area are available to buy from www.sustransshop.co.uk
- For more information on routes in Scotland, visit www.routes2ride.org.uk/scotland
- Scotland Tourist Information: 0845 225 5121; www.visitscotland.com

ROUTE DESCRIPTION
The route travels north to Balquhidder along the course of the old Caledonian railway line. Passing through woodland, alongside the swift waters and spectacular falls of the River Leny, you cycle through the Pass of Leny. It then follows the shores of Loch Lubnaig. Please note that halfway along there is a short section of zig-zag slopes and rough surfaces.

At the end of Loch Lubnaig, the route takes a quiet road to Balquhidder, where you can visit Rob Roy's grave. From here, you can continue through the spectacular Glen Ogle, once described by Queen Victoria as Scotland's Kyber Pass, with some excellent views of Loch Earn, to make your way to Killin and Loch Tay. This section of the route uses the old military road, two railway paths and two listed viaducts.

A shorter ride from Callander to Brig O'Turk follows a quiet road and cycle track along the shores of Loch Venachar, passing splendid isolated houses set above the water's edge and offering views across to Ben Ledi. The loch ends at Blackwater Marshes. You then follow a short section on forest roads to reach the refreshment stop/ turnaround point at Brig O'Turk.

NEARBY CYCLE ROUTES
From Killin, National Route 7 continues to Loch Tay,

Pitlochry, Aviemore, and Inverness. To the south of Loch Venachar, Route 7 crosses the Dukes Pass via forestry tracks, then passes through Aberfoyle and Drymen on its way to Loch Lomond and Glasgow.

There are plenty of forest routes in the Queen Elizabeth Forest Park. There is also a delightful ride on a traffic-free Scottish Water road along the northern side of Loch Katrine to Stronachlachar, which can be continued on minor roads as far as Loch Lomond or Aberfoyle.

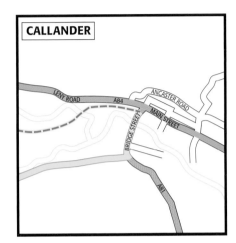

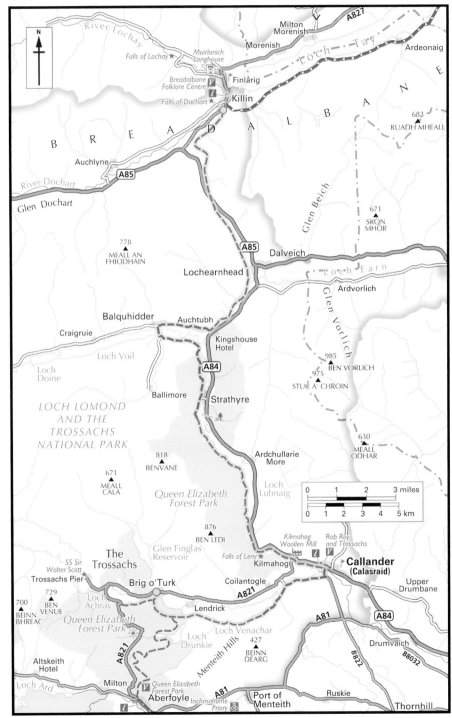

BOWLING TO THE FALKIRK WHEEL

Scotland's two principal cities, Glasgow and Edinburgh, are linked by two canals: the Forth & Clyde Canal from Glasgow to Falkirk and the Union Canal from Falkirk to Edinburgh. Together they offer a wonderful, level cycling route through Scotland's Central Belt, with the Falkirk Wheel representing the highlight of the whole route at the junction of the two canals. The ride described here follows the section along the Forth & Clyde from Bowling near Glasgow to the Falkirk Wheel.

The Forth & Clyde Canal was opened in 1790 and the Union Canal in 1822. They fell into disuse in the early 1960s, but then as part of the Millennium celebrations in 2000, the £78 million Millennium Link project was set in motion to restore navigability across Scotland on the Forth & Clyde and Union Canals.

A major challenge was to create a link between the two canals at Falkirk, as the Forth & Clyde Canal lay 35m (115ft) below the level of the Union Canal. Historically, the two canals had been joined by a flight of locks, but these were dismantled in 1933. The answer was the perfectly balanced structure known as the Falkirk Wheel – the world's first and only rotating boat lift – opened by the Queen in 2002. The Wheel is the height of eight double-decker buses and is capable of lifting loads equivalent to the weight of 100 elephants!

National Routes: 754 and 7

START Bowling Harbour on the Clyde estuary, Glasgow.

FINISH Falkirk Wheel.

DISTANCE 30 miles (48km).

GRADE Easy/Moderate.

SURFACE Gravel and tarmac.

HILLS None.

YOUNG & INEXPERIENCED CYCLISTS
Traffic-free, except for Stockingfield Junction, Glasgow, which involves negotiating the road for a short stretch.

REFRESHMENTS
• Lots of choice in Clydebank, Glasgow and Kirkintilloch.

• See www.scottishcanals.co.uk for details of eating places along the Forth & Clyde Canal.
• Boathouse pub, Auchinstarry Marina.
• Cafe at Falkirk Wheel.

THINGS TO SEE & DO
• Clydebank Museum: local, social and industrial history artefacts, especially relating to ship-building; 0141 562 2400; www.museumsgalleriesscotland.org.uk
• Auld Kirk Museum, Kirkintilloch: local history collection housed in a building dating from 1644: 0141 578 0144; www.museumsgalleriesscotland.org.uk
• Antonine Wall: name given to the Roman frontier in Scotland, which crossed the narrowest part of Britain, from Bo'ness, on the Firth of Forth, to Old Kilpatrick, on the River Clyde; passes very close to the Falkirk Wheel; www.antonine-way.co.uk
• Rough Castle Roman fort: small but well-preserved fort on the Antonine Wall; can be reached by footpaths

from the Falkirk Wheel; www.antonine-way.co.uk
- Falkirk Wheel: boat trips, cafe, picnic area and interactive exhibition; 0870 050 0208; www.thefalkirkwheel.co.uk
- Falkirk Museum: collections local to the Falkirk area,

including Roman archaeology relating to the Antonine Wall, iron-founding artefacts and items from the potteries in Bo'ness and Dunmore; 01324 503770; www.museumsgalleriesscotland.org.uk

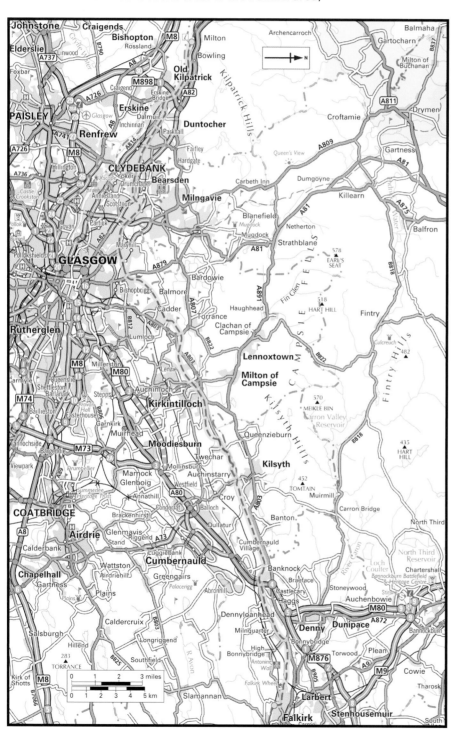

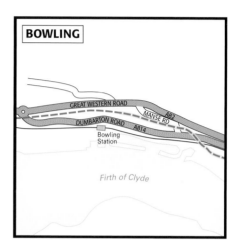

TRAIN STATIONS

Bowling and all stations into the centre of Glasgow; Croy; Camelon; Falkirk Grahamston; Falkirk High (access to the canal from the south station platform).

BIKE HIRE

- Magic Cycles, Bowling Harbour: 01389 873433; www.magiccycles.co.uk
- Billy Bilsland Cycles, Glasgow: 0141 552 0841; www.billybilslandcycles.co.uk

FURTHER INFORMATION

- To view or print National Cycle Network routes, visit www.sustrans.org.uk
- Maps for this area are available to buy from www.sustransshop.co.uk
- For more information on routes in Scotland, visit www.routes2ride.org.uk/scotland
- Glasgow Tourist Information: www.seeglasgow.com
- Scotland Tourist Information: 0845 225 5121; www.visitscotland.com

ROUTE DESCRIPTION

The ride is usually best done from west to east, as this is the direction of the prevailing wind. Start on National Route 7 at Bowling, where the Forth & Clyde Canal enters the Clyde. Pass through Clydebank, where Route 7 heads off alongside the River Clyde towards the centre of Glasgow, and Route 754 continues on the canal, passing the imposing Maryhill Locks.

Alternatively, if starting from central Glasgow, you can take the Kelvin Walkway to the locks at Maryhill or follow the branch canal north from Port Dundas for 2 miles (3km) until it meets the main canal at the Stockingfield Junction. Along this elevated section, there are fine views right across the city. Take care making the connection at Stockingfield, as you have to leave the canal for a short section on a difficult road – a bridge is planned to solve the problem here.

After Stockingfield, you reach Glasgow Road bridge, a bustling boating, eating and drinking centre. From here, you shortly come to the beautiful Kelvin Valley,

with the Kilsyth Hills to the north. Follow the canal through Kirkintilloch, the Auchinstarry Marina and on to Bonnybridge, from where it's only another 3 miles (5km) to the Falkirk Wheel.

From here, you can follow the path up beside the wheel until you pass through a short tunnel onto the Union Canal towards Linlithgow and eventually Edinburgh (the full distance from Bowling to Edinburgh is 62 miles/100km). Once you get onto the canal, it's hard to get lost!

To return, you can access the south platform of Falkirk High train station from the canal for trains back to either Glasgow or Edinburgh.

NEARBY CYCLE ROUTES

National Route 7 heads north from Bowling to Loch Lomond, Pitlochry and Inverness. In the other direction, it follows the canal to Clydebank and then carries on parallel to the Clyde to Bell's Bridge in the centre of Glasgow, before heading down to Ayr and Carlisle. National Route 75 intersects with Route 7 at Bell's Bridge – it runs between Gourock on the Clyde and Leith, Edinburgh on the Forth.

Other waymarked or traffic-free rides include the Kelvin Walkway, also a cycle route, which runs alongside the River Kelvin from Kelvinside to Milngavie. The Strathkelvin Railway Path runs from south of Muirhead, through Kirkintilloch to Strathblane.

AYR TO ARDROSSAN

This 28-mile (45-km) route takes in long stretches of the Ayrshire coastline between Irvine, Troon, Prestwick and Ayr, and has spectacular views across to the Isle of Arran. Passing through three nature reserves at Stevenston Beach, Garnock Floods and Shewalton Moss, it offers the opportunity to experience the varied landscapes of this part of Scotland. You can visit beaches or stop and explore the town centres along the way. It is also possible to organize shorter cycling trips by using the regular train service between Kilwinning and Ayr.

Ayr is the region's main coastal resort, dominated by the early 19th-century Town Buildings with their octagonal turret and 38-m (125-ft) steeple. Two bridges span the River Ayr: the Auld Brig dates from the 13th century and the New Bridge from 1788. Troon is famous for its golf courses (there are no fewer than five of them!) and its Victorian turreted red-sandstone buildings looking out over the sandy beach, marina and harbour to Ayr Bay. Ardrossan is the port serving the Isle of Arran, whose outline is a constant companion along the route.

National Routes: 7 and 73

START Southern end of Ayr esplanade.

FINISH Ardrossan ferry terminal.

DISTANCE
28 miles (45km).

Shorter options, from Ayr to Irvine: 19 miles (30.5km); from Irvine to Ardrossan: 9 miles (14.5km).

GRADE Easy.

SURFACE Tarmac.

HILLS None.

YOUNG & INEXPERIENCED CYCLISTS
Almost traffic-free with short on-road sections in Ayr, Prestwick, Troon and Irvine, and through residential streets in Barassie. About 2 miles (3km) on quiet roads between Kilwinning and Stevenston.

REFRESHMENTS
• Lots of choice in Ayr, Troon and Gailes.
• Cafe at the Maritime Museum, Irvine.
• The Ship Inn, Irvine.

THINGS TO SEE & DO
• Burns National Heritage Park, Alloway, just south of Ayr: museum dedicated to Robert Burns; 01292 443700; www.burnsheritagepark.com

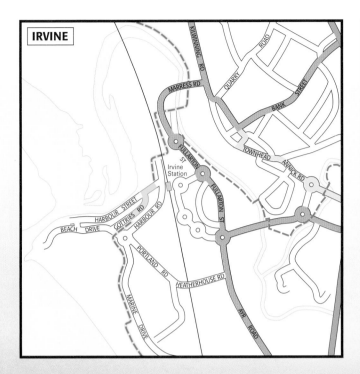

- Eglinton Country Park: developed around the ancient Eglinton Estate, with a visitor centre, cafe and children's play area; 01294 551776; www.north-ayrshire.gov.uk
- Golf courses at Troon: includes Royal Troon Golf Club, host to the Open Golf Championship; 01294 311555 www.royaltroon.co.uk
- Dundonald Castle: dating back to the 1370s; 01563 851489; www.dundonaldcastle.org.uk
- Irvine Beach Park: includes a lake and leisure centre; www.ayrshirescotland.com
- Scottish Maritime Museum, Irvine: a range of exhibits relating to Scotland's maritime history, including the Linthouse engine shop, a Victorian glass-roofed building dating from 1872; 01294 278283; www.scottishmaritimemuseum.org; www.museumsgalleriesscotland.org.uk
- Gailes Marsh Wildlife Reserve, Shewalton Wood Wildlife Reserve and Garnock Floods Nature Reserve: good birdwatching sites; www.swt.org.uk

TRAIN STATIONS

Ayr; Newton-on-Ayr; Prestwick Town; Prestwick International Airport; Troon; Barassie; Irvine; Kilwinning; Stevenston; Ardrossan.

FERRIES

Ardrossan to Brodick ferry: www.calmac.co.uk

BIKE HIRE

RT Cycles and Fishing, Glengarnock: 01505 682191; www.cyclerepairman.co.uk: delivers and collects cycles.

FURTHER INFORMATION

- To view or print National Cycle Network routes, visit www.sustrans.org.uk
- Maps for this area are available to buy from www.sustransshop.co.uk
- For more information on routes in Scotland, visit www.routes2ride.org.uk/scotland
- Ayrshire Tourist Information: www.ayrshire-arran.com
- Scotland Tourist Information: 0845 225 5121; www.visitscotland.com

ROUTE DESCRIPTION

Between Ayr and Troon, the route is either on or close to the coast. From Troon, it heads inland and through two Scottish Wildlife reserves, Shewalton Wood and Gailes Marsh, to return to the coast at Irvine Beach Park. It then follows the riverside path through Irvine towards Kilwinning, passing the Garnock Floods Nature Reserve. Eglinton Country Park is just off the route and offers extensive opportunities for walking, cycling, horse riding and angling, plus children's play areas.

At Kilwinning, the route turns west along minor roads to Stevenston, before rejoining a traffic-free path, which runs along the coast and gives sweeping views towards the isle of Arran. At Ardrossan, you can take your bike on the ferry to the Isle of Arran, known as 'Scotland in miniature', where the route continues from Brodick to Lochranza, or you can catch the train to Irvine.

NEARBY CYCLE ROUTES

National Route 7 heads north from Kilwinning to Lochwinnoch, Paisley and Glasgow. From Ayr, Route 7 continues to Newton Stewart, Dumfries and Carlisle. National Route 73 runs from Irvine to Kilmarnock.

The ferry from Ardrossan will take you to the Isle of Arran, where Route 73 heads north to Lochranza. Here, another ferry links to National Route 78, running from Campbeltown to Oban. The New Town Trail links Irvine, Kilwinning and Eglinton Country Park.

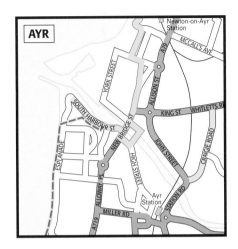

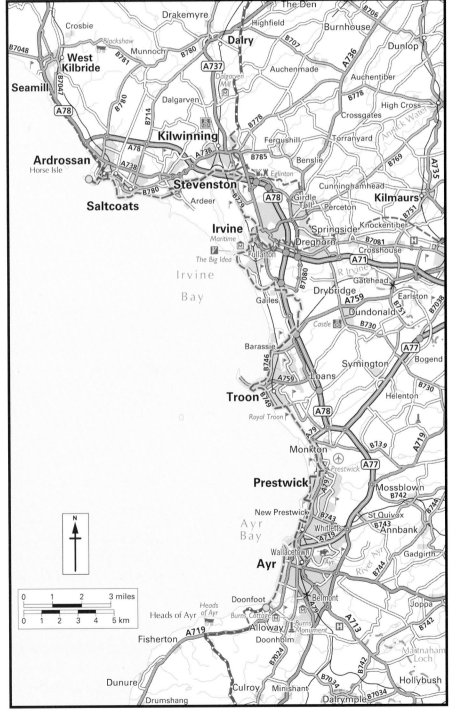

INVERNESS TO DINGWALL

Inverness, set at the mouth of the River Ness, the terminal of the Caledonian Canal and the junction of the Beauly Firth with the Moray Firth, is known as the capital of the Highlands. It is by some distance the largest settlement in the Highlands and lies at a junction of two National Cycle Network routes: Route 1 passes through the town on its way from Aberdeen to John O'Groats and it is also the terminus of Route 7, the Lochs & Glens Route, which starts in Carlisle. In the future, Route 78, with a starting point at Campbeltown on the Mull of Kintyre, will follow the Great Glen to finish at Inverness.

The route to Dingwall crosses the A9 Kessock Bridge on a cyclepath and passes beneath the Iron Age hill fort on Ord Hill on the north side of Beauly Firth. Quiet lanes and a newly built cyclepath alongside the A835 to the northwest of Tore lead to the bridge built by Thomas Telford in 1809 over the River Conon at Maryburgh, at the head of Cromarty Firth. Keep an eye out here for red kites, with their distinctive forked tails, which you may see wheeling overhead. Dingwall's oldest building, a former schoolhouse, dates back to 1650. There is good birdwatching from Dingwall's harbour foreshore.

National Route: 1

START Ness Bridge, over the river near Inverness train station.

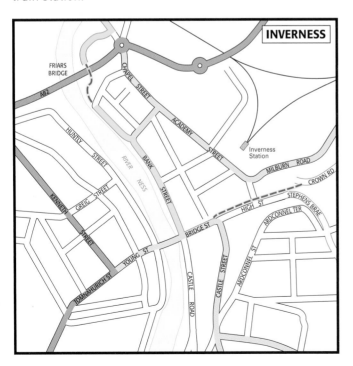

FINISH Dingwall town centre.

DISTANCE 14 miles (22.5km).

GRADE Moderate.

SURFACE Tarmac.

HILLS Some hills, with great views over Dingwall as a result!

YOUNG & INEXPERIENCED CYCLISTS
A combination of roads, cycle paths and quiet roads. There are a number of access roads across the A835 cycletrack and road crossings at the Tore roundabout and at Maryburgh, where care should be taken. There is a steep hill down to North Kessock.

REFRESHMENTS
- Lots of choice in Inverness and Dingwall.
- Cafe and North Kessock Hotel in North Kessock.

THINGS TO SEE & DO

INVERNESS:

- Inverness Museum and Art Gallery: covers the history and heritage of the capital of the Highlands; 01463 237114; www.museumsgalleriesscotland.org.uk
- Inverness Castle: dating from the1830s, overlooking the River Ness; www.undiscoveredscotland.co.uk
- Inverness Cathedral: dating from 1866; 01463 233535; www.invernesscathedral.co.uk
- North Kessock Dolphin and Seal Centre: one of the best places in Europe to observe dolphins and seals in their natural habitat; open June to September; 01463 731866; www.highland.gov.uk/leisureandtourism
- Dingwall Museum: local museum with pretty courtyard and picnic tables; 01349 865366; www.museumsgalleriesscotland.org.uk
- Black Isle Brewery: 1-mile (1.6km) detour off the route; small independent organic brewery; 01463 811871; www.blackislebrewery.com

TRAIN STATIONS

Inverness; Dingwall.

BIKE HIRE

- Highland Bicycle Company, Inverness: 01463 234935; www.highlandbikes.com
- Ticket to Ride, Culloden Moor: offers bike delivery; 07902 242301; www.tickettoridehighlands.co.uk

FURTHER INFORMATION

- To view or print National Cycle Network routes, visit www.sustrans.org.uk
- Maps for this area are available to buy from www.sustransshop.co.uk
- For more information on routes in Scotland, visit www.routes2ride.org.uk/scotland
- Inverness Tourist Information: 01463 234353
- Highlands Tourist Information: www.visithighlands.com
- Scotland Tourist Information: 0845 225 5121; www.visitscotland.com

ROUTE DESCRIPTION

Follow Route 1 north from the centre of Inverness along the River Ness to Kessock Bridge. A cycle track on the west side of the bridge takes you over the Beauly Firth to the Black Isle – despite its name, it is not an island. As you cross the bridge, you can see the village of North Kessock far below. Once over the bridge, you have a choice of routes.

Route 1 heads down to the left, but you can continue on the cycleway alongside the A9 to reach the Tourist Information Centre and the Dolphin and Seal Centre. To reach North Kessock, follow the signs for Route 1 down the hill and enjoy a pleasant cycle by the shore through this old village.

At the western end of the village, Route 1 heads uphill, where it rejoins the A9 cycleway and then goes under the A9 to join a cycle track for 0.5 mile (0.8km) followed by a minor road for 3.5 miles (5.6km) to Tore. As you head along the route, you'll see a sign for the Black Isle Brewery, a 1.25-mile (2-km) detour from Route 1. This road also leads to the Cromarty Ferry (open in summer only) if you want to do a circuit round the Cromarty Firth.

Use the cycle path to circumnavigate the Tore roundabout, turn sharp right through a narrow opening at the west side and pass some houses before joining a traffic-free cycle track that runs for just under 3 miles (5km) to where the route crosses the B9169. Another stretch of quiet road leads down to near Conan Bridge – red kites are frequently seen circling overhead along this section. From Conan Bridge, there's another stretch of cycle track leading over the bridge and to the roundabout at Maryburgh, where you cross the road and take a right turn along a stretch of traffic-free road, taking you almost into the centre of Dingwall.

NEARBY CYCLE ROUTES

National Route 1 heads north from Inverness to John O'Groats, and south to Aberdeen. National Route 7 heads south to Aviemore, Pitlochry and Glasgow.

The Great Glen Way is a signed, long-distance walking route heading west out of Inverness along the length of Loch Ness and the Caledonian Canal to Fort William. It is best suited to mountain bikes.

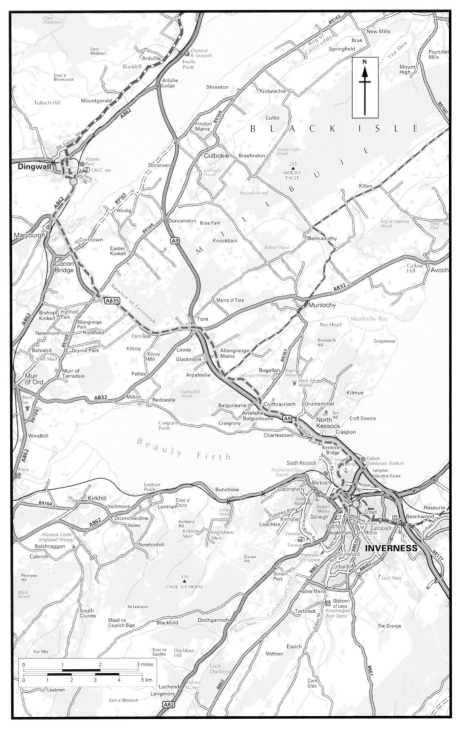

NORTHERN IRELAND

With its rich farmland and dramatic coastline, fine parks and country houses, prehistoric burial sites and iron age forts, Northern Ireland provides a range of cycling opportunities for everyone from novices and families to long-distance tourers. The region is full of pleasant, relaxed towns and you will of course encounter the legendary Irish welcome from the locals.

The Ballyshannon to Ballycastle Cycle Route starts on the Atlantic Ocean at Rossknowlagh Beach on Donegal Bay. Entering Northern Ireland at Belleek on Lower Lough Erne it continues to criss-cross the border. At Pettigo there are two options: a northern route to Newtownstewart and a southern one to Enniskillen, rejoining south of Strabane. Crossing the River Foyle at Lifford, the route follows quiet roads to Carrigans and a railway path along the river to Craigavon Bridge in Londonderry. Riverside paths lead to the historic walled city. Between Derry and Limavady it passes the northern slopes of the Sperrin Mountains. A short, steep climb towards Coleraine brings cyclists to the unmistakable profile of Binevenagh Mountain and the viewpoint overlooking Magilligan Point, Inishowen and the Atlantic Ocean. The route crosses Coleraine's Millennium Bridge and uses dedicated cycle routes through the resort towns of Castlerock, Portstewart and Portrush. At Bushmills, famous for its whiskey, a coastal path leads to the spectacular Giant's Causeway before turning inland on the Antrim Plateau towards Ballycastle, avoiding busy coastal roads.

The Belfast to Ballyshannon Cycle Route (Route 9) can be seen as the return coast to coast route. It starts in Whiteabbey on the shores of Belfast Lough and passes Belfast docks, famous as the birthplace of the *Titanic*. It follows the River Lagan towpath towards Lisburn and minor roads to Portadown before joining the Newry Canal heading south. The route passes through the cathedral city of Armagh with its ecclesiastical and educational heritage, Tynan with its famous cross, then follows the former Ulster Canal and grassy lanes towards the market towns of Dungannon and Cookstown. The magnificent landscape of the Sperrin Mountains has changed little since Stone Age people built their circles like those at Beaghmore. Heading towards Omagh via Gortin, the route passes the Ulster American Folk and History Parks and uses quiet roads through small country towns and villages towards Enniskillen. Passing loughs and rivers, the route continues towards Ballyshannon and the Atlantic Ocean.

The Kingfisher Trail is an amalgam of parts of the two trails described above, with an extra loop to the southwest from Upper Lough Erne to Leitrim, Drumshanbo and Carrick-on-Shannon. The North West Trail covers the same area with two extra loops from Ballyshannon, northeast to Donegal and Raphoe and southwest to Sligo and Manorhamilton. Added to this are the beautiful circuits of loughs: the Loughshore Trail follows the shores of Lough Neagh, the largest freshwater lake in the UK and Ireland; the Strangford Lough Cycle Trail explores the lough to the east of Belfast with spurs to Belfast, Bangor and Newcastle.

National Cycle Network traffic-free routes
National Cycle Network on-road routes
Cycling in the UK routes
3 National Route Numbers

Castlerock to Giant's Causeway

Castlerock
Portrush
Ballycastle
93
Coleraine
Cushendull
Cushendall
Limavady
Ballymoney
96
Londonderry
Foyle Valley
Claudy
Glenarm
97
Portglenone
93 Larne
Strabane
Balleymena
Newtownstewart
Gortin
Toome
Carrickfergus
95
95
Antrim
94
Pettigoe
Omagh
Cookstown
Whiteabbey
94
Bangor
Belleek
91
92
Dungannon
Belfast
Newtownards
93
Fintona
94
Lagan & Lough
Comber
91
Enniskillen
95
Lisburn
9
Comber Greenway
Tynan
Portadown
Craigavon
Armagh
Portaferry
91
Scarva
Downpatrick
93
Newry to Portadown
9
Newcastle
Newry

FOYLE VALLEY

Crossing between Northern Ireland and the Republic, this 21-mile (33.8-km) ride along the valley of the River Foyle links the historic walled city of Derry (Londonderry) with the border towns of Lifford and Strabane near the confluence of the River Mourne with the River Foyle.

Derry is the second largest city in Northern Ireland, and its defensive walls, built in the shape of a diamond and up to 5.5m (18ft) thick, date from the early 17th century and are the most complete of any city in the country. It is one of the few cities in Europe that never saw its fortifications breached. Many of the houses that you see along the course of the route are new, an indication of the tremendous rise in the economic fortunes of the Republic of Ireland in recent times. The end of the ride is marked by the magnificent stainless steel and bronze figure sculptures known as *Let the Dance Begin*. Standing 5.5m (18ft) high, the figures represent a merging of two cultures rich in music and dance.

National Route: 92

START Near City Hotel, Derry.

FINISH Tourist Information Centre, Strabane.

DISTANCE 21 miles (34km).

GRADE Easy at the start of the ride; moderate elsewhere.

SURFACE Tarmac.

HILLS
There are several climbs in the second half of the ride, most notably just before Lifford.

YOUNG & INEXPERIENCED CYCLISTS
The first 4.5 miles (7km) alongside the River Foyle are on a flat, well-surfaced, traffic-free path, and an excellent there-and-back ride for families and novices. The second section, down to Strabane, occasionally uses or crosses fairly busy roads.

REFRESHMENTS
• Lots of choice in Derry.
• Carrig Inn and stores in Carrigans.
• Pub and stores in St Johnston.
• Lots of choice in Lifford.
• Lots of choice in Strabane.

THINGS TO SEE & DO
DERRY:
• 17th-century city walls.
• Tower Museum: tells the history of Derry from geological formation to present day; 028 7137 2411; www.derrycity.gov.uk/museums
• St Columb's Cathedral: built in 1633; www.stcolumbscathedral.org
• Foyle Valley Railway Museum: with working diesel railcars that run on a 3-mile (5-km) track through Riverside Park; www.discovernorthernireland.com
• Gray's Printer's Museum, Strabane: 18th-century printing press and a reminder of Strabane's reputation as Ireland's capital of publishing at that time; attractive gardens; www.nationaltrust.org.uk
• Cavanacor House & Gallery, Ballindrait; 074 914 1143; www.cavanacorgallery.ie
• The Old Courthouse, Lifford: dates back to 1743; 074 914 1733; www.liffordoldcourthouse.com

TRAIN STATIONS
Derry (Londonderry).

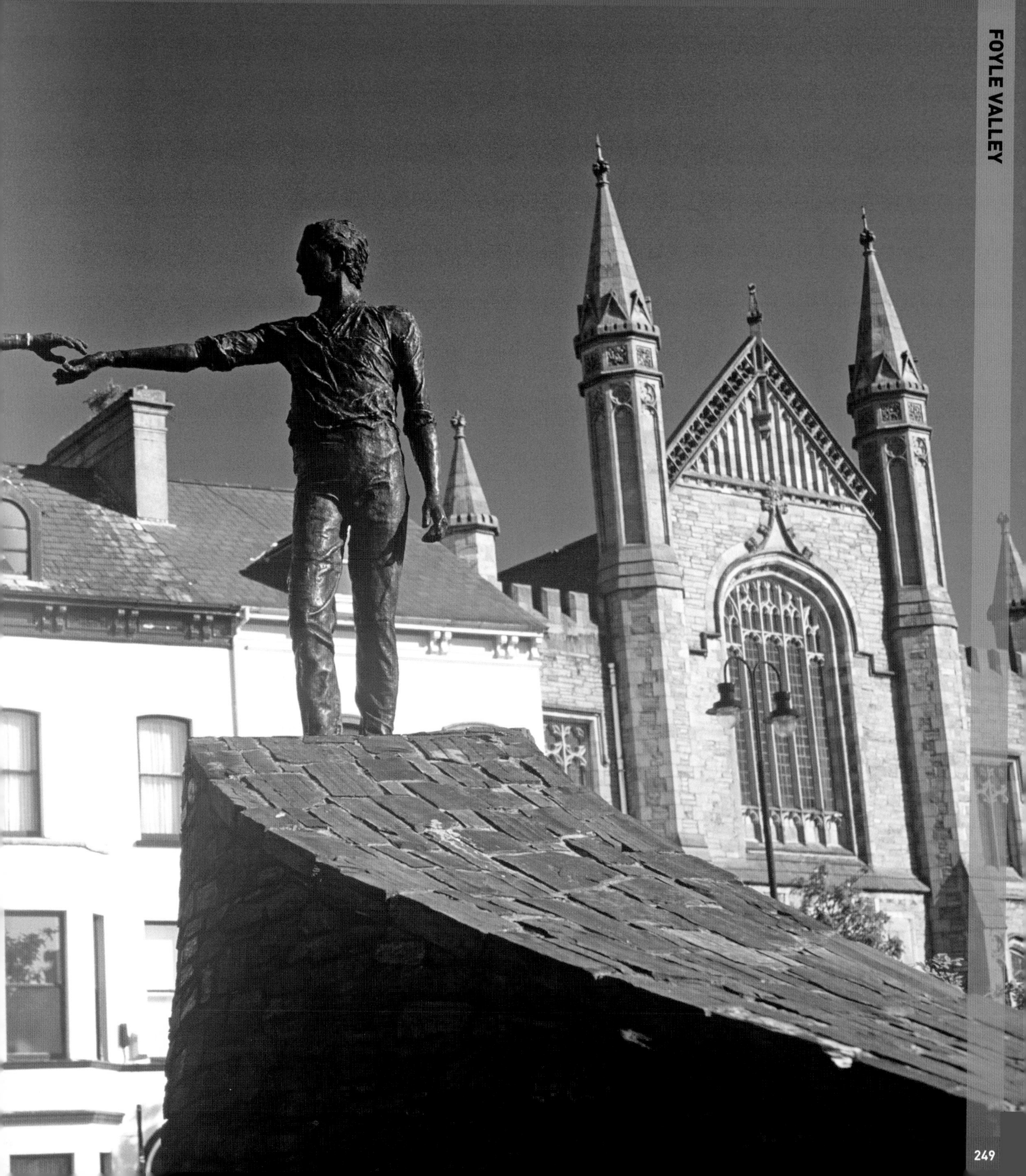

BUS SERVICES

Ulsterbus has direct express services connecting Belfast to Derry or via Omagh and Strabane. The cross-country buses can normally fit one or two bikes in the luggage storage areas: 028 7126 2261.

Bus Eireann operates express bus services from Dublin to Sligo, Donegal town and Letterkenny. Call Dublin Central Bus Station on 0353 1836 6111.

BIKE HIRE

Claudy Cycles: 028 7133 8128.

FURTHER INFORMATION

- To view or print National Cycle Network routes, visit www.sustrans.org.uk
- Maps for this area are available to buy from www.sustransshop.co.uk
- Derry Tourist Information: www.derryvisitor.com
- Strabane Tourist Information: 028 7188 4760; www.strabanedc.com
- Donegal Tourist Information: 0353 74 912 1160; www.donegaldirect.com
- Northern Ireland Tourist Information: www.discovernorthernireland.com

ROUTE DESCRIPTION

Interpretive panels have been located along the first 4.5-mile (7-km) traffic-free section of the route to illustrate the area's rich cultural, industrial and natural heritage. There is a newly built rest area and art sculpture approximately 2.5 miles (4km) from the start, with cycle parking, seating and a telescope for views of the east bank, and a matching rest area at Newbuildings.

Shortly after the end of the traffic-free section, you enter the Republic of Ireland. You then take minor roads near Carrigans, with a couple of short but busy road sections on the B236 through the village, and along the R236 just after St Johnston. A final climb leaves you with a long descent to Lifford and across the bridge over the River Foyle back into Northern Ireland.

NEARBY CYCLE ROUTES

Route 92 forms an integral part of the National Cycle Network's 236-mile (380-km) Ballyshannon to Ballycastle Cycle Route, which goes east from Ballyshannon on the Atlantic coast to Ballycastle (just beyond the Giant's Causeway) on the Irish Sea.

There is another traffic-free ride on the other side of the River Foyle, running for 3 miles (5km) from the double-decker Craigavon Bridge to New Buildings. This is the start of Route 93.

From Strabane, you can continue south on National Route 92 towards Sion Mills, Newtownstewart, Enniskillen and Ballyshannon.

While in Derry, you can follow the cycle path along the west bank of the River Foyle towards the Guildhall and Foyle Bridge.

The Foyle Valley Greenway forms part of the Inis Eoghain Cycleway, a 34-mile (55-km) loop connecting the River Foyle to Lough Swilly in Donegal: www.iniseoghaincycleway.com

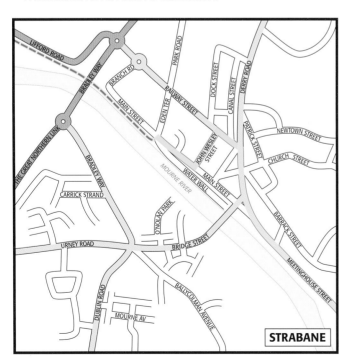

STRABANE

NEWRY TO PORTADOWN

The Newry to Portadown Canal was built to transport coal from Coalisland in County Tyrone to Dublin, via Lough Neagh, Portadown, Newry and the Irish Sea at Carlingford Lough. The canal was opened in 1742 and operated for almost 200 years. It was the first summit level canal in the British Isles. By 1777, Newry was the fourth largest port in Ireland, with a flourishing trade in coal, linen and glassware.

The canal rises to 24m (79ft) above sea level at Poyntzpass, with the section between Poyntzpass and Terryhooghan being the summit level. Fourteen locks were built along the canal, 11 of them south from Poyntzpass, to help the canal boats climb to the summit level from Newry, and three north of Scarva to assist the descent to Lough Neagh. The last lock before the canal joins the River Bann is known as Moneypenny's Lock. The Moneypennys were lock keepers for 85 years and operated the lock gates. With the growth of the railway network, the use of Newry Canal began to decline, and the last-known commercial journey through the lock was in 1936. The canal fell into disuse and is now in a state of benign neglect. There are frequent interpretation boards along the course of the canal relating its history.

This route is best followed south to north, from Newry to Portadown, for two reasons: to make best use of the prevailing winds, and because Newry train station is at the top of a hill and it's far easier to freewheel down to the canal than climb the hill up to the station!

National Route: 9

START Tourist Information Centre, Newry Town Hall.

FINISH Bann Bridge, Portadown.

DISTANCE 20 miles (32km).

GRADE Easy.

SURFACE Mainly tarmac, with sections of very good-quality gravel path.

HILLS None.

YOUNG & INEXPERIENCED CYCLISTS

The ride is flat and largely traffic-free. There are some stretches where it runs along minor roads parallel with the canal, but these carry very little traffic. Care should be taken at the road crossings. The cafe at Scarva Visitor

Centre is an ideal turnaround point for a shorter there-and-back ride from Portadown or Newry.

REFRESHMENTS

- Lots of choice in Newry.
- Rice Hotel, Railway Bar and stores in Poyntzpass.
- Excellent cafe at the Scarva Visitor Centre.
- Park Hotel and stores in Scarva.
- Lots of choice in Portadown.

THINGS TO SEE & DO

- Newry Cathedral; 028 3026 2586; www.newryandmourne.gov.uk/tourism.asp
- Craigmore Railway Viaduct: 18-arch viaduct designed by Sir John O'Neill; the highest arch is 38m (125ft), making the viaduct the tallest in Ireland; www.newryandmourne.gov.uk/tourism.asp
- Scarva Visitor Centre: includes exhibits about the canal and a good cafe; 028 3883 2163; www.banbridge.com
- Derrymore House, off the route near Newry: late 18th-century thatched house; 028 8778 4753; www.nationaltrust.org.uk
- Bagenal's Castle: the castle survived enveloped in the premises of McCann's Bakery until it was rediscovered in 1996; now serves as a museum and visitor centre; 028 3031 3182; www.bagenalscastle.com

TRAIN STATIONS

Newry; Portadown. Stations also at Scarva and Poyntzpass but very few trains a day and none on Sunday.

BIKE HIRE

Border City Cycles, Bessbrook: 028 3083 8432; www.bordercitycycles.com

FURTHER INFORMATION

- To view or print National Cycle Network routes, visit www.sustrans.org.uk
- Maps for this area are available to buy from www.sustransshop.co.uk
- Newry Tourist Information: 028 3031 3170; www.newryandmourne.gov.uk/tourism.asp
- Northern Ireland Tourist Information: www.discovernorthernireland.com

ROUTE DESCRIPTION

From Newry Town Hall, make your way northwards along Canal Quay to join the Newry Canal towpath. Follow this to Gambles Bridge, where you join a minor road under the railway bridge that runs parallel with the canal to Poyntzpass. Here, you rejoin the canal towpath, with the main railway line on your left to Scarva. The Scarva Visitor Centre is a good stopping or turnaround point for a shorter journey.

The canal towpath continues to Point of Whitecoat, where the canal joins the River Bann, and the trail runs parallel with the wide watercourse on its way through Portadown towards Lough Neagh. The ride ends just beneath the Bann Bridge – a stone's throw from the heart of Portadown.

For an easy return trip, you can catch one of the fast trains between Belfast and Dublin, which stop at both Portadown and Newry.

NEARBY CYCLE ROUTES

The northern part of the ride is on National Route 9, part of the Belfast to Ballyshannon cycle route, which goes east from Portadown to Lisburn and Belfast. To the west

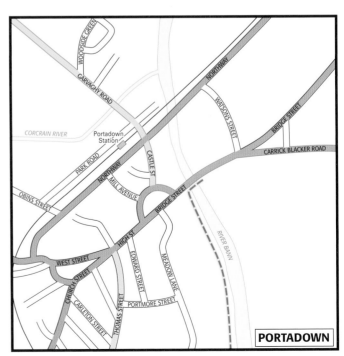

of the canal towpath, Route 91 goes to Armagh, then in a circuitous route via Dungannon, Cookstown and Omagh to Enniskillen and Ballyshannon. Route 94, meanwhile, is the Lough Neagh Circuit.

There are short, traffic-free trails on the east side of Craigavon Lake and, a little further east, between Moira and Aghalee. The Craigavon Cycle Trail uses Regional Route 10 and National Route 9 to form a circular ride.

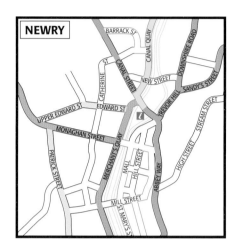

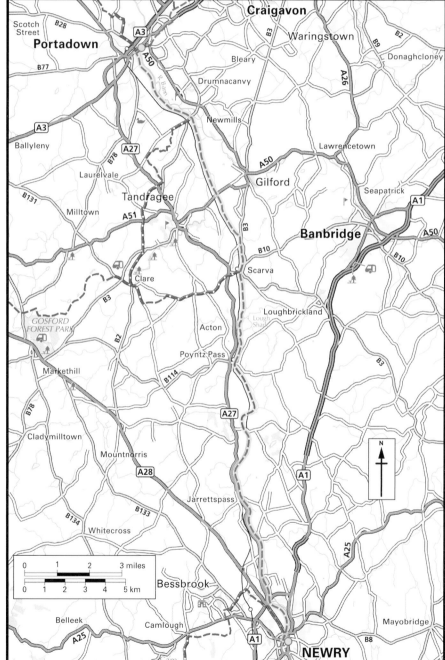

CASTLEROCK TO GIANT'S CAUSEWAY

Forming part of National Route 93, this stunning 23-mile (37-km) cycle route runs along the North Atlantic coast from Castlerock to the Giant's Causeway, via Coleraine. There are fine sea views from the Barmouth Viewpoint across the mouth of the River Bann, which flows out here into the Atlantic, and also over the white sandy beach of Portstewart Strand to the coast of Scotland and the Mull of Kintyre.

There are several recommended side trips from the main route. Just to the west of Castlerock lies the 18th-century Mussenden Temple, a small circular building located on the cliffs high above the Atlantic Ocean, with stunning views east and west along the coast. Between Portrush and Bushmills, there are the 500-year-old ruins of Dunluce Castle, located on a spectacular rock face setting. The Bushmills Whiskey Distillery offers guided tours and whiskey tastings.

From Bushmills, a delightful section of railway path takes you almost to the door of the Giant's Causeway Visitor Centre. The Giant's Causeway, a World Heritage Site and a designated Area of Outstanding Natural Beauty, was created by a volcanic eruption 60 million years ago and is famous for its 40,000 interlocking stones.

National Route: 93

START Castlerock train station.

FINISH Giant's Causeway.

DISTANCE
23 miles (37km).
Shorter options, from Castlerock to Coleraine: 7 miles (11km); Coleraine to Portrush: 7 miles (11km); Portrush to Giant's Causeway: 9 miles (14.5km).

GRADE Moderate.

SURFACE
All tarmac, except for the railway path into Giant's Causeway, which is high-grade stone.

HILLS
There are several short climbs and two longer hills of almost 91m (300ft): one between Castlerock and Coleraine, the other between Portrush and Bushmills.

YOUNG & INEXPERIENCED CYCLISTS
Most of the ride is on quiet roads, cycle lanes and segregated cycleways, where the route runs safely alongside busier roads. The final traffic-free section from Bushmills to Giant's Causeway is along the course of a disused railway.

REFRESHMENTS
- Pubs and a cafe in Castlerock.
- Lots of choice in Coleraine, Portstewart and Portrush.
- Cafe at the Giant's Causeway.

THINGS TO SEE & DO
- Mussenden Temple, just west of Castlerock: 18th-century ruins perched upon a precipitous cliff edge; 028 2073 1582; www.nationaltrust.org.uk
- Hezlett House, Castlerock: 17th-century thatched cottage and garden; 028 2073 1582; www.nationaltrust.org.uk

- Barmouth Viewpoint; www.nationaltrust.org.uk
- Portstewart Strand: 2-mile (3-km) long beach with dunes; www.nationaltrust.org.uk
- Mountsandel Fort, just outside Coleraine: site where the remains of settlements dating from before 7000 BC

were found; www.colerainebc.gov.uk
- Portrush coastal resort: popular holiday destination; www.portrush.org.uk
- Dunluce Castle: medieval castle on the coast; 028 2073 1938; www.northantrim.com

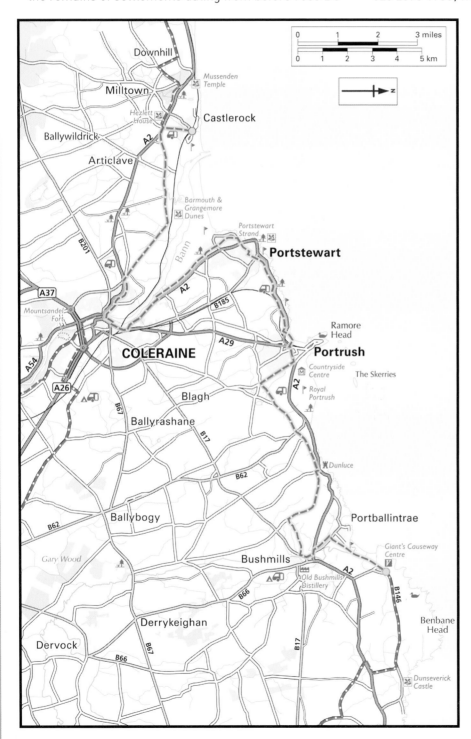

- Bushmills Irish Whiskey Distillery: the world's oldest licensed whiskey distillery has been making Irish malt whiskey for 400 years; 028 2073 1521; www.bushmills.com
- Giant's Causeway: unique geological formation; 028 2073 1582; www.nationaltrust.org.uk

TRAIN STATIONS
Castlerock; Coleraine; Portrush.

BIKE HIRE
Bushmills Bike Company: 028 207 30262

FURTHER INFORMATION
- To view or print National Cycle Network routes, visit www.sustrans.org.uk
- Maps for this area are available to buy from www.sustransshop.co.uk
- Coleraine Tourist Information: 028 7034 4723; www.discovernorthernireland.com
- Portrush Tourist Information: 028 7082 3333; www.northcoastni.com

ROUTE DESCRIPTION
From Castlerock station, follow the road out of the town to the short section along the A2, which has a shared-use path before you follow minor roads inland, parallel with the course of the River Bann towards Coleraine.
From Coleraine, the ride uses cycle lanes and segregated cycle tracks into the town centre and out towards Portstewart, where it continues on town roads. After Portstewart, join the shared-use path along the coast to Portrush, where there are fine sea views across to the Mull of Kintyre. From Portrush to Bushmills, the route follows quiet lanes parallel to the busy coast road, with a climb up to 91m (300ft) with wonderful views.

From Bushmills, a section of railway path adjacent to the narrow gauge tourist railway, with views over the beach, takes you almost to the door of the Giant's Causeway Visitor Centre. For safety reasons – a steep hill with a blind bend and lots of pedestrians – you are not allowed to cycle down to the Giant's Causeway from the Visitor

Centre. Please do not ignore this sensible and necessary safety precaution.

You could choose to break this ride up into several shorter sections, with Coleraine or Portrush as good starting points. Both are served by train stations.

NEARBY CYCLE ROUTES
West of Castlerock, National Route 93 climbs steeply on Bishop's Road to over 305m (1,000ft), with magnificent views to the Inishowen Peninsula and, on a fine day, to the Scottish Isles of Islay and Jura. It then drops down to Limavady, via Binevenagh Forest. East of Giant's Causeway, Route 93 continues inland towards Ballycastle and the ferries to Scotland and Rathlin.

West of Castlerock, there is a link route from National Route 93 that goes to the Lough Foyle ferry service, connecting Magilligan Point to Greencastle on the Inishowen Peninsula.

Rathlin Island, which is a ferry ride from Ballycastle, offers virtually traffic-free cycling and walking to famous birdnesting sites and dramatic cliffs.

LAGAN & LOUGH

Belfast is the capital city of Northern Ireland and seat of the legislative assembly. It has long been associated with the shipbuilding industry and, in the early 20th century, Harland & Wolff, who built the ill-fated *Titanic*, were known as the largest and most efficient shipyard in the world. The city stands at the eastern end of Belfast Lough and at the mouth of the River Lagan. In 1994, a weir was built across the river to raise the average water level, in order to cover the unsightly mud flats.

Since the Good Friday Agreement, Belfast has seen a long period of economic growth and urban development, including the Cathedral Quarter, Victoria Square and Laganside, with the Odyssey complex and the Waterfront Hall.

Belfast Lough is a large sea lake at the mouth of the River Lagan, popular for sailing, with two marinas, one at Bangor and the other at Carrickfergus. The Belfast Lough Nature Reserve is an important feeding area for a wide range of waders and wildfowl, including redshanks, oystercatchers and blacktailed godwits.

Belfast and the bicycle go back a long way: John Dunlop invented the world's first inflatable tyre behind the City Hall in 1888 for his son's bicycle!

This ride can be split easily into shorter sections by using trains, which carry cycles. There are several stations along the route, including one at each end.

National Routes: 9 and 93

START Lisburn Civic Centre, Lagan Valley Island.

FINISH Loughshore Park, Jordanstown at the edge of Belfast Lough.

DISTANCE
19 miles (30.5km).
Shorter options, from Lisburn to Waterfront Hall, Belfast: 12 miles (19.5km); Waterfront Hall, Belfast, to Loughshore Park, Jordanstown: 7 miles (11km).

GRADE Easy.

SURFACE Mainly tarmac, with a short section of cobbles at Clarendon Docks.

HILLS None.

YOUNG & INEXPERIENCED CYCLISTS
The route is almost totally traffic-free. The sections from Lisburn Civic Centre to Clarendon Dock, Belfast, and from Dargan Road in north Belfast to Loughshore Park, Jordanstown, are particularly good for young children.

REFRESHMENTS
- Plenty of choice in Lisburn, including a cafe at the Civic Centre.
- Tap Room, Hilden Brewery, Hilden.
- Cutters Wharf, Stranmillis.
- The Stables Tea Room, Sir Thomas and Lady Dixon Park (just off the route at Drumbeg).

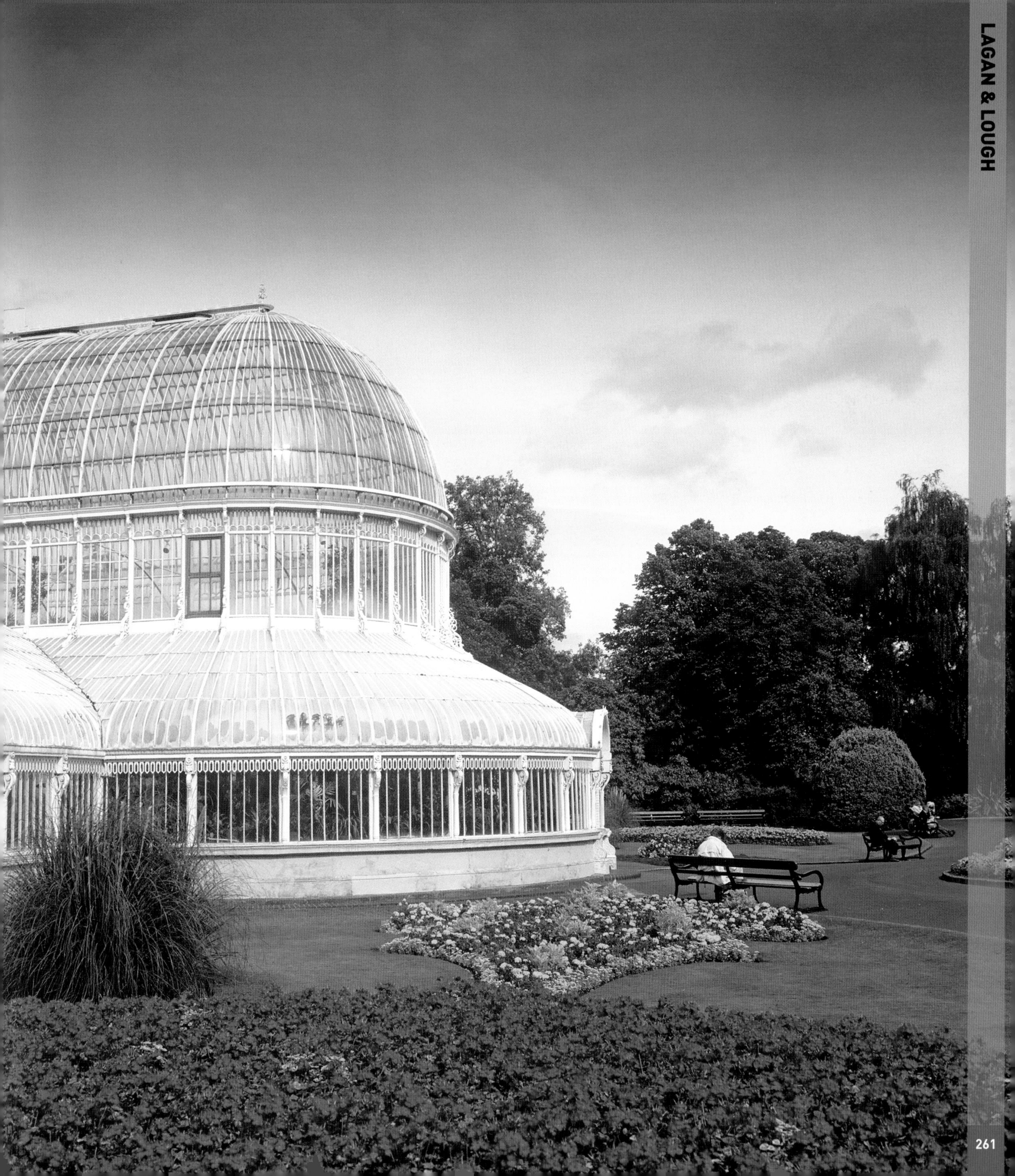

- Malone House Restaurant, Barnett Demesne (just off the route at Shaw's Bridge).
- Lots of choice in Belfast.
- Ice cream shops and tea shops in Whiteabbey and Jordanstown.

THINGS TO SEE & DO

- Lagan Valley Regional Park; 028 9049 1922; www.laganvalley.co.uk
- Minnowburn Beeches: 128 acres of naturally mixed countryside, 3 miles south of Belfast.

BELFAST:
- The Botanic Gardens: situated between Queen's University and the River Lagan; www.belfastcity.gov.uk
- Belfast Cathedral; 028 9032 8332; www.belfastcathedral.org
- Ormeau Park; www.belfastcity.gov.uk
- The Odyssey: Ireland's largest all-seater indoor venue; 028 9076 6000; www.theodyssey.co.uk
- The Crown Bar, Belfast: famous Victorian pub; 028 9024 3187; www.nationaltrust.org.uk
- Belfast Lough: haven for wading birds and ducks in autumn and winter, and breeding terns in summer; 028 9147 9009; www.rspb.org.uk

TRAIN STATIONS

Lisburn, Hilden, Yorkgate, Botanic, Belfast Central. Whiteabbey station is 0.5 mile (0.8km) from the route, and Jordanstown 1 mile (1.6km).

BIKE HIRE

- Bike Dock: 028 9073 0600; www.bikedock.com
- McConvey Cycles: 028 9033 0322; www.mcconvey.com

FURTHER INFORMATION

- To view or print National Cycle Network routes, visit www.sustrans.org.uk
- Maps for this area are available to buy from www.sustransshop.co.uk
- Belfast Tourist Information: 028 9024 6609; www.gotobelfast.com
- Lisburn Tourist Information: 028 9266 0038; www.visitlisburn.com
- Northern Ireland Tourist Information: www.discovernorthernireland.com

ROUTE DESCRIPTION

From Lisburn, a long wooded river and canalside section leads past former linen mills to Shaws Bridge. From here, the route passes through Clement Wilson Park and follows the river past the recently constructed cafe and renovated lough keeper's cottage, into the centre of Belfast, via safe crossings at the Ormeau and Albert Bridges. Along the way, you'll spot some great artworks (see photos left and right). The towpath between Lisburn and Stranmills is shared-use, narrow in places but mostly widened. It is popular and can be busy, so please give way to pedestrians and dismount if necessary.

After the ferry terminals and the dockland area, cross onto the North Foreshore Path, which will take you all the way to Hazelbank Park and Whiteabbey, with the vast shimmering expanse of Belfast Lough off to your right. The fence along the first part of this section was erected to protect the numerous wading birds from being disturbed by dogs and walkers.

NEARBY CYCLE ROUTES

From Lisburn, National Route 9 continues west over the Horseback Bridge at Union Locks, towards Lough Neagh at Oxford Island and on to Portadown, to follow the Newry Canal towpath.

In due course, National Route 93 will run east after crossing the River Lagan at the Queen Elizabeth Bridge and past the Odyssey complex before joining the Comber Greenway at Ballymacarrett. A second spur will head to Holywood and Bangor. Route 93 will also continue northwards via the Newtownabbey Way to the Newtownabbey Council Offices at Mossley Mill before continuing to Carrickfergus and Larne.

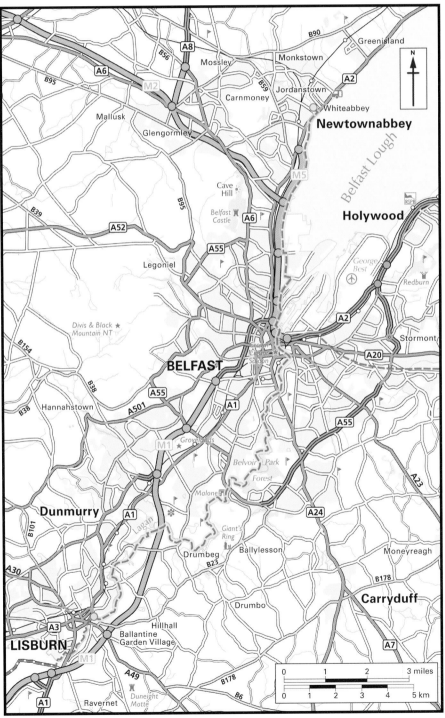

COMBER GREENWAY

From the Holywood Arches to Dundonald, the Comber Greenway provides a tranquil green corridor through East Belfast, with points of interest along the way, including the statue of CS Lewis, views of the Harland & Wolff cranes, Parliament Buildings at Stormont and the Belfast Hills. The trail runs along the course of an old railway, which closed in 1950. It gives the 150,000 people living in its vicinity a more attractive and safer route for walking and cycling than the busy nearby road.

The trail is also a haven for a diverse range of wildlife, and during the Greenway's construction, special care was taken at sites of nature conservation importance, such as the River Enler and areas of woodland and wetland. The Comber Greenway's environmental credentials have also extended into large-scale recycling: two bridges that form part of the route were originally a surplus temporary foot bridge spanning the River Bann in Portadown.

The Greenway links to the Strangford Lough Cycle Trail, an 82-mile (132-km) circuit of Strangford Lough on quiet country roads.

National Route: 99

START Dee Street, Belfast.

FINISH Comber town centre.

DISTANCE 7 miles (11km).

GRADE Easy.

SURFACE Tarmac.

HILLS None.

YOUNG & INEXPERIENCED CYCLISTS
This short, level ride along a disused railway line is traffic-free and suitable for families and novice cyclists.

REFRESHMENTS
• Lots of choice in Belfast.
• Variety of choices also along the route in Holywood Arches, Ballyhackamore, Kings Square, Tullycarnet, Dundonald and Comber.

THINGS TO SEE & DO

BELFAST:

- Belfast Cathedral: 028 9032 8332; www.belfastcathedral.org
- The Odyssey: Ireland's largest all-seater indoor venue; 028 9076 6000; www.theodyssey.co.uk
- The Crown Bar, Belfast: famous Victorian pub; www.nationaltrust.org.uk
- Statue of CS Lewis, East Belfast.
- View of Harland & Wolff cranes, East Belfast.
- View of Parliament Buildings and Stormont. Dundonald International Ice Bowl; 028 9080 9100; www.theicebowl.com
- View of Scrabo Tower: one of Northern Ireland's best-known landmarks; www.ni-environment.gov.uk/scrabo
- Killynether Wood; www.nationaltrust.org.uk
- Lisnabreeny & Cregagh Glen; www.nationaltrust.org.uk

TRAIN STATIONS
Belfast Dee Street; Belfast Central; Bridge End; Sydenham.

BIKE HIRE
- Bike Dock: 028 9073 0600; www.bikedock.com
- McConvey Cycles: 028 9033 0322; www.mcconvey.com

FURTHER INFORMATION
- To view or print National Cycle Network routes, visit www.sustrans.org.uk
- Maps for this area are available to buy from www.sustransshop.co.uk
- Belfast Tourist Information: 028 9024 6609; www.gotobelfast.com
- Ards Tourist Information: 028 9182 6846; www.ards-council.gov.uk
- Northern Ireland Tourist Information: www.discovernorthernireland.com

ROUTE DESCRIPTION
The Comber Greenway is a new traffic-free section of the National Cycle Network, which runs along the old Belfast to Comber railway line.

It begins in Dee Street, East Belfast, close to the Harland & Wolff shipyard. From the Holywood Arches to the Comber Road, Dundonald, the Greenway provides a traffic-free route through East Belfast.

At the Comber Road in Dundonald, the route diverts briefly from the old railway along a section of riverside path to Millmount Road before continuing to Comber through a rural landscape and wetland area. It passes the Billy Neill (MBE) Centre for Soccer Excellence, where it runs near to the River Enler and from where there are views of adjacent farmland and Scrabo Tower. Cyclists and walkers can cross the River Enler and farm lanes using a number of reinstated bridges before arriving at the Old Belfast Road, Comber.

NEARBY CYCLE ROUTES
National Route 99 travels northeast from Comber Square towards Scrabo Tower, while Regional Route 20

travels southeast from Comber Square to Castle Espie,
Whiterock and beyond.
The Strangford Lough Cycle Trail is an 82-mile (132-km)
circular cycle route in the Strangford Lough area.

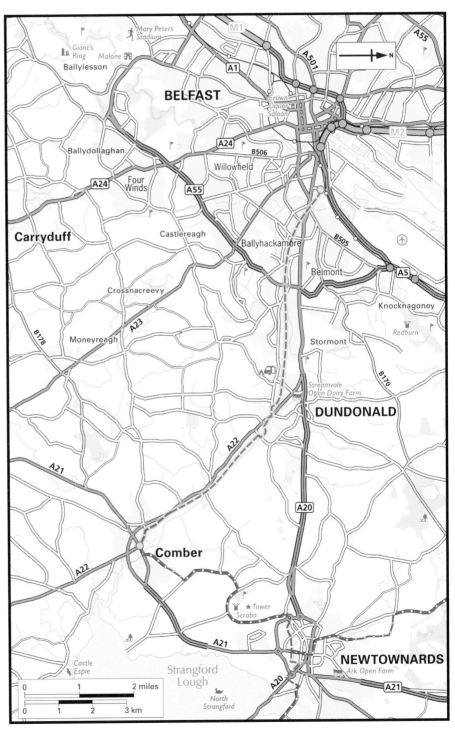

PRACTICAL HELP & CYCLING WITH CHILDREN

GETTING TO THE START OF A RIDE

The best rides are often those that you can do right from your doorstep, maximizing time on your bike and reducing travelling time. However, if you need to travel to the start of the ride, consider catching a train.

WHAT TO WEAR

For most of the easy day rides featured in this book you do not need any special clothing or footwear. Shoes suitable for walking are also fine for cycling. Looser-fitting trousers allow your legs to move more freely, while tops with zips let you regulate your temperature. If it's cold, pack some gloves and a warm hat; if it looks as though there may be rain, take a waterproof. If you are likely to be out at dusk, take a bright reflective top. If you start to cycle regularly, you may well appreciate the benefits of specialist equipment on longer rides, especially padded shorts and gloves.

WHAT TO TAKE

For a short ride on a fine dry summer's day, you will need, at the very minimum, a pump and a small tool bag with a puncture repair kit, just in case. However, it is worth considering the following: water bottle, spare inner tube, 'multi-tool' (available from cycle shops), lock, money, sunglasses, lightweight waterproof (some pack down as small as a tennis ball), energy bars, map, camera and a spare top, in case it cools down or to keep you warm when you stop for refreshments.
Rucksacks are fine for light loads but can make your back hot and sweaty. For heavier loads and for longer or more regular journeys, you are better off with panniers that attach to a bike rack.

MAKING THE MOST OF YOUR BIKE

There are three things that can make a real difference to almost any bike. First, don't use knobbly tyres unless you are riding on rough tracks – smooth tyres offer much less rolling resistance. Second, pump up the tyres hard so the bike rolls along more easily. Third, adjust the saddle so that it is at the right height – most 'occasional' cyclists have their saddles too low and waste a lot of energy. While bike shops are often the best places to have repairs done, it really is worth learning how to mend a puncture, as this can happen to anyone, anywhere, and walking several miles with a flat tyre is no fun. At least learn how to change a tube, and carry a spare one with you.

SAFETY

Build up your confidence on traffic-free trails and cyclepaths, and quiet streets and roads. Be aware of traffic around you, and make it clear to other road users if you intend to turn left or right. Be prepared to pull in and wait for traffic to pass. Get off and push your bike if you feel uncomfortable at busy road junctions. Be seen – wear bright clothing and use lights in gloomy conditions.

LOCKING YOUR BIKE

Unless you are sitting right next to your bike when you stop for refreshments, it is worth locking it up, preferably to something immovable like a post, fence or railings (or a bike stand, of course). If nothing else, lock it to a companion's bike. Bike theft is more common in towns

and cities, and if you regularly leave your bike on the streets, it is important to invest in a good-quality lock and to lock your bike up in a busy, well-lit location.

TOP TEN TIPS FOR CYCLING WITH CHILDREN

- Check that their bikes are ready to ride. Do the brakes and gears work? Is the saddle the right height? Are the tyres pumped up?
- Take enough clothes and waterproofs to keep them warm, as well as panniers to carry any clothes they may remove as they warm up. Check that trousers and laces can't get caught in the chain.
- Don't be overambitious. If your children don't enjoy the ride because they are exhausted, they won't want to go out cycling again.
- Choose a ride that holds plenty of interest for children, such as animals or playgrounds, and ensure you have a goal to aim for at the turnaround point, such as a pub, cafe or place of interest.
- Wrap toddlers in child seats up warm because, unlike you, they are generating no energy.

- If cycling in a group with children, make sure there is an adult at the front and one at the back. Take special care at road junctions. If you are the only adult, stay at the back and keep an eye on the children ahead of you.
- Take rewards (bribes!) in the form of sweets and drinks or other goodies.
- Carry some sticking plasters and antiseptic wipes - kids are far more likely to fall off and graze arms, hands or knees.
- Take care not to pinch their skin when helping your children put on their helmet. Place your forefinger between the clip and chin.
- Take a camera – memories are made of this.

FINDING OUT MORE – WWW.SUSTRANS.ORG.UK

Use the Sustrans website to find out where you can cycle from home or while you are away on holiday, and browse through a whole host of other useful information.

The websites of local authorities often have details of nearby rides – type 'Cycling' into the search engine.

INDEX

PICTURE CREDITS

The Automobile Association wishes to thank the following photographers and organisations for their assistance in the preparation of this book.

Abbreviations for the picture credits are as follows – (t) top; (b) bottom; (l) left; (r) right; (c) centre; (dps) double page spread; (AA) AA World Travel Library

2 Callander to Killin railway path, Jenny Baker/Sustrans; 5 Alistair McGowan, Yves Salmon; 6 John Grimshaw, J Bewley/Sustrans; 6-7 Sunlit Loch Venacher, John Grimshaw/Sustrans; 8 Malcolm Shepherd, J Bewley/Sustrans; 10t Fishponds, Bristol & Bath Railway Path, J Bewley/Sustrans; 10c Okehampton town centre, AA/G Edwardes; 10b Weymouth Beach, AA/M Jourdan; 12/13 Bridge over Camel Estuary, AA/R Moss; 14/15 Padstow harbour AA/J Wood; 16/17 Okehampton Castle, AA/N Hicks; 17 Ham Green viaduct, J Bewley/Sustrans; 18 Foxgloves near Okehampton, J Bewley/Sustrans; 19 White Lady Falls, AA/N Hicks; 20/21 Pulteney Bridge, Bath, AA/C Jones; 22/23 Fishponds, Bristol & Bath Railway Path, J Bewley/Sustrans; 24/25 Frampton on Severn, AA/S Day; 26/27 Flamingos at Slimbridge, AA/D Hall; 28/29 Thatchers Cider visitor centre, J Bewley/Sustrans; 30/31 Entrance arch, Yatton Station, J Bewley/Sustrans; 32/33 Sea Cow Pub, Weymouth, AA/M Jourdan; 34 & 35 Weymouth Beach, AA/M Jourdan; 37(i) Lanhydrock, Cornwall, NTPL/Ross Hoddinott; 37(ii) Lanhydrock, Cornwall, NTPL/Andreas von Einsiedel; 37(iii) Causeway below Lindisfarne Castle, NTPL/Joe Cornish; 37(iv) Huts at Lindisfarne Castle, NTPL/Joe Cornish; 37(v) Statue of shepherd by John Van Nost, NTPL/David Levenson; 37(vi) Powis Castle, NTPL/Andrew Butler; 37(vii) Kings Room, Falkland Palace, Douglas MacGregor/National Trust for Scotland; 37(viii) Falkland Palace and gardens, David Robertson/ National Trust for Scotland; 38t Chalk and Channel Way, David Young/Sustrans; 38c Wooden doorway at Canterbury, AA/M Busselle; 38b Winged Shelter by Angus Ross, J Bewley/Sustrans; 40/41 & 43 Cowes, AA/S McBride; 44/45 Cuckoo wire sculpture, Ian Chamberlain/Sustrans; 47 Millennium milepost, Cuckoo Trail, Ian Chamberlain/Sustrans; 48/49 Detail in Canterbury Cathedral, AA/M Busselle; 50/51 Bookshop, Canterbury, AA/M Busselle; 52 Milton Keynes Cows, AA/M Moody; 53 Beacon point in Campbell Park, AA/M Moody; 54/55 Grand Union Canal, AA/C Jones; 56/57 St Mark's church, Thame, AA/S Day; 58l Simplicity Bench by Yumiko Aoyagi, Katy Hallett/Sustrans; 58r Three characters on poles by Lucy Casson, Katy Hallett/Sustrans; 59 Marker Posts by Patrick O'Riordan, J Bewley/Sustrans; 60/61 Samphire Tower by Jony Easterby & Pippa Taylor, David Young/Sustrans; 62l Dover Castle, AA/M Busselle; 62r Flora Calcarea by Rob Kesseler, David Young/Sustrans; 63 Saxon Shore Way, AA/N Setchfield; 64(i) Sandwell Valley RSPB, AA/C Jones; 64(ii) Langstone Harbour, Jason Crook/RSPB; 64(iii) London Wetland Centre, AA/R Harris; 64(iv) Portmore Lough, Andy Hay/ rspb-images.com; 64(v) Common Shelduck, Roger Tidman/FLPA; 64(vi) Sandwell Valley Park, AA/C Jones; 64(vii) Langstone harbour, Tony Hamblin/rspb-images.com; 65 North Kent Marshes, Robert Canis/FLPA; 66t Regents Canal at Mile End, AA/L Hatts; 66c Royal Observatory, London, AA/N Setchfield; 66b Albert Bridge, London, AA/S Montgomery; 67 London Eye, AA/C Sawyer; 68-69 & 70-71 Hampton Court Palace, AA/R Turpin; 72 Deer at Richmond Park, AA/N Setchfield; 73 Royal Observatory, London, AA/N Setchfield; 74-75 Millennium Dome, AA/N Setchfield; 76 The River Ravensbourne, www.white-windmill.co.uk/Alamy; 77 Sign on Waterlink Way, J Bewley/Sustrans; 78-79t Sculpture in Mile End Park, AA/J Hatts; 79cl Sculpture at Hackney Marshes, AA/J Hatts; 80/81 Docklands, London, AA/N Setchfield; 82 Salmon Lane Lock at Mile End, AA/L Hatts; 83 & 84-85 Blue plaque by Jemima Burrill, J Bewley/Sustrans; 86-87 Flowers along Wandle Trail, J Bewley/Sustrans; 88t Marriots Way, Sue Coulson/Sustrans; 88c Genome Double Helix by Katy Hallett & John Sulter, Katy Hallett/Sustrans; 88b Willington Dovecote, John Grimshaw/Sustrans; 90-91 Hatfield House, AA/M Birkitt; 92 Hertford Castle, Colin Palmer Photography/Alamy; 93 River Lee near Ware, Tony Eveling/Alamy; 94/95 River Nene, Peterborough, Ethel Davies/Robert Harding; 96 River Nene, Peterborough, Dave Porter; 96/97 Peterborough Cathedral, Bildarchiv Monheim GmbH/Alamy; 98/99 Elm Hill, Norwich, AA/R Ireland; 100 Marriotts Way, Sue Coulson/Sustrans; 101 Norwich Cathedral AA/R Ireland; 102-103 King's College, Cambridge, James Thomson/Sustrans; 104 Genome artwork, Katy Hallett/Sustrans; 105 Punting in Cambridge, James Thomson/Sustrans; 106-107 Bedford Park, Stephen Griffiths; 108/109 Footbridge over River Great Ouse, Bedford, Greg Balfour Evans/Alamy; 109t River Great Ouse Bedford, David Martyn Hughes/Alamy; 110-111 Writtle village pond, Essex, John Wheeler/ Alamy; 112 Meadow Brown butterfly, John Carter/Alamy; 113 Aythorpe Roding Windmill Essex, Colin Palmer Photography/Alamy; 114 Twisted Arch by Cod Steaks, J Bewley/Sustrans; 115l Keyhole Arch by Jeremy Cunningham, Julia Bayne/Sustrans; 115tr Cycle Arch by Dominic Clare, Julian Cram/Sustrans; 115cr Tredegar Chimes by Jony Easterby, Jony Easterby/ Sustrans; 116tl Reflection by Tony Eastman, David Martin/Sustrans; 116tc Signal seats by Angus Ross, J Bewley/Sustrans; 116tr Bird Trio by Katy Hallett & Dolton school, Sustrans; 116cr Elks by Sally Matthews, Patrick Davis/Sustrans; 117 Lincoln Red Shorthorns by Sally Matthews, David Martin/Sustrans; 118t Centenary Square, Birmingham, Steve Morgan/ Sustrans; 118c Oxendon Tunnel, J Bewley/Sustrans; 118b High Peak Trail, AA/J Beazley; 120/121 & 122/123 Gas Street Basin, Birmingham, AA/C Jones; 124-125 Melbourne Lake, Robin Weaver/Alamy; 126 Arms of the Coke family, Melbourne Hall, M-dash/Alamy; 127 Rock Drills by Mike Evans, Patrick Davis/Sustrans; 128-129 Lincoln Cathedral, AA/C Coe; 130/131 Boston Pendulum Hi-Views by Paul Robbrecht, David Martin/Sustrans; 132/133 Tissington village, AA/T Mackie; 134/135 View over Cromford, AA/T Mackie; 136 High Peak Trail, AA/N Coates; 137 Cottage and pond in Tissington, AA/T Mackie; 138-139 Worcester, J Bewley/Sustrans; 140/141 Worcester Cathedral, AA/M Moody; 141br View from Worcester, AA/M Moody; 142/143 Millennium Commission Sign Post, J Bewley/Sustrans; 143br Limestone wall and dog-rose, AA/J Sparks; 144/145 Brampton Valley Way, J Bewley/Sustrans; 147(i) Hewenden viaduct, John Grimshaw/Sustrans; 147(ii) Harland and Wolff's twin cranes, Robert Ashby/Sustrans; 147(iii) Ironbridge, Shropshire, John Grimshaw/Sustrans; 147(iv) Cullen viaduct, Julia Bayne/Sustrans; 147(v) Hastings, AA/J Miller; 147(vi) Hengoed viaduct, Julian Cram/Sustrans; 147(vii) Little Venice, J Bewley/Sustrans; 148t Cardiff Opera House, J Bewley/Sustrans; 148c Rhayader Gateway by Reece Ingram, Julian Cram/Sustrans; 148b Afon Mawddach Estuary, AA/W Voysey; 150/151 Millennium Stadium, Cardiff, AA/N Jenkins; 151 Bay front carving, Cardiff, AA/N Jenkins; 152/153 Cardiff Opera House, J Bewley/Sustrans; 154/155 Burry Port Lighthouse, Andrew Kneath/Alamy; 156/157 Kidwelly Castle, AA/I Burgum; 158/159 Caernarfon Castle, AA/P Aithie; 161 Lôn Eifion gateway, Julian Cram/Sustrans; 162/163 Blorenge Mountain, The Photolibrary Wales/Alamy; 164tr Clydach Gorge, Robert Gray/Sustrans; 164/165 Clydach Gorge, Graham Morley/Alamy; 166/167 Haverfordwest Castle, AA/I Burgum; 168/169 Haverfordwest, AA/I Burgum; 170/171 Garreg Ddu viaduct, AA/N Jenkins; 172l Rhayader Gateway by Reece Ingram, Julian Cram/Sustrans; 172/173 Below the Craig Goch Dam, AA/N Jenkins; 174/175 Toll bridge at Penmaenpool, AA/R Newton; 176/177 Afon Mawddach Estuary, AA/W Voysey; 177br Mawddawch Trail sign, Julian Cram/Sustrans; 178 Beach at Budleigh Salterton, AA/N Hicks; 179(i) St Michael's Mount, AA/A Besley; 179(ii) Chalk and Channel Way, David Young/Sustrans; 179(iii) Brighton, Sarah Gardiner/Sustrans; 179(iv) Margate, AA/M Busselle; 179(v) To The Lighthouse by Michael Fairfax with Walk the Sea earthwork by Richard Long behind, Tim Snowdon/Sustrans; 179(vi) Blackpill, Swansea, Sustrans; 179(vii) Saundersfoot Harbour, AA/C Warren; 180(i) Cocklawburn Beach, Sustrans; 180(ii) Llandudno, AA/N Jenkins; 180(iii) Holy Island causeway, John Grimshaw/Sustrans; 180(iv) St Hilda's Abbey, AA/M Kipling; 180(v) Warkworth Castle, AA/R Coulam; 180(vi) Stonehaven beach, David Gold/Sustrans; 180(vii) Aberdeenshire coast, David Gold/Sustrans; 181 Crawfordsburn shoreline, J Bewley/ Sustrans; 182t Gateshead Millennium Bridge, Ian Cheatle/Sustrans; 182c Jason Lane waymarker, Spen Valley Greenway, Paul Kirkwood/Sustrans; 182b Whitehaven harbour lighthouse, Cass Gilbert/Sustrans; 184/185 East Gate, Chester, AA/A Midgley; 186 The Rows, Chester, AA/A Midgley; 187 Hawarden Bridge, AA/T Marsh; 188/189 Hebden Bridge, Paul Kirkwood/Sustrans; 191 Statue of Harold Wilson, Mike Kipling Photography/Alamy; 192-193 St Peter's cathedral, Lancaster, AA/S Day; 194 Lune bridge, Lancaster, John Grimshaw/ Sustrans; 195 Ashton Memorial, Lancaster, J Bewley/Sustrans; 197 Florist in Georgian buildings, Whitehaven, AA/A Mockford & N Bonetti; 198 Carved seat by Gilbert Ward, John Grimshaw/Sustrans; 1 of 13 steel route images by Richard Farrington, C2C, Cumbria, Anthea Truby/Sustrans; 200-201 York Minster, AA/P Bennett; 202 York Millennium Bridge, John Grimshaw/Sustrans; 203 Station clock York, AA/R Newton; 204-205 Souter Lighthouse, AA/R Coulam; 206-207 Lizard Point, AA/R Coulam; 207tr Red Robot or Groyne Lighthouse, Paul Kirkwood/Sustrans; 208/209 Millennium Bridge, Newcastle upon Tyne, AA/R Coulam; 210 Tyne Bridge, Newcastle upon Tyne, AA/R Coulam; 210-211 Gateshead promenade, Cass Gilbert/Sustrans; 213 Porth Moina, AA/J Wood; 214(i) Allonby Beach, Nikki Wingfield/Sustrans; 214(ii) Bridge Seats by John Naylor & John Grimshaw, G L Jones/Sustrans; 214(iii) C2C Start Sculpture by Chris Brammall, Whitehaven harbour, Anthea Truby/Sustrans; 214(iv) Highest millennium milepost on the Lôn Las Cymru, Julian Cram/Sustrans; 214(v) Tynemouth Beach, Cass Gilbert/Sustrans; 214(vi) Bodmin Moor, Anthea Truby/Sustrans; 214(vii) Okehampton, J Bewley/Sustrans; 215 Land's End, AA/R Tenison; 216t Lifebuoy at Scottish Maritime Museum, Irvine, AA/S Anderson; 216c Norham, Cass Gilbert/Sustrans; 216b Red rider over rural river bridge, J Bewley/Sustrans; 218/Forth Rail Bridge, AA/J Smith; 221 South Queensferry town centre, AA/J Smith; 222/223 RSPB Reserve; Lochwinnoch, Mike Booth/Alamy; 224/225 Blue tit at RSPB Lochwinnoch, Arron Barnes/Alamy; 226/227 Unicorn figurehead on the frigate *Unicorn*, Dundee, AA/J Smith; 228 Arbroath, Julia Bayne/Sustrans; 229 Statue of Desperate Dan, AA/J Smith; 230/231 Falls of Dochart, AA/S Anderson; 233 Glen Ogle viaduct, Jenny Baker/Sustrans; 234/235 Falkirk Wheel, AA/J Smith; 236r Falkirk Wheel detail, AA/J Smith; 237 Falkirk Wheel aqueduct Annette Price, H20 Photography/Alamy; 238 Brig o' Doon, Alloway, AA/K Paterson; 239 West Kilbride, John Grimshaw/Sustrans; 240/241 Burns Monument, Alloway, AA/P Sharpe; 242/243 View over Dingwall, AA/S Whitehorne; 244 Inverness, Andrew North/Sustrans; 245tl High street, Dingwall, AA/S Whitehorne; 245bl The Castle, Inverness, AA/J Smith; 246t Barmouth Reserve, J Bewley/Sustrans; 246c Thanksgiving Square Belfast angel, Robert Ashby/Sustrans; 246b Dividers by Vivien Burnside, Robert Ashby/Sustrans; 248-249 Peace statue, Londonderry, AA/C Coe; 250/251 Bogside mural, Londonderry, AA/C Coe; 252-253 Moneypenny's Lock, courtesy of Craigavon Borough Council; 256/257 Giant's Causeway, AA/C Coe; 258 Barmouth Reserve, J Bewley/Sustrans; 259 Barrels at Old Bushmills Distillery AA; 260-261 Palm House, Belfast Botanic Gardens, AA/G Munday; 262 Giant fish at Lagan-side, Belfast, AA/I Dawson; 263 Thanksgiving Square artwork, Belfast, Robert Ashby/Sustrans; 264/265 Comber Greenway, J Bewley/Sustrans; 265r CS Lewis statue, J Bewley/Sustrans; 266/267 Comber Greenway, Robert Ashby/Sustrans; 268l Aberystwyth, Pru Comben/Sustrans; 268r Whatever the weather, Robyn Hughes/Sustrans; 269 Locking bike, J Bewley/Sustrans.

Every effort has been made to trace the copyright holders, and we apologise in advance for any unintentional omissions or errors. We would be pleased to apply any corrections in the following edition of this publication.